Modern Military Strategy

M000248703

This textbook provides a coherent introduction to post-Cold War and post-9/11 military theory for upper-level students seeking an initial understanding of strategic studies.

In the contemporary period there has been significant and growing interest among students about international security issues. While many publications focus on one particular aspect of military strategy, there is no single volume that provides a comprehensive yet accessible overview of strategic thought in this new era.

Modern Military Strategy fills this gap in the literature, with chapters on the conduct of war in each of the naval, land, air, space and cyber dimensions, and on nuclear strategy, and irregular war and counterinsurgency. The text concludes by identifying cross-cutting trends, statements and principles which may form the basis of a modern, general theory of war.

This book will be essential reading for students of strategic studies, war studies and military history, and is highly recommended for students of security studies and international relations in general.

Elinor C. Sloan is Associate Professor of International Relations at Carleton University, Ottawa and a former defence analyst with Canada's Department of National Defence. Her previous books include *Military Transformation and Modern Warfare* (2008), *Security and Defence in the Terrorist Era* (2005), and *The Revolution in Military Affairs* (2002).

Modern Military Strategy

An introduction

Elinor C. Sloan

Routledge
Taylor & Francis Group

LONDON AND NEW YORK

First published 2012
by Routledge
2 Park Square, Milton Park, Abingdon, Oxon OX14 4RN

Simultaneously published in the USA and Canada
by Routledge
711 Third Avenue, New York, NY 10017

Routledge is an imprint of the Taylor & Francis Group, an informa business

© 2012 Elinor C. Sloan

The right of Elinor C. Sloan to be identified as author of this work has been
asserted by her in accordance with sections 77 and 78 of the Copyright, Designs
and Patents Act 1988.

All rights reserved. No part of this book may be reprinted or reproduced or utilised in
any form or by any electronic, mechanical, or other means, now known or hereafter
invented, including photocopying and recording, or in any information storage or
retrieval system, without permission in writing from the publishers.

Trademark notice: Product or corporate names may be trademarks or
registered trademarks, and are used only for identification and explanation
without intent to infringe.

British Library Cataloguing in Publication Data
A catalogue record for this book is available from the British Library

Library of Congress Cataloging-in-Publication Data
Sloan, Elinor C. (Elinor Camille), 1965-
Modern military strategy: an introduction / Elinor C. Sloan.
p. cm.
Includes bibliographical references and index.
1. Strategy. 2. Military art and science. I. Title.
U162.S57 2012
355.4 – dc23
2011038384

ISBN: 978-0-415-77770-4 (hbk)
ISBN: 978-0-415-77771-1 (pbk)
ISBN: 978-0-203-12446-8 (ebk)

Typeset in Times
by Taylor & Francis Books

Printed and bound in Great Britain by
TJ International Ltd, Padstow, Cornwall

Contents

Boxes

Introduction

"What about today?" asked a graduate student in a seminar on strategic thought some years ago, after discussing the likes of Sun Tzu, Clausewitz, Mahan and Douhet. "Aren't there any contemporary strategic thinkers?" The question formed the genesis of this book. In 1943 Edward Meade Earle published *Makers of Modern Strategy from Machiavelli to Hitler*, an edited volume covering the range of strategic thought over the previous four centuries that ultimately became a modern classic. Four decades later Peter Paret's edited book *Makers of Modern Strategy from Machiavelli to the Nuclear Age*, published in 1986, significantly revised and updated the earlier version and took us through much of the Cold War era. But "Where are the great military minds of our [present] day?" lamented one commentary on military strategy in the latter half of the 1990s, "Are there any?"[1] And why does it matter?

In the contemporary era the conduct of war remains one of the most important acts of the state. While the overall trend in numbers of conflicts is downward, there are still many wars between states, between states and non-state actors, and among non-state actors. A number of issues that impact on the security of citizens today—ultimately a country's primary responsibility—are non-military in character or require broader, comprehensive, whole of government, civilian activities. But for those that are military in nature, or require a military response, strategic thought remains imperative. "Our ability simply to cope with—much less shape—a future of pronounced complexity, uncertainty, and turbulence," notes one scholar, "will depend in large measure on the prevalence of strategic thinkers in our midst."[2] In our present age of almost continual conflict, and on occasion outright war, our ability to think strategically may be more important than ever.

Our search for strategic thinkers requires a prior understanding of what we mean by strategy and strategic thought. The word "strategy" is derived from the Greek *strategos*, normally translated as "general". Therefore, notwithstanding the increasing application of the word strategy to a range of human activities over the last several decades—from education to healthcare to business and industry—the term itself remains fundamentally military in character. Most discussions of strategy begin with Clausewitz's classic text *On War*, in which he defined strategy as "the use of an engagement for the purpose of the war,"[3] with "engagements" often interpreted as meaning not only actual battles and campaigns but also tacit and explicit threats of the use of force.

Clausewitz's definition lends itself to a wider interpretation of strategy that encompasses policy instruments other than the military. Once we do that, what we are really talking about is not strategy per se but grand strategy. The role of grand strategy, argued Sir Basil Liddell Hart, "is to coordinate and direct all of the resources of a nation, or band of nations, toward the attainment of the political objective of the war."[4] Others go still broader, arguing that grand strategy is a state's theory about how it can best "cause" security for itself, and that there may be military, political and/or economic strategies within an overarching grand strategy.[5] There is a great deal of merit to this broadest perspective, in that it can help to explain the overall foreign and security policy actions of a state. It is a valuable big-picture perspective. But it is not the focus of this book. Rather, this book takes as its starting-point the original Clausewitzian definition of strategy, noted above, and paraphrased in the 1986 *Makers* volume as "the use of armed force to achieve the military objectives and, by extension, the political purpose of the war."[6]

Strategic thought or strategic thinking, argues Bernard Brodie, can be roughly equated to strategic theory.[7] Theory may be defined as a set of statements or principles devised to explain a group of facts or phenomena. But theory in the area of strategy cannot be static, as this definition would suggest; it must always be forward looking. "The essence of strategy," argues Colin Gray, "lies in the realm of the consequences of actions for future outcomes."[8] Strategic theory must be transferable to the world of action. Yet at the same time its components cannot be overly linked to the practical world, lest they be rendered irrelevant in a different time and place. An important characteristic of a theory of war is that its ideas must also be able to transcend "time, environment, political and social conditions, and technology."[9] The challenge is to find the appropriate balance between practicality and enduring applicability.

A further factor to consider is whether the strategic thought accounts for all dimensions of warfare—sea, land, air, space, and now cyber—or whether it focuses on just one (or two) element(s). It is the distinction between a general theory of war and partial theories like the works of Alfred Thayer Mahan on seapower and Guilio Douhet on airpower. These provide valuable insight into the nature of war, so long as no one "mistakes their partial theories for whole theories of war and strategy."[10] At first glance Clausewitz also presents a partial theory of war, but Clausewitzian concepts like friction, the political nature of war, and the centre of gravity, originally formulated for land warfare, have been applied to all dimensions of warfare, thereby demonstrating that a partial theory can contain the seeds of a general theory.

As for who may be considered a strategic thinker, at the most rudimentary level we might ask whether we are looking for the ideas of a military person or a civilian. Some argue for the former. "It is ironic and disappointing that virtually all the reputed 'experts' on strategic and military affairs familiar to the public are civilian academicians, consultants, and journalists ... To be effective in the strategic realm, the military must produce its own strategic thinkers."[11] Others argue that "the civilian writers with something important to say have usually been well received by the professionals," and have often been closer to the mark than their military contemporaries in making predictions about the future.[12] Thus it would seem that a maker of modern strategy can come from the ranks of the military or civilian society. The real problem is the relatively small number of strategists of any stripe. "The field of potential strategic theorists is exceeding small because soldiers tend not to be scholars, civilians tend not to be comfortable theorizing about strategy, and strategy as a vocation falls between the political and military realms."[13]

Thus strategic thought matters. It matters because it helps us to cope with the uncertain and turbulent world around us, and because it helps us to understand the contemporary role of military force in a nation's security policy. "Although its effects on international politics are profound," notes one scholar, "the conduct of war is often neglected [by members of the academic community] who instead focus chiefly on its causes. This overlooks a rich—if under-theorized—literature by historians, soldiers, and strategists."[14] To this end, this book centers on strategic thought in the post-Cold War and post-9/11 eras. In our search for modern strategic thinkers we are looking for military strategists and practitioners, civilian strategists and scholars, and military and civilian historians who have written in the decades since the end of the Cold War about the conduct of war in the contemporary period, and who have put forth statements or principles that are at a sufficient level of generality, so as to present, at a minimum, a partial theory of war.

For simplicity's sake the book is organized functionally. Chapter 1, Seapower, chronicles the move from the blue-water, open-ocean strategic thinking of the Cold War to the post-Cold War emphasis on operations in littoral regions "from the sea" onto land, to today's integration of the two approaches to include operations in the littorals and throughout the sea lines of communications. Chapter 2, Landpower, focuses on state-to-state combat in the land dimension, drawing out perspectives on the conduct of war that first emerged in the latter Cold War period with AirLand battle, were later refined in military vision statements, and saw application in the 2003 Iraq War. Chapter 3 examines strategic thinking on the value and use of airpower, debates that were sparked in the contemporary era by the 1991 Gulf War and continued through to the 2011 operation in Libya. Chapter 4, on joint theory, examines strategic thought on themes that cannot be neatly categorized into the sea, land or air dimensions of warfare, but include all three services as well as force enhancement from the space domain. Packages of discrete but to some degree overlapping ideas are captured by the terms Revolution in Military Affairs, system of systems, network-centric warfare, military transformation, effects-based operations, rapid decisive operations, and "shock and awe."

The most prevalent form of conflict today, irregular war involving a state and at least one non-state entity, is the subject of Chapter 5, which considers strategic thinking on insurgency and counterinsurgency and includes concepts like fourth-generation warfare, non-trinitarian war, and New War. Chapter 6 centres on cyberwar, a topic that sparked some discussion in the mid-1990s but, with the growing number of cyber-attacks against states in the 2000s, has been an area of increasing attention. Chapter 7, on nuclear power and deterrence, highlights strategic thinking on the current role of nuclear weapons in deterrence and how best to make threats credible in light of new actors, while Chapter 8 turns to strategic thought on spacepower, including "traditional" spacepower themes like space force enhancement, as well as space control and some fledgeling ideas (at least in the unclassified domain) about war in, through, and from space.

In each chapter I attempt to identify the significant contemporary strategic thinkers in a particular area, recognizing of course that the most strategic of strategic thinkers—those who move beyond partial theories to approach a general theory of war—cannot fit neatly into one chapter or another. Some names appear in several places. A further constraining factor is that some notable thinkers—Marine Corps General (retired) Charles Krulak comes to mind—published few works and thus it was not possible to cover their strategic thought in as great detail as their actual contribution would warrant. Many chapters begin with a brief opening discussion of the ideas of classical, mainly pre-World War Two, strategists within the functional theme in order to provide historical context. Specific to a particular geopolitical circumstance, and available in innumerable places, the vast Cold War literature on most topics is only briefly raised.

The focus and added value of this volume is the post-Cold War period. One exception is Irregular War, which includes an examination of Cold War literature, since the end of the Cold War arguably had little impact on the conduct of war at that level. Finally, some functional areas are almost purely post-Cold War in nature and thus have little or no prior body of literature.

Each chapter concludes by drawing together principles of a theory of war within a particular functional area as revealed by the scholarship of the strategic thinkers in our midst. A holistic consideration of these partial theories may make it possible to draw out themes that collectively approach a general theory of war in the contemporary era. This is a tall order—and the one to which the book aspires.

Elinor Sloan
Ottawa

Notes

1 Gregory D. Foster, "Research, Writing, and the Mind of the Strategist," *Joint Forces Quarterly* (Spring 1996), 115.
2 Ibid., 111.
3 Carl von Clausewitz, *On War*, ed. and trans. Michael Howard and Peter Paret (Princeton, NJ: Princeton University Press, 1976), 177.
4 B. H. Liddell Hart, *Strategy: The Indirect Approach* (London: Faber and Faber Limited, 1954), 335–36.
5 Barry R. Posen, *The Sources of Military Doctrine* (Ithaca, NY: Cornell University Press, 1984), 13.
6 Peter Paret, "Introduction," in Peter Paret et al., eds., *Makers of Modern Strategy from Machiavelli to the Nuclear Age* (Princeton, NJ: Princeton University Press, 1986), 3.
7 Bernard Brodie, *War and Politics* (New York: Macmillan Publishing Co., Inc., 1973), 452.
8 Colin S. Gray, *Modern Strategy* (Oxford: Oxford University Press, 1999), 18.
9 Ibid., 125.
10 Ibid., 126.
11 Foster, "Research, Writing, and the Mind of the Strategist," 115.
12 Brodie, *War and Politics*, 437 and 473.
13 Gray, *Modern Strategy*, 114.
14 Stephen Biddle, "Strategy in War," *Political Science & Politics* 40, no. 3 (July 2007), 461.

Further reading

Earle, Edward Mead, ed. *Makers of Modern Strategy: Military Thought from Machiavelli to Hitler* (Princeton, NJ: Princeton University Press, 1943).
Gray, Colin S. *Modern Strategy* (Oxford: Oxford University Press, 1999).
Handel, Michael I. *Masters of War: Classical Strategic Thought* (London: Frank Cass, 2001).
Paret, Peter, ed. *Makers of Modern Strategy from Machiavelli to the Nuclear Age* (Princeton, NJ: Princeton University Press, 1986).

1 Seapower

For the student of strategic studies an examination of seapower is the first and arguably most important step in achieving a present-day understanding of how a country can best employ military force to further its national security goals. This is because naval forces, unlike land and air forces—but perhaps similar to present and future space capabilities—are inextricably linked to the predominant phenomenon of our age: globalization. "Seapower," notes the preeminent contemporary maritime strategist, Britain's Geoffrey Till, "is at the heart of the globalization process in a way that land and air power are not."[1]

Globalization refers here to the growing interconnectedness of the world and the resultant effect, such that activities in distant locations increasingly directly impact on circumstances at home and vice versa. The phenomenon is not new: the first great era of globalization lasted from about 1870 to 1914 and spawned the "father" of the concept of seapower, Alfred Thayer Mahan. His was essentially a "blue-water" vision of naval forces, that is, one that saw forces operating well offshore and countering one another to secure maritime trade routes. Yet even in these early years (albeit toward the end of the era) there was an alternate vision, one expressed by Sir Julian Stafford Corbett, of the use of naval forces to assist the army in its operations on shore. The ideas of Mahan and Corbett, history's best-known seapower strategists, provide a useful framework through which to view modern ideas about the role of naval forces in a nation's security policy.

This chapter examines contemporary strategic thought in the maritime dimension. It begins by highlighting the key ideas of Mahan and Corbett with respect to a nation's use of naval power. It then presents through the Mahan–Corbett conceptual lens the strategic thinking of those who have written about seapower in the post-Cold War (including post-9/11) period. They include, among others, British scholar Geoffrey Till and American analyst Robert Work, as well as several US Navy admirals and Marine Corps generals who were instrumental in furthering US naval doctrine and strategy during the 1990s and 2000s, including General Charles Krulak, Admiral Arthur Cebrowki and Admiral Michael Mullen. The chapter concludes with some thoughts on the components of contemporary seapower theory.

Alfred Thayer Mahan[2]

A US naval officer who served during the American Civil War, Alfred Thayer Mahan remained in the US Navy for more than two decades after the war's end. In 1886 he was given as his final posting the position of lecturer in naval history and strategy at, and president of, the US Naval War College in Newport, Rhode Island. He subsequently went on to a prodigious writing career, but is best known for the lectures he turned into a two-part volume on seapower: *The Influence of Sea Power upon History* (1890) and *The Influence of Sea Power upon the French Revolution and Empire* (1892). The goal of these two works, which cover the periods 1660–1783 and 1793–1812 respectively, was to examine the "effect of sea power upon the course of history and the prosperity of nations."[3] Mahan presents his findings early, stating in the preface to the first volume that "mastery of the sea rested with the victor."[4] Most of the remaining pages are devoted to naval histories of various battles, Mahan's own "collection of special instances in which the precise effect [of superior naval power] has been made clear."[5] Unfortunately the combined works lack a chapter that draws together conclusions, and only "from time to time, as occasion offers"[6] does Mahan relate the narrative back to his original thesis. It is therefore left to others to concisely state the *Influence* volumes' overall argument: "Their central theme is simple," writes Philip A. Crowl in the pages of the 1986 *Makers of Modern Strategy*, "in every phase of the prolonged contest between France and England, from 1688 to the fall of Napoleon, command of the sea by naval domination, or lack of it, determined the outcome."[7]

Seapower in Mahan's conceptualization had two essential meanings, the first relatively narrow and the second comparatively broad, both of which pertain to the sea as a great highway of important trade routes. The first meaning centers on straightforward naval capability, that is, "military strength afloat, that [*sic*] rules the sea or any part of it by force."[8] A second, broader meaning of seapower includes "peaceful and extensive commerce," elaborated to involve (1) production; (2) shipping; and (3) colonies and markets.[9] A seapower must produce and exchange goods, carry out this exchange through shipping and, significantly, have access to secure "stations along the road"—in Mahan's age, colonial possessions—from which "armed shipping" could facilitate trade by protecting the "peaceful vessels of commerce."[10] Contemporary definitions similarly encompass a narrow and broad understanding of the term. Seapower, argues Sam Tangredi, entails not only the operations of navies in war, but also the control of international trade and commerce, the use and control of ocean resources, and the use of navies as instruments of diplomacy, deterrence, and political influence in peacetime.[11]

For Mahan, the aim of naval strategy was to support and increase seapower, and the purpose of seapower, in turn, was to enable sea control. The latter meant ensuring that the great sea commons through which trade flows was open to a nation's own use and interests at all times, and deprived to its enemies in wartime. Along these lines, contemporary British maritime doctrine has defined sea control as "the condition in which one has freedom of action to use the sea for one's own purpose in specified areas and for specified periods of time and, where necessary, to deny or limit its use to the enemy."[12] But, as will be seen below, the notion of sea control has, at least in some quarters, undergone a subtle change in recent years. "In a globalized world [sea control] is less a question of 'securing' the sea in the sense of appropriating it for one's own use," notes Till, "and more of 'making it secure' for everyone but the enemies of the system to use."[13]

Although Mahan acknowledged that sea traffic was at times threatened by piracy, his view of the history of seapower was largely one of a contest between nations—and this contest took place on the open oceans. The requirement was for overbearing power on the sea to drive the enemy's fleet from the sea; such power would have to come from capital ships, meaning armoured battleships, but Mahan left open whether this was better obtained through a few very big ships or more numerous medium ships. It follows that he discounted the use of naval forces in coastal operations in support of land forces, something he had witnessed and observed to be generally ineffectual during the Civil War. "On no point is Mahan more emphatic," states Crowl, "the primary mission of a battle fleet is to engage the enemy's fleet."[14]

Sir Julian Stafford Corbett

The failure to incorporate power projection from the sea onto land, and the inter-dependence of armies and navies in wartime, have been identified by scholars as notable shortfalls in Mahan's thinking. This was evident during the Cold War, but is even more apparent in the twenty-first century as "joint" warfare—incorporating sea, land and air forces—has become all but mantra in the Western world. For early thinking about joint warfare we can turn to a second naval strategist of the early twentieth century, and our first non-military strategic thinker, Sir Julian Stafford Corbett.

A contemporary of Mahan's, Corbett was a British scholar, a civilian naval historian who lectured at the British Naval War College and is best known for his 1911 book *Some Principles of Maritime Strategy*. The book itself examines a broad set of concepts, including, among others, the concentration of forces at sea and the notion of a decisive battle (both of which he refuted), maritime communications, command of the sea, blockades, and an extensive discussion of limited war. But of most interest here, because of its applicability to the present era, is his discussion of the integration of naval and landpower in the context of expeditionary warfare.

The first indication of the importance Corbett attributed to what he refers to as "combined warfare," but is today called joint warfare, lies in the book's title and the use of the term "maritime strategy". A maritime strategy encompasses naval strategy, but is broader in nature. For Corbett, a maritime strategy is necessary whenever there is a war in which the sea is a substantial factor, but that strategy must necessarily include other elements because, as he pointed out, "it is almost impossible that a war can be decided by naval action alone … [s]ince men live upon the land and not upon the sea."[15] In his view, "the paramount concern … of maritime strategy is to determine the mutual relations of your army and navy in a plan of war."[16] "Naval strategy," in turn, "is but that part of [maritime strategy] which determines the movements of the fleet when [the] strategy has determined what part the fleet must play in relation to the action of the land forces."[17]

Just as naval power cannot determine the outcome of a war, nor can landpower effectively operate without the assistance of the navy. Unless by happenchance troops are being transported to friendly territory, the role of the navy must go beyond the simple transport of troops. "[A]n army acting overseas against hostile territory is an incomplete organism incapable of striking its blow in the most effective manner without the assistance of the men of the fleet," he argues. "Alone and unaided the army cannot depend on getting ashore, it cannot supply itself, it cannot secure its retreat, nor can it avail itself of the highest advantages of amphibious force."[18] For Corbett, one scholarly expert has concluded, "In order for war to be decisive … military force must be projected ashore, and this is most effectively done from the sea."[19]

Although Corbett discussed joint and combined operations, his analysis was comparatively brief. Indeed, most of *Some Principles* is devoted to other concepts; the United States Naval War College describes Corbett's contribution on joint and combined military operations as being one of "partial insights."[20] Nonetheless, his views provide an important set of contrasting ideas to those of Mahan, and therefore help to establish a useful framework through which to analyze the evolution of strategic thought in the area of seapower since the end of the Cold War.

The first post-Cold War decade

Navy strategy

With the end of the Cold War and the demise of the Soviet Union, the predominant seapower of the day, the United States, prevailed over the predominant land-based power, Russia and its satellites—just as Mahan would have predicted. Yet throughout the Cold War the Soviet Union was also a significant seapower. US naval doctrines and strategies centered on capabilities, scenarios, and operations both for sea control and power projection. Western naval forces maintained open the sea lines of communications between North America and Europe; patrolled the chokepoints between Soviet naval outlets and the wider ocean; assisted in opening up relations with China (since the existence of the Pacific Fleet convinced China that the West could back it in any confrontation against the Soviet Union); and helped in arming forces battling the Soviets in Afghanistan (because supplies were shipped first to Pakistan by sea and then overland to Afghanistan). When it entered power the Carter administration questioned the value of power projection forces, producing *Seaplan 2000*, which focused on sea control and downgraded the power projection mission. But the Reagan administration reversed the trend, focusing first on sea control through strikes and decisive battles in the Norwegian Sea, and then on naval power projection against Soviet ground targets. By including the land dimension, the new strategy, which was ambitious and expensive and credited with assisting in bringing about the Soviet implosion, was not just a naval strategy but also a *maritime strategy*.[21]

Rendered moot by the dramatically new security environment, US naval strategy underwent a substantial change in the 1990s. The overall context was one of unpredictable risks to security, brought on by failed states, ethnic conflict, the resurgence of old hatreds, humanitarian crises, and the proliferation of weapons of mass destruction. Western navies were called on to assist crisis management efforts on land by bringing power to bear in support of ground forces. The attendant shift in strategic focus, notes Till, was away from what navies do *at* sea, and toward what they can do *from* the sea.[22]

For strategic thinking about seapower in the early to mid-1990s we can look not only to scholars like Geoffrey Till and Norman Friedman, but also to early strategy documents produced by the US Navy as it adjusted to the nature of the post-Cold War security environment. Jointly drafted by the US Navy and the US Marine Corps, "From the Sea" (1992) and *Forward … from the Sea* (1994) defined a vision for the Navy and Marine Corps that was largely Corbettian in nature. The 1992 document makes explicit that the direction it provides "represents a fundamental shift away from open-ocean warfighting on the sea toward joint operations *from* the sea,"[23] while the 1994 elaboration confirms that "[t]he new direction for the Naval Service remains focused on our ability to project power *from the sea* in critical littoral regions of the world" (emphasis added).[24] Rather than seeking to achieve command of the seas in a Mahanian sense, the idea was to use the command of the seas enjoyed by the United States as a result of its competitor's demise to achieve other goals.

The implicit and underlying premise of the two documents is that while events happen at sea, people ultimately live on land, and thus in order to have strategic impact the navy must be able to exert at least a measure of influence on activities ashore. Moreover, the vast majority of humanity, it is noted in several places, lives within close proximity of the sea or waters that reach the sea. The combination of these factors meant that navies would have to operate in the "littoral" regions, defined by "From the Sea" as (1) areas of the open ocean that are close to shore and have to be controlled if one is to support operations ashore (a "close to land" version of sea control); and (2) areas of land close to shore that can be defended directly from the sea. As usefully elaborated by Friedman, "the littoral is distinguished from a much narrower coastal strip ... The landward part of the littoral includes most of the world's population and most of the major cities," while the seaward portion may be considered the two-hundred-mile exclusion zone established under the United Nations Treaty on the Law of the Sea.[25] At the same time, disorder at sea is often linked to events ashore—the contemporary piracy off the coast of Somalia being a case in point. Therefore, even if the goal were to maintain open the sea lines of communication it would be necessary to focus on instabilities and conflicts in the littoral regions, rather than the direct defense of shipping at sea.

For the US Navy, operations would thus take place in the littorals, and they would be in response to a whole range of "regional challenges," ranging from the "chief" danger of aggression by regional powers to the far more common instance of intra-state civil war. The two strategy documents discuss a number of sea concepts, many of which are shaped by the fact that such challenges were unlikely to take place next door. The first is Naval Expeditionary Forces, a clear echo of Corbett's emphasis on naval support to army "Expeditions." Just as expeditionary operations are (land-based) military operations abroad, far from the homeland, naval expeditionary operations are meant to respond to crises "in distant lands."[26] While expeditionary warfare takes place on land, naval expeditionary warfare takes place in the littorals (landward or seaward). Significantly, the term "expeditionary" in contemporary usage also implies a rapid response time. It is not enough to get over there—one must get over there quickly. "'Expeditionary'," states "From the Sea," "implies a mind set, a culture, and a commitment to forces that are designed to operate forward and to respond swiftly."[27]

The Navy's answer to a rapid response time is the second sea concept of forward presence. Briefly discussed in "From the Sea," forward presence is highlighted as imperative in *Forward ... from the Sea*. "Our most recent experiences ... underscore the premise that the most important role of naval forces in situations short of war is to be *engaged* in forward areas" (emphasis in original).[28] The building blocks of forward presence operations are stated as Carrier Battle Groups and Amphibious Ready Groups, thereby providing one answer to Mahan's unanswered question of whether it is best to focus on a smaller number of big ships or a larger number of medium ships.

Should a crisis response be necessary, this would be taken in the context of joint operations, a third area of conceptual emphasis. Examples include the Navy and Marine Corps seizing an enemy's coastal bases to allow the entry of friendly ground and air forces, and strikes from carrier-based aviation against land targets in the context of power projection. "Just as the complementary capabilities of Navy and Marine Corps forces add to our overall strength," notes *Forward ... from the Sea*, "combining the capabilities and resources of other services ... will yield decisive military power."[29] In separate scholarly work, General Carl E. Mundy, Commandant of the US Marine

Corps at the time these documents were written, stressed that the ability to wage littoral warfare would be dependent on the services waging effective joint warfare.[30] Naval fighter training during this time period took a "pronounced swing" toward precision ground-attack operations, enabling carrier-based aviation to participate in joint strike operations ashore as part of an overall strategic bombardment campaign.[31] Box 1.1 provides one example of such an operation.

Box 1.1 **Naval ground attack operations in Bosnia**

- At the end of the Cold War the six republics of former Yugoslavia broke away to form their own states. Civil war broke out in many areas, but especially in the Bosnian republic, which further disintegrated into its three major component nationalities or cultures.
- To enforce a No Fly Zone over Bosnia, provide close air support to United Nations peacekeepers trying to deliver humanitarian aid, and conduct strategic strikes against Serbian tanks and mortars shelling Croats and Muslims in Sarajevo, NATO and the United Nations agreed to the use of precision airpower. By the summer of 1993 NATO aircraft were on station on NATO bases in Italy and on US aircraft carriers in the Adriatic.
- NATO airpower was used on several occasions in 1994 and 1995, culminating in a sustained air campaign against Serb positions and facilities throughout Bosnia in the late summer of 1995, and leading to a balance of power among the factions that paved the way to the Dayton Peace Accords.
- Precision strikes by carrier-based aircraft and sea-launched cruise missiles in Bosnia marked the US Navy's first major use of force "from the sea" against land targets as means of post-Cold War crisis management.

Thus with the publication of "From the Sea" and *Forward … from the Sea*, notes Till, the Navy's area of focus shifted from one of sea control—which remained important but was maintained by default—to one of land control.[32] The US Navy's early strategy documents center on littoral operations in crisis areas around the world, and on the interrelated sea concepts of naval expeditionary operations, forward presence, joint operations, and power projection from sea to land. They are broad themes. Moreover, for all the talk of joint operations among the sea, land and air elements, the more immediate issue was jointness among the Sea Services, especially the Navy and the Marine Corps. For greater detail on how the US Navy and Marine Corps would operate jointly one must look to the Marine Corps' *Operational Maneuver from the Sea* (1996) and *The Navy Operational Concept* (1997).

Operational implementation

As a service historically designed to project power from the sea onto shore, the US Marine Corps arguably faced little adjustment in responding to the post-Cold War security environment. Nonetheless, the intellectual push for the Navy and Marine Corps to work more closely together in a joint environment came from the latter service. Described in positive terms as an iconoclast in US defence circles in the mid- to late 1990s, General Charles Krulak, Commandant of the US Marine Corps, spear-headed *Operational Maneuver from the Sea* and was an instigating force behind the Navy's parallel undertaking. "The threat of the next century," Krulak argued prolifically in a 1999 article that summarized his thinking, "will not be the 'son of Desert Storm'—it will be the 'stepchild of Chechnya',," meaning that it would predominantly feature warfare waged by non-state entities.[33] He also introduced the notion of a "three block war," wherein within three contiguous city blocks the Marines might have to execute a range of missions from humanitarian assistance, to armed peacekeeping, to combat operations against a "tenacious and ferocious" adversary.[34]

In this new environment the Navy had to maintain open the sea lines of communication, but it also had to work with the Marine Corps to project power ashore across the spectrum of warfare from low- to high-combat intensity. How the Sea Services would do so was through a new concept that reflected a marriage between maneuver and naval warfare. Naval maneuver warfare, *The Navy Operational Concept* points out, means: "using the advantages we gain by operating on and from the sea to establish operational and strategic advantage over enemy forces ashore. We do this by … providing unimpeded use of strategic sea lanes and freedom of operation in littoral waters."[35] It means, in short, ensuring and taking advantage of sea control in littoral waters.

A manifestation of this was the Marine Corps' *Operational Maneuver from the Sea* or OMFTS, a doctrine for the projection of power ashore. As a long-standing amphibious warfare organization, the Marine Corps' traditional practice had been to establish a secure presence on shore, build up heavy combat power, and then move inland. Under the new construct, the Marine Corps would take advantage of the benefits enabled by sea control, notably sea-based logistics and sea-based fire support. These two things would allow the Marines to skip the "buildup" phase on shore, moving directly from the sea to targets far inland "in a single decisive maneuver directly from amphibious shipping"[36] known as Ship-To-Objective Maneuver. The change was made possible in large part because of improvements in the precision of long-range weapons, since with advanced communications the force ashore could call the ships for support that otherwise might have come from its own artillery. The increased precision of weapons also reduced ammunition requirements, thereby contributing to a lighter logistics tail.

The overall objective was to create a force that was based at sea and could project force inland without first having to establish a foothold on land. It was, and is, a concept with substantial historical precedent. Notes Till, "A brief review of the military experience of the 20th century shows that the notion that navies can base military power at sea and can support forces ashore directly is by no means new."[37] Nonetheless, *Forward … from the Sea* sparked a revitalized undertaking, notably raising for the first time the idea of "highly mobile 'sea bases' in forward areas."[38] Except for a brief period in the late 1990s, when a sea base was promoted as a massive floating island, a sea base has been consistently described not as a "thing" but as an approach or concept for organizing and using seapower to influence events ashore. That concept includes "a collection of ships and aircraft that can exploit the maneuver space of the ocean."[39] According to a Pentagon report, the collection itself would be flexible, "scaled to fit the needs of specific operations, allowing their use in a spectrum of applications, from humanitarian relief and non combatant evacuation operations to employment in large, full-war scenarios."[40]

A decade and a half after the Sea Basing concept was first introduced it was still being refined, having achieved, according to the Dean of the Center for Naval Warfare Studies at the Naval War College, a "quasi-paradigm" status.[41] The concept's longevity and continued elaboration may be explained by the persistence of the key factor behind its introduction: the fact that in the post-Cold War era, US access to land bases in likely crisis areas is extremely restricted, if not entirely non-existent (by contrast, during the Cold War, US forces were based close to the likely crisis area, the inter-German border). "[T]he tyranny of distance [to] the Pacific-Indian Ocean and Persian Gulf littorals," Krulak pointed out in 1999, "challenges the response time of land forces, making the forward deployment of naval forces necessary."[42] Introduced as a navy concept, Sea Basing took on departmental importance in the post-9/11 era as a contributing element to the Pentagon's change in overseas force posture, under which massive US overseas bases were significantly downsized in favor of a greater number of smaller sites close to crisis spots around the world.

Thus the naval strategy documents "From the Sea" and *Forward … from the Sea*, along with the Navy and Marine Corps operational concepts, did much to push forward strategic thinking about seapower in the 1990s. The centerpiece was expeditionary warfare in a maritime (and Corbettian) sense, and the requirements were sea control on the open ocean and in the littorals, the projection of power ashore (including troops and precision strike), and the provision of sea-based logistical support. But could this be done using existing assets, incorporating advanced technology? Or were new assets and approaches necessary? At least one strategic thinker answered the latter question in the affirmative.

Admiral Arthur Cebrowski and littoral warfare

It is difficult to know where to place Admiral Arthur Cebrowksi in the annals of strategic thinkers. As an academically inclined US Navy admiral who, like Mahan before him, became President of the US Naval War College, he was very interested in seapower. But much of his thinking is more properly placed in a chapter on "joint warfare" (as was, to a certain degree, that of General Krulak), and some of his later thinking could even be placed in a chapter on landpower or counterinsurgency. Cebrowski thus appears several times in this volume; this chapter highlights his thinking as it pertains to seapower. (The ideas of another academically minded admiral and colleague of Cebrowski, William Owens, fit squarely within a discussion of strategic thinking about joint warfare and are discussed in Chapter 4.)

In 1998 a group of naval officers led by then Vice Admiral Arthur Cebrowski began to argue that the Navy's new strategic focus required a new set of assets. Increasingly sophisticated land-based anti-ship cruise missiles would put at risk the large ships and carriers, holdovers from the Cold War era, that were now expected to ensure sea control in littoral areas. Even small coastal navies, especially those featuring diesel-electric submarines, could force the US Navy to operate some distance from shore, fighting for access to coastal waters. For the reformers the answer to Mahan's unanswered question on fleet composition was not a combat fleet of large, multi-mission surface combatants but rather, numerous smaller, cheaper platforms. These vessels, dubbed "Streetfighter," could operate independently to conduct a wide range of missions, from drug, piracy, and terrorism patrols to support to humanitarian assistance and disaster-relief operations. Or, their combat effectiveness could be dramatically enhanced by being tightly integrated into a "network-centric" force.

Cebrowski is considered the father of the network-centric warfare (NCW) concept, a vision of the conduct of war that is fundamentally "joint" in nature and is therefore discussed in Chapter 4. Whereas "platform-centric warfare" focuses on the individual attributes of a particular military platform (bigger and better tanks, for example), NCW centers on the combat power generated by having many (perhaps smaller and less capable) platforms linked together through advanced technologies. In a naval environment the concept translated into "the small, the fast, the many"; it "eschew[ed] big ships and major weapons for a diffuse, ever changing and adaptable military force that shares information instantly."[43] The concrete manifestation of the approach was the Streetfighter, which also responded to the littoral warfare requirements of the post-Cold War strategic environment.

To a service organized since the early 1940s around "big deck" aviation platforms, the move toward smaller, networked vessels proved a difficult sell. But the idea survived in the form of the larger and more capable Littoral Combat Ship (LCS). Now entering service, the LCS is designed to operate in highly contested waters near shorelines to counter mines, submarines, and fast-attack boats. The Pentagon's 2002 decision to develop the LCS concept, argues Robert Work of the Center for Strategic and Budgetary Assessments, indicated the acceptance at the highest levels of the US Navy of new thinking that had originated with Cebrowski. Leaders had embraced a future that was "all about assuring joint force access into and from coastal waters," and they had endorsed a move from a battle fleet organized around carriers, to one characterized by a network of tightly connected carriers, ships, and submarines.[44]

The second post-Cold War decade

Admiral Michael Mullen and the Global Maritime Partnership

"In 1992," notes one assessment of US seapower, "the US Navy, after one hundred years, closed its book on seapower doctrine in the image of Mahan. For how long remained to be seen."[45] One could argue that the book remained closed for only a decade and a half. In 2007 Mahanian ideas reemerged, in adjusted form, in a new strategy that had its intellectual origins in the ideas of Chief of Naval Operations, and subsequently Chairman of the Joint Chiefs of Staff, Admiral Michael Mullen. In Mullen's view, seapower is about more than projecting force ashore in the context of joint littoral warfare. This remains important, but it is only one component of a more expansive view of seapower. For Mullen it is not a case of prioritizing the high seas, blue-water domain of Mahan, or the littoral, brown-water domain of Corbett. Rather, there is only one domain—the maritime—a product of the ubiquitous nature of accelerated globalization.

In such an environment, warfighting may be necessary, but other activities are also important, such as securing sea lanes and delivering humanitarian aid. Moreover, there are a whole host of threat scenarios that fall well short of actual war but nevertheless need to be addressed. "I'm here to challenge you first to rid yourself of the old notion ... that maritime strategy exists solely to win wars at sea and the rest will take care of itself," he argued in 2006, "in a globalized, flat world, the rest matters a lot."[46] Piracy, for example, "can no longer be viewed as someone else's problem ... It is a global threat to security because of its deepening ties to international criminal networks, smuggling of hazardous cargoes, and disruption of vital commerce."[47] Securing the seas is in the interests of all nations, and the benefits of free markets should be spread to everyone. This formulation leads naturally to the changed understanding of sea control noted earlier. In Mullen's view, "the economic tide of all nations rises not when the seas are controlled by one but rather when they are made safe and free for all."[48]

But "the rest" is expansive, and governing or exerting influence across the globe is far beyond US naval capabilities. The necessity is therefore for a cooperative approach, a Global Maritime Partnership among nations. In 2006 Admiral Mullen put forward a naval concept he called "the 1,000 ship navy," not a literal notion but rather a metaphor for "a free-form, self-organizing network of maritime partners" cooperating to halt or divert the movement of threats on the high seas, or address concerns in the littorals.[49] Concrete examples included coordinated operations by Malaysia, Indonesia, and Singapore to counter piracy and terrorist movements in the Strait of Malacca; the Proliferation Security Initiative, under which nations voluntarily intercept ships in international or (more likely) local waters suspected of transporting weapons of mass destruction; humanitarian assistance operations in the Indian Ocean after the 2004 tsunami and along the US Gulf Coast after Hurricane Katrina; and maritime evacuation operations, like off the coast of Lebanon in 2006. All of these reflected an informal maritime coalition to address common threats (manmade or natural) to common interests. As articulated by Mullen, America's future participation in similar such endeavors could be facilitated by the creation of Global Fleet Stations. This is considered a "fresh approach" to sea basing that would include assets like modularly configured ships, unmanned aerial vehicles and helicopters, as well as forces suited to the mission at hand, such as medical teams for humanitarian crises and natural disasters. The overall idea is to enable the US Navy "to operate everywhere there [is] a requirement across the maritime security spectrum, without the high overheads of the overtly-aggressive carrier battlegroups."[50]

Mullen's ideas found formal expression in *A Cooperative Strategy for 21st Century Seapower*, jointly prepared by the US Navy, US Marine Corps and—uniquely—the US Coast Guard, and released in Fall 2007. The strategy is premised on an expansive notion of the maritime environment that is consistent with Mullen's perspective. The maritime domain, it argues, includes coastal areas, bays, estuaries, islands, and littorals, but it also encompasses the world's oceans and seas, and all the airspace above them. It thus straddles the Mahanian and Corbettian perspectives, explicitly reaffirming "the use of seapower to influence actions and activities *at sea and ashore*" (emphasis added). The unifying theme running throughout the *Cooperative Strategy* is that "preventing wars is as important as winning wars." The goal is to prevent or contain wars that would otherwise disrupt the maritime domain, "an area covering three quarters of the planet," and representing "the lifeblood of a global system that links every country on earth." The focus is on "the system" and systemic security, rather than on any particular units or components. Specific missions for the maritime services include "selectively controlling the seas, projecting power ashore, and protecting friendly forces and civilian populations from attack." A particular concern is to mitigate threats to good order at sea, such as piracy, terrorism, weapons proliferation, and drug trafficking. The ability to do all this in a timely fashion requires "maritime forces that are persistently present" and therefore "globally postured," although the concept does not specifically mention global fleet stations or sea basing. Moreover, it requires, above all, working in cooperation with multinational partners along the lines of Mullen's original 1,000-ship navy vision, now renamed the Global Maritime Partnership initiative.[51] Box 1.2 gives an example of a set of operations that fit within Mullen's conceptualization.

Box 1.2 Anti-piracy operations off the coast of Somalia

- Growing piracy off the coast of Somalia in the mid-2000s sparked the UN World Food Program to request assistance in escorting cargo vessels from Kenya to Somalia delivering humanitarian aid.
- A 2008 UN resolution authorized all states with vessels in the region to use force to suppress piracy.
- Since that time, three multinational naval task forces have been deployed off the Horn of Africa and in the Gulf of Aden: a European Union contingent, Operation Atalanta; a NATO standing maritime group, Operation Ocean Shield; and a wider international effort under US command, Combined Joint Task Force 151. All these operations and their component vessels have a general anti-piracy role, as do the naval forces from several other countries—including China, India, and Japan, among others—that are operating in the region under national command.
- The existence of multiple players united by a common mission fits well with Mullen's vision of a self-organizing network of maritime partners cooperating to address threats on the high seas.
- The combined naval forces have had some success. World Food Program supplies are getting through and the strategically important Gulf of Aden has experienced significantly fewer attacks.
- But the overall effect of anti-piracy operations, which address the symptom and not the cause, has been not so much to stop piracy but to push it further out into the ocean. Ultimately, long-term solutions to these sorts of maritime threats lie on shore with functioning states that offer pirates and their families a better way of life.

A Cooperative Strategy for 21st Century Seapower is not without its critics. Robert Work questions the strategy's unifying theme, noting that saying "preventing wars is as important as winning wars" is far different from saying "preventing wars *is preferable to* winning wars." In Work's view, the latter formulation is the better one, coupled with the unambiguous assertion that *nothing* is more important than winning wars (emphasis in original).[52] The crux of the issue may be that the new strategy is a post-modern document in a largely modern world. Geoffrey Till has made a useful distinction between post-modern and modern navies and states. The navies of post-modern states pursue sea control, especially in the littoral regions; they are engaged in expeditionary operations; and they focus on the system, promoting general good order and the conditions for globalization that benefit one and all. Modern states and their navies, by contrast, "will be warier about the implications of globalization for their own security ... and less inclined to collaborate with others in the maintenance of the world's trading system."[53] For Till, there is much evidence that countries are focusing on their own defense and immediate interests, not those of the system—and this suggests a future involving more traditional Mahanian concepts of sea control, including fleet-on-fleet engagements.

Conclusion

Thus a handful of scholars, analysts and practitioners are associated with post-Cold War strategic thought on seapower. They include scholar Geoffrey Till and analyst Robert Work, and practitioners Charles Krulak, Arthur Cebrowski and Michael Mullen, among others. Their ideas have helped to modernize, elaborate and push forward the limits of those of history's best-known seapower strategists, Alfred Thayer Mahan and Julian Corbett. Leaning variously toward one or the other perspective—but always incorporating a degree of both—post-Cold War strategic thinking in the maritime dimension has done much to fill out the partial insights of an earlier era.

Taken together, contemporary views on the use of naval forces reveal a theory of seapower that might include the following tenets: the primary purpose of seapower is to enable sea control *both* in littoral areas and in the open ocean; seapower working in conjunction with land forces, whether through precision strike or logistic support, can help to achieve strategic effects in war; by extension, effective littoral warfare requires effective joint warfare; sea control in the littorals can significantly impact on the course of intra-state conflicts and is necessary for effective naval support of humanitarian and disaster-relief operations; navy expeditionary warfare is required to respond to distant crises and is facilitated by naval forward presence, including sea-basing concepts; and sea control on the open ocean is necessary to maintain open the sea lanes for all those operating lawfully in the context of the globalized system.

Much of the post-Cold War, including post-9/11, theorizing about seapower centered on the littorals and seapower's impact on shore. In an environment where the demise of the Soviet Union had granted, by default, American control of the open oceans, Mahanian themes about fleet-on-fleet tactics found little or no place or relevance. But threats and competitors are beginning to emerge that hark back to an earlier time, whether these may be piracy on the open seas or concern about China's growing blue-water fleet. As unipolarity gives way to multipolarity this trend—already reflected in the strategic thought of Geoffrey Till and implicitly flagged in *A Cooperative Strategy*—is likely to instigate scholarly debate and, in doing so, push forward the boundaries of contemporary strategic thought on seapower. The next chapter examines post-Cold War strategic thinking with regard to landpower.

Notes

1 Geoffrey Till, "New Directions in Maritime Strategy? Implications for the U.S. Navy," *Naval War College Review* 60, no. 4 (Autumn 2007), 30.
2 For a more detailed discussion of Mahan's work, see Margaret Tuttle Sprout, "Mahan: Evangelist of Sea Power," in Edward Mead Earle, *Makers of Modern Strategy: Military Thought from Machiavelli to Hitler* (Princeton, NJ: Princeton University Press, 1943); Philip A. Crowl, "Alfred Thayer Mahan: The Naval Historian," in Peter Paret, ed., *Makers of Modern Strategy from Machiavelli to the Nuclear Age* (Princeton, NJ: Princeton University Press, 1986); and Jon Sumida, *Inventing Grand Strategy and Teaching Command: The Classic Works of Alfred Thayer Mahan Reconsidered* (Washington, DC: Johns Hopkins University Press, 1999).
3 A. T. Mahan, *The Influence of Sea Power upon History 1660–1783* (New York: Dover Publications, 1987), v–vi.

4 Ibid., iv.
5 Ibid., iii.
6 Ibid., 89.
7 Crowl, "Alfred Thayer Mahan," 451.
8 Mahan, *The Influence of Sea Power*, 28.
9 Ibid., 28, 50, 71.
10 Ibid., 28, 82.
11 Sam J. Tangredi, "Globalization and Sea Power: Overview and Context," in Sam J. Tangredi, *Globalization and Maritime Power* (Washington, DC: National Defense University Press), 3.
12 J. J. Widen, "Julian Corbett and the Current British Maritime Doctrine," *Comparative Strategy* 28, no. 2 (March/April 2009), 176.
13 Till, "New Directions in Maritime Strategy?," 31.
14 Crowl, "Alfred Thayer Mahan," 458.
15 Julian S. Corbett, *Some Principles of Maritime Strategy* (New York: Longmans, Green and Co., 1911), 14.
16 Ibid.
17 Ibid., 13.
18 Ibid., 300–301.
19 Widen, "Julian Corbett," 172.
20 US Naval War College, Strategy and Policy Course Outline, Spring 2011.
21 Important works on Cold War seapower include George Baer, *One Hundred Years of Seapower: The US Navy, 1890–1990* (1994); Bernard Brodie, *A Guide to Naval Strategy* (1965); Norman Gorshkov, *Navies in War and Peace: Navies and National Interests* (2001); Sergie Gorshkov, *Navies in War and Peace* (1974) and idem, *The Seapower of the State* (1979); and Wayne Hughes, *Fleet Tactics: Theory and Practice* (1986). See also R. Castex, *Strategic Theories* (1993, original 1935); and Colin S. Gray, *The Navy in the Post-Cold War World* (1994).
22 Till, "New Directions," 32.
23 US Navy, "From the Sea: Preparing the Naval Service for the 21st Century," reprinted in John B. Hattendorf, ed., *U.S. Naval Strategy in the 1990s* (Newport, RI: Naval War College Press, 2006), 90.
24 US Navy, *Forward … from the Sea* (Washington, DC: Department of the Navy, 1994), 8.
25 Norman Friedman, *Seapower as Strategy: Navies and National Interests* (Annapolis, MD: Naval Institute Press, 2001), 220.
26 US Navy, "From the Sea," 90.
27 Ibid.
28 US Navy, *Forward … from the Sea*, 1.
29 Ibid., 8.
30 Carl E. Mundy, "Thunder and Lightning," *Joint Force Quarterly* (Spring 1994), 50.
31 Benjamin Lambeth, "Air Force–Navy Integration in Strike Warfare," *Naval War College Review* 61, no. 1 (Winter 2008), 32–33.
32 Geoffrey Till, *Seapower: A Guide for the Twenty-First Century* (London: Routledge, 2009), 67.
33 Charles C. Krulak, "Operational Maneuver from the Sea," *Joint Force Quarterly* (Spring 1999), 79.
34 Charles C. Krulak, "Ne Cras: Not Like Yesterday," in Richard H. Shultz, Jr. and Robert L. Pfaltzgraff, Jr., eds., *The Role of Naval Forces in 21st-century Operations* (Washington, DC: Brassey's, 2000), xiv.
35 US Navy, "The Navy Operational Concept," in Hattendorf, ed., *U.S. Naval Strategy in the 1990s*, 167.
36 Krulak, "Operational Maneuver," 82.
37 Geoffrey Till, *Naval Transformation, Ground Forces, and the Expeditionary Impulse: The Sea-Basing Debate* (Carlisle, PA: US Army War College Strategic Studies Institute, 2006), vii.
38 US Navy, *Forward … from the Sea*, 5.
39 Jason Sherman, "Pentagon Group Details Sea Base Concept," *Defense News*, October 27, 2003, 6.
40 Defense Science Board Task Force, *Sea Basing* (Washington, DC: Department of Defense, 2003), vii.
41 Robert C. Rubel, "The Navy's Changing Force Paradigm," *Naval War College Review* 62, no. 2 (Spring 2009), 15.

42 Krulak, "Operational Maneuver," 81.
43 Christopher P. Cavas, "Cebrowksi's Legacy: Think Outside the Pentagon," *Defense News*, November 21, 2005, 8.
44 Robert O. Work, "Small Combat Ships and the Future of the Navy," *Issues in Science and Technology* (Fall 2004), 63–64.
45 George Baer, *One Hundred Years of Seapower: The US Navy, 1890–1990* (Stanford, CA: Stanford University Press, 1994), 451.
46 Stephen Trimble, "US Seeks Wider Seapower Definition," *Jane's Navy International*, July 1, 2006.
47 Admiral Michael Mullen, "A Global Network of Nations for a Free and Secure Maritime Commons," in John B. Hattendorf, ed., *Seventeenth International Seapower Symposium: Report of the Proceedings 19–23 September 2005* (Newport, RI: U.S. Naval War College, 2006), 4.
48 Trimble, "US Seeks Wider Seapower Definition."
49 As quoted in Christopher P. Cavas, "Spanning the Globe: U.S. Floats Fleet Cooperation Concept to Allies," *Defense News*, January 8, 2007, 11.
50 Stephen Trimble, "New Dawn for US Global Strategy?" *Jane's Navy International*, November 1, 2006.
51 All references in this paragraph are taken from *A Cooperative Strategy for 21st Century Seapower* (Washington, DC: The Pentagon, 2007). The document has no page numbers.
52 Robert A. Work and Jan van Tol, *A Cooperative Strategy for 21st Century Seapower: An Assessment* (Washington, DC: Center for Strategic and Budgetary Assessments, March 2008), 23–24.
53 Till, *Seapower*, 14.

Further reading

Corbett, Julian S. *Some Principles of Maritime Strategy* (New York: Longmans, Green and Co., 1911).
Friedman, Norman. *Seapower as Strategy: Navies and National Interests* (Annapolis, MD: Naval Institute Press, 2001).
Gray, Colin S. *The Navy in the Post-Cold War World* (University Park, PA: The Pennsylvania State University Press, 1994).
Hattendorf, John B., ed. *U.S. Naval Strategy in the 1990s* (Newport, RI: Naval War College Press, 2006).
Mahan, A. T. *The Influence of Sea Power upon History 1660–1783* (New York: Dover Publications, 1987).
Tangredi, Sam J. *Globalization and Maritime Power* (Washington, DC: National Defense University Press, 2002).
Till, Geoffrey. *Seapower: A Guide for the Twenty-first Century* (London: Routledge, 2009).
United States Navy. *Forward … from the Sea* (Washington, DC: Department of the Navy, 1994).
United States Navy, Marine Corps and Coast Guard. *A Cooperative Strategy for 21st Century Seapower* (Washington, DC: Department of Defense, 2007).
Work, Robert A. and Jan van Tol. *A Cooperative Strategy for 21st Century Seapower: An Assessment* (Washington, DC: Center for Strategic and Budgetary Assessments, March 2008).

2   Landpower

Throughout much of recorded history, until Alfred Thayer Mahan emerged as a strategist of seapower, the study of strategic thought was all but synonymous with military strategy in the land dimension of warfare. Two names are familiar to even the most casual reader of military affairs: Sun Tzu, the fifth-century BC Chinese general who lived during the "period of the warring states" and wrote *The Art of War*; and Carl von Clausewitz, the Prussian general who served during the Napoleonic Wars and whose *On War* was published posthumously. Two others, somewhat less well known but whose ideas are usefully included in any volume on strategic thought, are: Baron Antoine Henri Jomini, a Swiss national who served as a general in both the French and Russian armies (including on Napoleon's staff), and whose *Summary of the Art of War* in many ways documented Napoleonic warfare; and Sir Basil Henry Liddell Hart, a captain in the British Army during World War One who retired in the 1920s to a life of military writing, including a volume on *Strategy: The Indirect Approach*.

Although elements of some of these works, notably Sun Tzu's *The Art of War*, are relevant to irregular warfare, and indeed to other walks of life, in general it can be said that the ideas of these theorists pertain primarily to conventional warfare. While definitions vary, conventional warfare can be understood as warfare between or among two or more roughly symmetrical organized groups (normally states) whose objective is the destruction of enemy forces, while irregular warfare features at least one non-state actor, a materially weaker and often difficult-to-locate opponent who, in operating against the stronger one, seeks not the annihilation of enemy forces (which is not possible) but rather the control of the population. Means and methods will also differ—the use of improvised explosive devices is one of the most prevalent contemporary "strategies of the weak"—but the main distinction lies in the overall objective.

Responding to irregular warfare is arguably more difficult, and at a minimum more complex, than to conventional warfare. Rather than developing principles in this area, for example, Jomini simply advised states to avoid involvement in civil or religious "wars of opinion."[1] But such advice was not particularly tenable in the decades after World War Two and is even less so in the post-Cold War and post-9/11 eras. Strategic thinking as it pertains to irregular warfare will be discussed in Chapter 5. Conventional warfare can also be contrasted with unconventional warfare involving weapons of mass destruction, that is, nuclear, biological or chemical weapons. Strategic thinking with respect to nuclear weapons and other weapons of mass destruction will be discussed in Chapter 7.

This chapter examines strategic thought on conventional landpower. It begins by briefly highlighting the key ideas of Sun Tzu, Liddell Hart, Clausewitz and Jomini.

Their strategic thought, particularly that of Clausewitz but also the others, has been discussed and interpreted in innumerable places; the purpose here is only to outline the parameters of strategic thinking about conventional landpower up until the early post-World War Two period. The chapter goes on to discuss some ideas that emerged in the latter part of the Cold War, notably that of AirLand battle, before examining in greater detail strategic thought on conventional landpower in the post-Cold War era. The first two post-Cold War decades were dominated by stabilization and counterinsurgency missions, for example, in Bosnia, Afghanistan and Iraq (the 2003 Iraq War, along with the 1991 Gulf War in the dying days of the Cold War, being the only truly "conventional" wars). Nonetheless, there have been strategic thinkers who have focused on the conventional use of force. Notable among them are scholars and former US Army officers Lieutenant-Colonel (retired) Andrew Krepinevich, Colonel (retired) Douglas MacGregor and Major-General (retired) Robert Scales. Official vision statements by the Pentagon and the US Army during this period also offer important insights on the use of conventional landpower in the post-Cold War era.

Sun Tzu[2]

Sun Tzu opens his treatise by arguing that war is a matter of vital importance to the state, a matter of life or death, of survival or ruin, and that it therefore must be thoroughly studied. A proponent of an "indirect" approach to warfare, Sun Tzu advised generals to prepare the battlefield using deception and maneuver, with the goal of reducing the amount of warfare as much as possible—and ideally to none at all—in the achievement of one's objectives. "All warfare is based on deception," he argues in his opening chapter, therefore "[w]hen capable, feign incapacity; when active, inactivity; when near, make it appear you are far away; when far away, make it appear you are near. Offer the enemy bait to lure him, feign disorder and strike him. When he concentrates prepare against him; where he is strong, avoid him. Confuse him. Pretend inferiority and encourage his arrogance. Keep him under strain and wear him down." Maneuver, in turn, is an important part of this strategy. To achieve deception, a commander must be able to "make the most devious route the most direct … march by an indirect route and divert the enemy … One able to do this understands the strategy of the direct and indirect."

Sun Tzu did not conceive the object of military action to be the annihilation of the enemy's army or the destruction of his cities and countryside. Rather, the ultimate goal was "to take All-under-Heaven intact"—ideally by "subduing the enemy without battle." "Generally in war the best policy is to take a state intact; to ruin it is inferior to this. To capture the enemy's army is better than to destroy it … For to win a hundred victories in a hundred battles is not the acme of skill. To subdue the enemy without fighting is the acme of skill." Tactically he advised deception and maneuver, while strategically he advised first targeting the enemy's overall approach. "What is of supreme importance in war is to attack the enemy's strategy. Next best is to disrupt his alliances. The next best is to attack his army. The worst policy is to attack his cities. Attack cities only when there is no other alternative." Finally, Sun Tzu drew attention to the importance of moral influences and leadership in war. For effective command, he argued, a general must exhibit qualities of wisdom, sincerity, humanity, courage, and strictness, and this, in turn, would give him the respect necessary for soldiers to follow him into war.

Liddell Hart

Writing in the aftermath of first one and then a second world war, B. H. Liddell Hart was an admirer of Sun Tzu who felt that civilization "might have been spared much of the damage of the world wars" had there been a greater knowledge of Sun Tzu's approach.[3] Liddell Hart's ideas and works are voluminous and centered to significant degree on theoretical development regarding mechanized warfare. What is of most interest here, however, is his refinement at both a strategic and tactical level of Sun Tzu's views with respect to an indirect conventional strategy. Strategically, Liddell Hart argues that the purpose of a military strategy is to diminish as much as possible the likelihood of resistance. A strategist's true aim, he argues, is to seek a strategic situation so advantageous that if this does not produce a decision, its continuation by battle is sure to do so. The approach, he argues, is one that will limit hostilities: "For even if a decisive battle be the goal, the aim of strategy must be to bring about this battle under the most advantageous circumstances. And the more advantageous the circumstances, the less, proportionately, will be the fighting." "The perfection of strategy," he states in words that echo those of Sun Tzu, "would be ... to produce a decision without any serious fighting."[4]

Tactically, diminishing resistance involves exploiting the elements of movement and surprise. For Liddell Hart, movement lies in the physical sphere, while surprise lies in the psychological sphere. The two elements react on one another in that movement generates surprise, and surprise gives impetus to movement. Physically, the approach should be to take the line of least resistance. Unlike Clausewitz, and even more so Jomini (see below), Liddell Hart advises against "the tendency ... to treat war as mainly a matter of concentrating superior force."[5] Superior weight at the decisive point, he argues, rarely suffices unless that point is also weakened morally.

Liddell Hart introduces the term "dislocation," which is created in the physical sphere by a combination of compelling the enemy to change his front, separating his forces, endangering his supplies, and menacing his routes of retreat. In the psychological sphere, dislocation is the result of the impression on the commander's mind of these physical effects. The impression is stronger if the enemy's realization of being at a disadvantage is sudden, and if he is unable to counter the enemy's move. "Psychological dislocation," he argues, "fundamentally springs from this sense of being trapped."[6] For Liddell Hart, only when physical and psychological aspects are combined is the strategy truly an indirect approach, calculated to dislocate the enemy's balance.

Clausewitz[7]

The strategic thought of Sun Tzu and Liddell Hart can be contrasted with that of Carl von Clausewitz. Whereas Sun Tzu and Liddell Hart advocate an indirect conventional strategy, Clausewitz is associated with a direct conventional strategy. He opens his work by arguing that violence is the essence of war. War is an act of force, it involves bloodshed and brutality, and the impulse to destroy the enemy is central to its very idea. "Kindhearted people might of course think there was some ingenious way to disarm or defeat an enemy without too much bloodshed, and might imagine this is the true goal of the art of war. Pleasant as it sounds it is a fallacy that must be exposed."

Warfare's nature involves some important intangible, or subjective, factors. Chance and luck, for example, are a big part of war. Whereas Sun Tzu talks about calculation,

Clausewitz argues that in "the whole range of human activities war most closely resembles a game of cards." So too are the inaccuracies of intelligence. "Many intelligence reports in war are contradictory," Clausewitz notes, "even more are false, and most are uncertain." Although Clausewitz did not use the term, the inadequacies and inaccuracies of intelligence are today referred to as the "fog" of war. To this must be added Clausewitz's famous concept of "friction" in war. The conduct of war, he argues, resembles the workings of an intricate machine with many parts, each everywhere in contact with one another, leading to friction and chance. As a result, outcomes cannot be predicted or measured, and combinations that are easily planned on paper can be executed only with great effort. "Friction," he argues, "is the force that makes the apparently easy so difficult ... [It] more or less corresponds to the factors that distinguish real war from the war on paper."

For Clausewitz, war demands the maximum use of force to work directly against the powers of the enemy's resistance and ultimately disarm him. But later on he introduces the idea of proportionality in warfare, arguing that the scale of the political demands on either side should determine the degree of force to be used. Belligerents should "act on the principle of using no greater force, and setting himself no greater military aim, than would be sufficient for the achievement of his political purpose." It follows, therefore, that "[n]o one starts a war—or rather, no one in his senses ought to do so—without first being clear in his mind what he intends to achieve by that war." In his view "the political object is the goal, war is the means of reaching it, and means can never be considered in isolation from purpose." The logic leads directly to Clausewitz's best-known phrase, that war is simply a continuation of politics, with the addition of other means.

Also at the strategic level, Clausewitz talks about warfare as comprising a "trinity" of interacting forces made up of the people, the commander and his army, and the government. He explains them as follows: first, there is the primordial violence, hatred, and enmity among the people. These are the blind natural forces that must already be inherent in the people; second, there is the courage and talent of the commander of the army, his creative spirit, and the chance and probability that surrounds him; third, there is the subordination of war to the government's political aims and the use of war as a political instrument. These three elements exist in a shifting relationship with one another and they affect the progress of war.

When it comes to the actual conduct of war, Clausewitz identifies "two basic principles that underlie all strategic planning": utmost concentration and utmost speed. For Clausewitz, secondary and subsidiary theaters do not matter. The main decision always comes on the main battlefield and any unnecessary expenditure of time, every unnecessary detour, is a waste of strength. "Endless discussions about moving left or right, about doing this or that"—in short, about maneuver—"serve no practical purpose." As for the object of this concentration and speed, Clausewitz calls attention to the "centre of gravity" in warfare—the enemy's "hub of all power and movement, on which all depends." In order to be successful in battle one must identify and direct all energies against the enemy's center of gravity. Based on his experience, Clausewitz believed the center of gravity was most often the enemy's army, then his capital, and then his allies. In modern times we can find the center of gravity in other areas. For example, during the Vietnam War America's center of gravity was found in the domestic population and on university campuses.

Finally, Clausewitz developed the concept of "military genius." By this he meant qualities of mind and temperament that are necessary in a military leader, and that must be held in combination. They include courage in the face of personal danger, a determination that can overcome doubt, and a certain presence of mind. In contrast to Sun Tzu, Clausewitz's overall emphasis is on simplicity and directness, rather than maneuver and calculation.

Jomini[8]

Against the largely philosophical approach of Clausewitz, Jomini's strategic thought is more scientific, almost mathematical, in nature. Influenced by the eighteenth century's Age of Enlightenment, where science and reason were predominant, Jomini sought to identify certain principles that, if followed, would most likely lead to success in war. Although he looked at many campaigns, his most important case study was the Napoleonic Wars, which he witnessed at first hand and which indicated to him some important maxims. In several theoretical works over the years, culminating in the *Summary of the Art of War*, published in 1838 (a few years after Clausewitz's *On War*), Jomini analyzed and effectively codified the Napoleonic way of war.

Jomini believed that the practice of warfare could be reduced to a general set of rules, more or less applicable to all battles. "There exists a small number of fundamental principles of war," he argued in the *Summary*, "which [can] not be deviated from without danger, and the application of which, on the contrary, has been in almost all time crowned with success." First, like Clausewitz, Jomini stressed the principle of the concentration of force. This idea he elaborated with the subordinate maxim that for success in war it was important to throw the mass of one's forces on the successively decisive points of the battlefield in the theater of war and to do so "at the proper time and with ample energy." Jomini is silent on civil wars, where "the enemy is everywhere and yet nowhere to be seen," making it difficult to identify "decisive points."[9]

Second, for an army to be in a position to mass forces at the decisive points it must position itself along the "interior lines of operations." Jomini argued that a friendly force should seek to separate an enemy army into two sides, rendering it weaker than if it were united. Situated in the middle—that is, operating along the "interior" lines—the friendly force can then strike at the heart of first one enemy component and then the other, defeating each in turn. This he had observed as being Napoleon's approach in the 1790s. "If *the art of war* consists in bringing into action upon the decisive point of the theatre of operations the greatest possible force," Jomini sums up, "the choice of the line of operations (as the primary means of attaining this end) may be fundamental in devising a good plan for a campaign."

Unlike Clausewitz, Jomini was able to step outside his predominate area of experience, land warfare, also contributing strategic thought on the maritime dimension of warfare. He argues, for example, that control of the sea is important in determining the outcome of war. "If the people possess a long stretch of coast and are masters of the sea, or in alliance with a power which controls it, their power of resistance is quintupled." In his own work, Alfred Thayer Mahan was influenced by Jomini's strategic thought, including the principle of "interior lines" and the importance of lines of communication, as well as the concentration of naval force as a maritime counterpart to Jomini's concentration of force. Finally, the Swiss made a notable contribution to amphibious warfare theory. Notes one observer, Jomini's general rules for the conduct of amphibious operations, including such things as deception and the expeditious seizure of necessary points, remained relevant into the post-World War Two period.

Conventional strategic thought during the Cold War

Strategic thought on the use of conventional landpower during the Cold War centered in the early years on how land warfare would operate in conjunction with nuclear weapons, and later as a first step in an escalation of warfare that would, hopefully, stop short of all-out nuclear war, a strategy known as flexible response. There was also significant strategic thinking about counterinsurgency, low-intensity conflict, and wars of liberation, notably by Mao Tse-tung, founder of the People's Republic of China and French scholar David Galula (see Chapter 5). What is of interest here is new ideas with respect to conventional landpower that emerged toward the end of the Cold War period. The notion of "AirLand battle," especially, was a forerunner to contemporary strategic thought on the employment of conventional landpower.

In their 1993 book, *War and Anti-War*, Alvin and Heidi Toffler document the genesis, promotion, and eventual institutionalization of AirLand battle, a concept that can be seen as a precursor to post-Cold War strategic thought encompassing long-range precision strike and jointness in warfare. Struggling to address the problem of NATO's vastly outnumbered ground forces as compared to the Soviet Union, and having previously been sent to investigate Israel's dramatic victory over Syria's much larger forces on the Golan Heights in the 1973 Yom Kippur War, US General Donn Starry, commander of the US Army in Germany in the mid-1970s and later commander of US Training and Doctrine Command (TRADOC), set out to promote—even force—a complete rethink of the role of mass in US Army doctrine. To address the waves of Soviet forces that were expected to form in echelons and march through the Fulda Gap in Germany, Starry emphasized moving away from combat at the "front," as it had existed since Napoleon, and instead striking over the heads of the first wave, far into the battle zone. Deep strikes would be used to "knock out the adversary's command centers, logistic lines, communications links, and air defenses," and prevent "subsequent echelons from reaching the scene of the battle," an approach that would "require the closest integration of air and ground forces."[10] AirLand Battle, later updated as AirLand Operations to reflect a new emphasis on preventing rear echelons from even forming, became US Army official doctrine in August 1991, just months before the Soviet Union disintegrated.

More recent theoretical work on AirLand Battle has been done by the US Air Force, with new concepts for AirLand Battle placing greater emphasis on the air component than the original as expressed by Starry. The US Army has been restructured into more numerous, smaller units called Brigade Combat Teams (see below), many of which—because they rely on precision airpower—are built around platforms that are lighter and more mobile, but offer less protection than the heavy tanks of yesterday. Similar patterns are underway in all Western nations. In a future conventional war ground forces could therefore find themselves facing a numerically superior and possibly heavier foe. In this new environment, contemporary AirLand theorists argue, "the innovative application of airpower will be central to success."[11] The case is made that airpower should be used not just in close air support of ground forces and air interdiction against enemy lines of supply and communication, but also to strike enemy ground forces directly. The use of airpower in these scenarios is discussed in Chapter 3.

Strategic thought since the end of the Cold War

Although futurists, the Tofflers were two of the first thinkers to put forward ideas on the nature of conventional landpower in the post-Cold War era. In line with the increased precision of a knowledge-based economy, they argued, there would be a "de-massification" of warfare—a reversal of the massed warfare trend that had started more than two centuries before with the Industrial Revolution and the Napoleonic Wars. Against the divisional structure established by Napoleon, there would be smaller-scale units, featuring more flexible formations armed with more firepower. "[T]he day is fast approaching," the Tofflers argued, "when a capital-intensive Third Wave brigade of 4,000–5,000 troops may be able to do what it took a full-size division [of about 15,000 troops] to do in the past."[12] The troops themselves would have to be better educated and more technically expert than ever before as the changing nature of war placed a growing premium on intellectual capacity.

Andrew Krepinevich

For more detailed insight in this early period on the nature of conventional land warfare we can look to strategic thinking by Andrew Krepinevich. A former US Army officer who is now director of the Center for Strategic and Budgetary Assessments, Krepinevich's range of scholarly work covers both conventional and irregular (counterinsurgency) warfare. What is notable here is his work on the "Military Technical Revolution" or MTR, an early term that later formed the core of 1990s thinking about a "Revolution in Military Affairs" or RMA (see Chapter 4).

In a seminal assessment of the MTR for the Pentagon's Office of Net Assessment, written in 1992 but released publicly in 2002, Krepinevich made a number of observations that pertained to or were relevant to landpower. Ground forces, he argued, would likely be centered on highly mobile formations of extended line-of-sight systems—armored forces and helicopters, rather than heavy tanks. These forces, in turn, would be less likely than in the past to "close with" and destroy the enemy on a traditional front. In a conflict between peer competitors, extended range strikes by air and sea-based assets would become an increasingly decisive element in combat, and there would be a progressive blurring of the distinction between, and increasing fusion of, air, land, and maritime operations. Operations would, in other words, be increasingly "joint" in nature—meaning involving all three (or in America's case, four) services—as air- and seapower are brought to bear in support of land-power. Finally, there would be a continuing trend toward simultaneous, *vice* sequential, military operations,[13] a concept that would later be characterized as "dispersed" operations.

Krepinevich's later work on conventional landpower elaborated on all of these ideas. At the end of the 1990s he highlighted the need for ground forces to place greater emphasis on mobility, physical dispersion of forces, and extended-range precision-strike systems. Writing in the aftermath of the 2003 Iraq War, he argued that the Army's ability to develop distributed, networked forces would be critical to its future dominance. "[N]ew information systems offer the prospect of an Army that can violate the principle of mass to disperse its forces … mov[ing] the Army beyond the heavy, mechanical air-land era of warfare that began with the blitzkrieg, enabling the Expeditionary Army."[14] And at the end of the millennium's first decade he stressed that high-end conventional warfare of the future would require a combined-arms battle network (i.e. armored, artillery, and infantry forces digitally linked together) that, critically, was also jointly networked with the air and sea services.

Douglas Macgregor

The scholarly work of Douglas Macgregor, a former US Army Colonel who fought in the 1991 Gulf War and is now a fellow with the Center for Defense Information, reflects several of these ideas, and also contributes new elements. Along the lines of "de-massification," for example, Macgregor argued in an early post-Cold War article that "smaller combined-arms formations with advanced indirect and direct-fire weapons systems [will] dominate larger areas than in the past."[15] Explicitly questioning "whether the division structure is the appropriate combat formation" of the future warfighting environment, in his ground-breaking 1997 book, *Breaking the Phalax*, Macgregor gave a detailed articulation of how "de-massified" ground forces should be organized.[16] Rather than relying on the "cumbersome mobilization and massed firepower arrangements of the Cold War," he argued, the US Army should be reorganized into mobile combat groups rendered "distinctly more effective by cooperation with American airpower and unchallenged American control of the sea."[17] The effect, controversial at the time, would be to create a warfighting organization that was both smaller in size and more numerous in quantity than the existing division organizations but, with the advantages of new technologies that allowed for sensing and engaging the enemy at long ranges, could dominate a much larger area.[18] In a follow-on work, *Transformation under Fire* (2003), he elaborated that the units themselves should be made up of smaller, self-contained units, specialized modules that could be integrated as necessary into joint forces.

Jointness among the services was clearly central to Macgregor's vision, but he also went further. Not only would the traditional distinction between ground, sea, and air campaigns appear increasingly anachronistic, as Krepinevich would have it, but so too would the familiar conceptual framework of the three levels of war—strategic, operational, and tactical. In the future, Macgregor argued, technology would have the effect of altering time and space on the battlefield such that the three levels of war "will merge ... into a single new structure for the integration of complex air-land-sea combat operations."[19]

US military visions

These themes and others could be found in several official United States military documents of the late 1990s and early 2000s. Indeed, taken together, the Pentagon's *Joint Vision 2010* of 1996, the US *Army Vision* of 1999, and the US Army's subsequent White Paper on *Concepts for the Objective Force* provide perhaps the most comprehensive elaboration of strategic thought on landpower during this period. Although *Joint Vision 2010* gave guidance to all four US military services—Army, Navy, Air Force and Marine Corps—many of its aspects were especially relevant to operations on land.

One characteristic of warfare identified in these documents is that ground-force operations would shift from being linear to nonlinear in nature, with units—much more mobile than in the past—being dispersed throughout the battlefield. "Increased dispersion and mobility will be possible offensively," *Joint Vision 2010* argued, "because each platform or individual warfighter carries higher lethality and greater reach."[20] Combining land with maritime and air forces would allow for still greater agility and a more dispersed footprint. The *Army Vision*, too, stressed that modern technologies, including inputs from manned and unmanned (satellites and unmanned aerial vehicles) sensors would enable combat organizations to synchronize highly lethal activity from dispersed locations. *Concepts for the Objective Force* speaks of nonlinear operations as being "distributed" in time, space, and purpose, and increasingly joint in nature.[21] According to the Concept, operations would be decentralized and "non-contiguous," with forces distributed across the battlefield and employed simultaneously. In contrast to the "phased, attrition-based, linear operations of the past" that "rolled up" enemy forces sequentially, the approach would be one of "exposing the entire enemy force to air/ground attack."[22]

In the new construct massed effects would be achieved with massed firepower from dispersed forces, rather than from massed forces. Whereas Jomini advised throwing the mass of one's forces on the decisive points of the battlefield at the proper time and with ample energy, *Joint Vision 2010* foresaw the US military being "increasingly able to accomplish the effects of mass—the necessary concentration of combat power at the decisive time and place—with less need to mass forces physically."[23] The notion of creating "mass effects without massing forces" is reiterated in *Concepts for the Objective Force*, which, notably, stated that de-massification would come in the form of creating smaller but more capable formations.[24] Thus was set in train a process that culminated in the US Army transforming, by the early 2010s, from a 10-division entity to an "Objective Force" made up of 45 brigade combat teams as the basic organizational unit.

Joint Vision 2010 also stated that new technologies would allow for increased capability at lower echelons—capabilities that had previously been reserved for more senior commanders at the operational or strategic level. *Concepts for the Objective Force* elaborated the point made earlier by Macgregor, that new sensor and command-and-control technologies were providing "common situational understanding [to all levels]," thereby "compressing the strategic, operational and tactical echelons" and "increasing the importance of the tactical level of war to strategic outcomes."[25]

Deployability is a further characteristic of land forces, highlighted especially in the army documents. As stated in the *Army Vision*'s accompanying briefing, future ground forces would be just as "deployable" as light forces, without jeopardizing any lethality. "As technology allows, we will begin to erase the distinctions between heavy and light forces."[26] The notion of being "rapidly deployable," as expressed by *Concepts for the Objective Force*,[27] is captured in another familiar term of the era, that of having ground forces that are "expeditionary" in nature. The idea reflects the view that it is not enough for ground forces to be mobile, agile, and versatile *in* theater; ground forces also have to be able to get *to* theater on relatively short notice, within days or weeks.

A unique contribution of *Joint Vision 2010* is its call for "full spectrum dominance." The US military should strive to be a dominant force not only in traditional, conventional landpower operations against a peer competitor, it argued, but across the "full range of military operations from humanitarian assistance, through peace operations, up to and into the highest intensity conflict."[28] The range of operations, *Joint Vision 2020* later elaborated, included major theater war, regional conflict, and smaller-scale contingencies, as well as those "ambiguous situations residing between peace and war" such as peacekeeping, peace enforcement, and humanitarian relief.[29] The implications of this ambition are discussed in Chapter 5 as part of Krepinevich's strategic thought on irregular warfare.

While these documents identified the necessity of broadening the focus of US military operations—an important departure from previous defense statements—they did little to indicate an accompanying broader range of capabilities. The logical disconnect is apparent in the statement that "the overarching focus of this vision [*Joint Vision 2020*] is full spectrum dominance—achieved through dominant maneuver [and] precision engagement"—concepts of little relevance to, for example, humanitarian assistance.[30] Guidance is limited to the *Army Vision*'s call for "agile" forces that have "the mental and physical agility to ... move forces from stability and support operations to war-fighting and back again."[31] Similarly, *Concepts for the Objective Force* stresses the need for "mentally and physically agile" forces, "able to transition rapidly across the spectrum of operations."[32]

Overall, the picture of landpower that emerged from US joint and Army vision statements of this period was one of a mixture of the clever maneuvering of Sun Tzu with the more visceral warfare of Clausewitz. The hallmarks of future ground force operations, argued *Concepts for the Objective Force*, would be "maneuvering to positions of advantage; engaging enemy forces beyond the range of their weapons; [and] destroying them with precision fires and maneuver."[33] But warfare remains "brutal" in nature and warfare from afar may not be enough. In those situations, "the only way to guarantee victory is to put our boots on the ground ... and destroy him in his sanctuary."[34]

Robert Scales

In a precursor of things to come, *Joint Vision 2010* was careful to caution that many military missions would continue to "require occupation of the ground and intensive physical presence."[35] Historian and military strategist Major-General Robert Scales was one high-ranking army officer who stressed at the time that warfare in the post-Cold War era, as in all periods in history, would continue to require "boots on the ground." As commandant of the US Army War College he wrote, in a 1997 issue of *Parameters*, of concerns about recent claims that technology and advanced precision weaponry could be used in place of combat forces. As he noted, the debate about force size and structure was quintessentially one about the future nature of war. Predictions that new technologies could permit friendly forces to defeat enemies from afar "with no need to risk lives in the maelstrom of land combat" did not account for the fact that conventional warfare against states would still center on the control of territory, and that defeating terrorist and non-state actors would demand the control of populations— both landpower-intensive tasks. Scales agreed that future war would be "non-linear" in nature, but "non-linear" he equates to "inherently chaotic," the game of chance identified by Clausewitz in which the character of war changes in ways that cannot be predicted.[36]

Scales subsequently refined his views on the nature and conduct of war in two scholarly works. *Yellow Smoke: The Future of Land Warfare for America's Military* (2003) was completed in the wake of the Afghanistan War of 2001–2, while *The Iraq War* (2003) with Williamson Murray was one of the first accounts of that conflict. Although the nature of war remained unchanged, Scales conceded that technology was impacting on the character of conventional landpower such that it resembled the distributed, nonlinear attributes identified by earlier strategic thinkers. Wargaming revealed the dramatic effect of giving soldiers the ability to see all friendly forces and most enemy forces, that is, of giving them "dominant situational awareness." As Scales recollected: "Freed from the need to maintain visual contact, the digitized brigade footprint expanded by a factor of four or more ... Linear formations began to break apart ... The ability to see the enemy from greater distances allowed the more clever commanders to engage the enemy at greater distances. The close fight was becoming less close."[37]

Meanwhile, precision technology was having the effect of increasing tempo and speed on the battlefield because platforms did not have to be as weighted down with ammunition as was previously the case.

For Scales, the 2003 Iraq War (see Box 2.1) highlighted a number of important signposts about conventional landpower, many of which echoed early strategic thinking. The fighting revealed a greater degree of interdependence between air and land forces, that is, jointness, than had ever previously been achieved; it suggested the need for smaller, brigade-sized units that could fight independently; it "reinforced the observation that the modern battlefield continues to empty and expand"; it approached "simultaneity" in operations to give the Iraqi high command the perception it was under attack from everywhere; and it pointed to the imperative of mobility and speed on the battlefield, as well as to the need for forces to be "agile" in the sense of adapting quickly to changing circumstances. At the same time, the war underscored that precision in weapons was not enough to ensure precision of effects. As Scales reminds us in his earlier work, in this new era of "firepower-centered warfare" there will still be limitations in achieving stand-off massed effects—limitations that in the end cannot obviate the true nature of war. "[N]o matter how efficient the network, coordinating the firepower from many dispersed locations will involve friction, confusion, and delay."[38] Indeed, the Iraq experience was such that advanced technologies, on occasion, actually exacerbated or intensified friction on the battlefield.

Box 2.1 The 2003 Iraq War

- The 2003 Iraq War demonstrated many themes about the conduct of conventional land war that have been identified by today's strategic thinkers.
- The war began at nightfall on March 20, 2003 when US forces crossed the border from Kuwait to strike Iraqi observation posts. Events moved quickly and within 18 hours the US Army's 3rd infantry division had moved almost 60,000 troops to within 100 miles of Bagdad, an unprecedented distance for such a large force.
- The division was divided up into three smaller brigade combat teams, each a highly mobile self-contained close combat unit that was able to command as much ground as could an entire division during the Cold War. The overall size of Coalition ground forces in the Iraq War was also substantially smaller, an attribute made possible by the radically increased precision and lethality of weapons.
- Contrary to strategic thinking, heavy tanks still played a key role in the conflict, but they were backed up by numerous tank-killer helicopters armed with precision-guided munitions, along with transport helicopters capable of moving combat soldiers hundreds of miles to strike deep within enemy territory. A quintessentially "joint" operation, the Iraq War was characterized by significant Coalition air support to ground forces. The war also highlighted an unprecedented role for special operations forces, and cooperation between these forces and conventional ground forces.
- The 2003 Iraq War was not without its mishaps; at times, much-vaunted advanced situational awareness technology failed to reveal the true size of an

Iraqi force, or when US commanders did have up-to-date information they could not transmit it quickly enough to front-line troops.

- Overall, the war was swift, agile, decisive, and employed overpowering technology in many dispersed locations at once—attributes that exemplified much of the strategic thinking about contemporary conventional landpower. Launched with the goal of regime change, the Iraq War itself ended in April 2003 when Bagdad fell to Coalition hands.
- With the fall of the regime a whole new phase of low-level conflict emerged, one that required the application of strategic thought on irregular warfare.

Perhaps the most notable aspect of Scales's strategic thought is his emphasis on the indirect, intellectual attributes of the contemporary warfighter. In contrast to the direct, action-oriented leadership of yesterday, he argues, the nature of warfare today is such that it requires "indirect leadership," that is, "the ability to think in real time and influence the battlefield by intent rather than directly by touch."[39] The current military system, he laments, tends to promote the promising tactician, the "go-to, can-do" types who can get things done, when what is needed is officers who understand the complexities of war.[40] The requirement is to imbue soldiers at lower and lower levels with an understanding of the art of war at the strategic level, thereby inculcating mental agility and the ability to be creative. "More than ever war is a thinking man's game. Wars ... are won as much by creating alliances ... reading intentions, building trust, converting opinions and managing perceptions" as by firepower and technology.[41] Thus, where Clausewitz spoke of genius in war and Sun Tzu spoke of the qualities for effective command as they pertained to generals, today these attributes—as the Tofflers would have predicted—must be inculcated even among junior and non-commissioned officers.

Conclusion

In the first two decades after the end of the Cold War scholarly minded practitioners like Andrew Krepinevich, Douglas Macgregor and Robert Scales undertook significant strategic thinking on the use of conventional landpower. Notable contributions were also made by the Pentagon and the US Army in official government documents. Taken together, post-Cold War strategic thought on landpower in conventional war reveals a theory of landpower that might contain the following tenets: conventional landpower is best employed using smaller, more mobile units that are dispersed on the battlefield and linked together through information technology; conventional land battles will feature simultaneous and synchronized operations that are nonlinear in nature; massed effects can be achieved using information and precision technologies, thereby reducing the footprint (and therefore vulnerability) of ground forces; conventional ground war is a joint endeavor with land forces closely linked to other elements of the joint force; advanced technologies dramatically improve the land force commander's ability to "see over the next hill," but they cannot eliminate the fog and friction of war; and decision making will be pushed to lower echelons, increasing the importance of a strategic understanding of warfare at the junior and non-commissioned officer level.

The nature of the actual conflicts that have taken place in the post-Cold War, and especially post-9/11, eras is such that strategic thinking about landpower has focused significantly on irregular warfare and counterinsurgency. Liddell Hart had stressed the importance of weakening the enemy morally and warned against the tendency of treating war as merely a matter of concentrating superior force; many of these lessons had to be relearned in the course of post-9/11 counterinsurgency operations. General David Petraeus, author jointly with General James Mattis of the US military's new counterinsurgency doctrine, is a person whom Scales identifies as the "archetype strategic warrior,"[42] that is, one who embodies the "can do" attitude appropriate for conventional warfare with the subtle, strategic, multifaceted approach necessary for the chaotic environment of unconventional, irregular warfare. His ideas and those of others on irregular warfare are examined in Chapter 5. But first we turn to strategic thought on the use of airpower.

Notes

1 John Shy, "Jomini," in Peter Paret, ed., *Makers of Modern Strategy from Machiavelli to the Nuclear Age* (Princeton, NJ: Princeton University Press, 1986), 170–71.
2 References in this section are taken from Sun Tzu, *The Art of War*, trans. Samuel B. Griffiths (New York: Oxford University Press, 1963), 66–69, 77–79, 102.
3 Ibid., v.
4 B. H. Liddell Hart, *Strategy: The Indirect Approach* (London: Faber and Faber Limited, 1954), 338–39.
5 Ibid., 342.
6 Ibid., 340.
7 References in this section are taken from Carl von Clausewitz, *On War*, ed. Michael Howard and Peter Paret (Princeton, NJ: Princeton University Press, 1976), 75, 86–87, 89, 100–103, 117, 119–21, 579, 585, 595, 605, 617 and 624.
8 References in this section are taken from Antoine Henri Jomini, *The Art of War*, ed. J. D. Hittle (Harrisburg, PA: Military Service Publishing Company, 1947), 43, 50, 67, 79 and 81.
9 J. Mohan Malik, "The Evolution of Strategic Thought," in Craig A. Snyder, ed., *Contemporary Security and Strategy* (New York: Routledge, 1999), 23–24.
10 Alvin Toffler and Heidi Toffler, *War and Anti-war* (New York: Warner Books, 1973), 60.
11 Ellwood P. Hinman IV, "Counterair and Counterland Concepts for the 21st Century," *Joint Force Quarterly* 48, 1st quarter (2008), 91.
12 Toffler and Toffler, *War and Anti-war*, 83, 89.
13 Andrew F. Krepinevich, *The Military Technical Revolution: A Preliminary Assessment* (Washington, DC: Center for Strategic and Budgetary Asssessments, 2002), 17, 20 and 26.
14 Andrew F. Krepinevich, *Transforming the Legions: The Army and the Future of Land Warfare* (Washington, DC: Center for Strategic and Budgetary Assessments, 2004), 12.
15 Douglas A. Macgregor, "Future Battle: The Merging Levels of War," *Parameters* (Winter 1992–93), 41.
16 Douglas A. Macgregor, *"Breaking the Phalanx": A New Design for Landpower in the 21st Century* (Westport, CT: Praeger, 1997), 62.
17 Ibid., 4.
18 Ibid., 74.
19 Macgregor, "Future Battle," 33.
20 US Joint Chiefs of Staff, "Joint Vision 2010: America's Military Preparing for Tomorrow," *Joint Force Quarterly* (Summer 1996), 40.
21 US Army, *Concepts for the Objective Force*, White Paper (Washington, DC: US Army, November 2001), 3.
22 Ibid., 13.
23 US Joint Chiefs of Staff, "Joint Vision 2010," 42.
24 US Army, *Concepts for the Objective Force*, 9 and 13.
25 Ibid., 4.
26 US Army, *The Army Vision Briefing*, www.army.mil/armyvision/armyvis.htm accessed January 30, 2001, no longer available on web.

27　United States Army, *Concepts for the Objective Force*, 1
28　US Joint Chiefs of Staff, "Joint Vision 2010," 46.
29　US Joint Chiefs of Staff, *Joint Vision 2020* (Washington, DC: Joint Chiefs of Staff, 2000), 3.
30　Ibid.
31　US Army, *The Army Vision Briefing*.
32　US Army, *Concepts for the Objective Force*, 1, 4.
33　Ibid., v.
34　Ibid.
35　US Joint Chiefs of Staff, "Joint Vision 2010," 40.
36　Paul van Riper and Robert H. Scales, Jr., "Preparing for War in the 21st Century," *Parameters* (Autumn 1997).
37　Robert H. Scales, Jr., *Yellow Smoke: The Future of Land Warfare for America's Military* (Lanham, MD: Rowman & Littlefield Publishers, Inc., 2003), 10.
38　Scales, *Yellow Smoke*, 3, 23.
39　Ibid., 13.
40　Robert H. Scales, Jr., "Return of the Jedi," *Armed Forces Journal* (October 2009).
41　Robert H. Scales, "The Second Learning Revolution," in Anthony D. McIvor, ed., *Rethinking the Principles of War* (Annapolis, MD: Naval Institute Press, 2005), 43.
42　Scales, "Return."

Further reading

Clausewitz, Carl Von. *On War*, ed. Michael Howard and Peter Paret (Princeton, NJ: Princeton University Press, 1976), books 1 & 8.
Gordon, Michael R. and Bernard E. Trainor. *Cobra II: The Inside Story of the Invasion and Occupation of Iraq* (New York: Pantheon Books, 2006).
Jomini, Antoine Henri. *The Art of War*, ed. J. D. Hittle (Harrisburg, PA: Military Service Publishing Company, 1947).
Krepinevich, Andrew F. *Transforming the Legions: The Army and the Future of Land Warfare* (Washington, DC: Center for Strategic and Budgetary Assessments, 2004).
Liddell Hart, B. H. *Strategy: The Indirect Approach* (London: Faber and Faber Limited, 1954).
Macgregor, Douglas A. *"Breaking the Phalanx": A New Design for Landpower in the 21st Century* (Westport, CT: Praeger, 1997).
——. *Transformation Under Fire: Revolutionizing how America Fights* (Westport, CT: Praeger Publishers, 2003).
Murray, Williamson and Robert H. Scales, Jr. *The Iraq War: A Military History* (Cambridge, MA: Harvard University Press, 2003).
Scales, Robert H., Jr. *Yellow Smoke: The Future of Land Warfare for America's Military* (Lanham, MD: Rowman & Littlefield Publishers, Inc., 2003).
Sun Tzu. *The Art of War*, trans. Samuel B. Griffiths (New York: Oxford University Press, 1963).
Toffler, Alvin and Heidi Toffler. *War and Anti-war* (New York: Warner Books, 1973).
United States Joint Chiefs of Staff. *Joint Vision 2010* (Washington, DC: Department of Defense, 1996).

3   Airpower

Not much more than a century old, airpower and airpower theory have already provided a compelling and varied narrative. The emergence of a third dimension to warfare in the first decades of the twentieth century sparked some theorizing as to the role, promise, and potential of airpower in warfare. The theorists included American General William Mitchell and Russian air theorist Alexander de Seversky, but the name that is most associated with early airpower theory is Italian General Guilio Douhet. His was a grand vision of airpower as being revolutionary in nature, and many of his key tenets were proven wrong by the events of World War Two. There followed four decades of Cold War during which conventional airpower theory received relatively little attention, dominated as the era was by nuclear strategy. But beginning with the 1991 Gulf War, which seemingly vindicated some of Douhet's ideas, the post-Cold War period's first two decades contained numerous conventional airpower cases and examples. This resulted in a significant degree of strategic thinking about the role and utility of airpower.

This chapter examines contemporary strategic thought in the air dimension. It begins by highlighting the key ideas of Guilio Douhet, and touches on various critiques of his thinking. It then examines new ideas about airpower, some of which can be viewed through the prism of Douhet's framework and many of which are substantively new. Notable post-Cold War airpower theorists, all civilian scholars but some with military backgrounds, include Stephen Biddle, James Corum, Benjamin Lambeth and Robert Pape, among others. The chapter concludes with some thoughts on the components of contemporary airpower theory.

Guilio Douhet

A general in the Italian army in the 1920s,[1] Guilio Douhet was the earliest and arguably history's most ardent proponent of what may be called the "promise" of airpower. This is the idea that wars can be won by airpower alone, or almost so, eliminating or substantially reducing the need to send in soldiers (or sailors), thus making warfare almost bloodless from the perspective of the predominant airpower. Douhet's views were premised on the strongly held belief that the airplane as a military instrument was qualitatively new, rendering obsolete or at least substantially less important old modes of warfare based on land or at sea. His reasoning was simple: while armies had to contend with the uneven configuration of the earth, and navies were bound by coastlines, airplanes had "complete freedom of action and direction ... Nothing a man can do on the surface of the earth can interfere with a plane moving freely in flight ... All the influences which have conditioned and characterised warfare from the beginning are powerless to affect aerial action."[2] From the beginning this perspective had its critiques, notably from Douhet's own superiors in the Italian army. His ideas thus set in train "the fundamental debate, never resolved, of whether airpower is unique and revolutionary, or whether it is just another arrow in a soldier's or sailor's quiver."[3]

Douhet was the author of many works on airpower, but the volume for which he is best remembered is *Command of the Air*, first published in 1921, expanded in 1927, and later translated into several languages. The book sets forth what may be called the "Douhet model" of warfare, with several key tenets. The first, reflected in the title of the book, is that victory in warfare absolutely depends on achieving "command of the air," what today we would call "air supremacy."[4] For Douhet, command of the air meant "to be in a position to prevent the enemy from flying while retaining the ability to fly oneself."[5] Douhet spoke in absolute terms, arguing that those with command of the air would enjoy "complete protection of one's own country," while those without could be subject to "offensive power so great it defies human imagination."[6] A second tenet centered on how a nation should go about achieving command of the air. Although he devotes some space to aerial combat, Douhet stressed that an enemy air force should be dealt with primarily by destroying it while it was still on the ground, and by targeting the industries and factories from which the air force would get its materials.

But military forces and installations were not where Douhet saw a nation's center of gravity. Rather, it lay in the population, and this led to a third and perhaps most controversial tenet of his thought. Douhet was the first to argue that the target of overwhelming offensive airpower should be centers of population. The fundamental premise and resulting logic train behind this view was that airpower was a military instrument of such a qualitatively new—and terrifying—character that its utilization would create panic among the population, have a devastating impact on civilian morale, lead to the population's uprising against the government, and thereby bring about the enemy's capitulation and an end to the war even, perhaps, before the army and navy had time to mobilize. He drew no distinction between soldiers and civilians, arguing that in the age of aerial offensives, all citizens become combatants. The attacks themselves should be mass attacks, the use of overwhelming force as opposed to individual strikes, and they should be against large area targets, including industrial, commercial, and civilian sites, using explosive, incendiary, and (remarkably) poison gas bombs. In Douhet's view, bombing accuracy was not a concern because "if targets were so small as to require high accuracy, then they were probably not worthwhile targets."[7]

Douhet's contemporary, William Mitchell, a general in the US Air Service, shared Douhet's belief in paralyzing a nation through command of the air and the use of airpower against economic and industrial sites. "To gain a lasting victory in war, the hostile nation's power to make war must be destroyed," he argued in his 1925 book *Winged Defense*; "this means the manufactories, the means of communication, the food products, even the farms, the fuel and oil and the places where people live and carry on their daily lives."[8] In addition, unlike Douhet, Mitchell continued to believe in the value of targeting an enemy's surface forces. His strategic thought included the importance of attacking the enemy's most important ground positions, menacing his airplanes on the ground, and striking his sea-craft. Today, the use of airpower against fixed military, industrial, or civilian targets in and near political and economic centers is known as strategic bombing, while the use of airpower against military forces, including supply lines and fielded forces, is known as theater air attack.

Douhet thus presents command of the air as *the* requirement for guaranteeing a nation's security: "*In order to assure an adequate national defense, it is necessary—and sufficient—to be in a position in case of war to conquer command of the air*" (emphasis in original).[9] In his analysis he was not unlike Mahan, arguing that whoever controls a particular dimension of warfare, sea or air, will surely triumph. At a time when air forces were a component of the army, Douhet was an adamant advocate of an Independent Air Force, which would significantly increase in importance, just as the navy and army would proportionately decrease in importance. To the extent that surface forces had a role, it would be a defensive one, designed to hold a front and prevent an enemy force from seizing one's own air force establishments. Thus a final tenet of the Douhet model was that not only institutionally but also as an actor on the battlefield, airpower should operate independently of the other dimensions of warfare. Douhet argued strongly against "auxiliary aviation," defined as "that mass of air power which facilitates or integrates land and sea actions"[10]—what today we might call joint warfare. In his view, the strength of airpower lay in the strategic dimension and not in the support of surface forces. Auxiliary aviation, he argued, was "worthless, superfluous, harmful" because it did not contribute to command of the air.[11]

Much of what Douhet argued was subsequently proven wrong by the character of World War Two. The advent of radar removed the freedom of action and direction of a plane moving freely in flight that Douhet had spoken of (in fact, ground-based artillery had done so even earlier); air forces destroyed one another largely in the air; no power submitted to using poison gas bombs; victory required far more than command of the air and the use of air forces; and over time precision in airpower has become one of its most useful attributes. Perhaps most glaringly, the German strikes on London civilians demonstrated the degree to which Douhet had underestimated the toughness with which civilians will endure bombardment, and overestimated the degree to which aerial strikes would create panic. Nonetheless, Douhet's strategic thought is an important starting-point in examining contemporary theory on the role and value of airpower because it created categories of debate and areas of focus that have endured into the contemporary age and that have framed much of the theorizing about airpower in the post-Cold War era.

The first post-Cold War decade

The first decade of the post-Cold War era started and ended with conflicts that seemingly vindicated Douhet's view that wars could be won with airpower almost or entirely alone. Those who watched the 1991 Gulf War live on CNN could not help but be awed by the apparent offensive power of precision strikes from the air. Immediate post-war assessments centered on the view that precision in airpower, pursued for decades, had with this conflict reached a qualitatively new level such that airpower had finally become the decisive force in battle. Even more convincing was the argument, a decade later, that NATO's 1999 air war in and around Kosovo represented a "clear victory for air power" and perhaps the first time in history that airpower alone had achieved military and political objectives.[12] But what stands out most significantly about the evolution of airpower theory in the first post-Cold War decade is the degree to which the role and value of this dimension of warfare was questioned and qualified. As the decade went on, airpower scholars added a degree of rigor to theorizing about conventional airpower, thereby pushing forward the boundaries of existing airpower theory.

John Warden

The starting-point in discussing post-Cold War strategic thought on airpower lies with the ideas of US Air Force Colonel (retired) John Warden, considered the architect of the 1991 Gulf War's air campaign. As deputy director of the US Air Force Directorate of Warfighting Concepts when Iraq invaded Kuwait in August 1990, Warden was tasked to put together a plan for a retaliatory air response. The outcome was Instant Thunder, a strategy that called for simultaneous air strikes against Iraq's centers of gravity, including its leadership; command, control, and communications apparatus; and on key infrastructure sites and facilities. In his view, airpower could attack ground forces directly, paralyzing the enemy in relatively bloodless fashion and avoiding the need for a large ground campaign. In the end, of course, a short ground campaign was necessary; nonetheless, Warden's intellectual contribution was recognized as central to Desert Storm's success.

When Warden was asked to draw up an airpower response to the Iraqi invasion he had already spent several years thinking about airpower strategy and theory. In his 1988 book, *The Air Campaign*, Warden set forth his ideas on planning and executing an air campaign at the operational level, including air superiority, offensive, and defensive operations, and the use of airpower for interdiction and in close air support of ground forces. His views on close air support, in particular, proved somewhat controversial because of the central role and potential he accorded to airpower. "[T]he soldier on the ground," he argued, "will find close air support useful in almost every conceivable situation, from pursuit to retreat." In fact, he argued, "The air campaign, under some circumstances, may be far more important than the ground campaign."[13]

Nonetheless, the clarity of his thinking in *The Air Campaign* brought Warden the appointment as deputy director of the warfighting concepts directorate. Although the book had focused on the operational level of war, Warden immediately turned his attention to the strategic application of airpower and it is this strategic thinking for which he is best remembered. In a summer 1988 essay called "Global Strategy Outline" Warden argued that the enemy was a "system," dependent for its effective functioning on certain centers of gravity that, if successfully targeted, would bring about his surrender. He depicted the centers of gravity as five strategic rings in concentric circles (much like an onion). According to his Five Rings Model, the circle at the very center was strategically the most important. It was the bull's eye or the "command ring" of the nation-state and it included the country's leadership and key command and control centers. The circle surrounding this inner core Warden identified as the infrastructure critical to the prosecution of war, such as energy, oil, and gas; the third circle also comprised infrastructure, but of a somewhat less critical nature, including bridges, roads, and railways; the fourth circle represented the population and agriculture, the citizens and their food sources; finally, the fifth circle, the least vital in war, was the state's fielded military forces.

Ideally, in war one would successfully target the leadership and central command and control centers, compelling the adversary to make concessions—a strategy that has been characterized by Robert Pape and others (see below) as "decapitation." But Warden also argued that the effect of a simultaneous attack on multiple target sets within each of the five rings would be exponential and would bring about surrender. This strategy he later labeled "parallel attack," a term that first emerged immediately after the 1991 Gulf War. "The most important requirement of strategic attack is to understand the enemy system," Warden argued in a 1995 article. The enemy has a number of "vital targets," and if a significant percentage were to be struck in parallel then the damage would become "insuperable." For Warden serial warfare—maneuver and counter-maneuver, attack and counterattack, reaching the culminating point in campaigns—was the historical experience. But technological advances had now made possible parallel warfare, the near-simultaneous attack of the enemy's strategic and operational-level vulnerabilities.

Robert Pape

Many of the ideas of a second notable airpower theorist of the post-Cold War, Robert Pape, are set out in opposition to those of Warden. In his 1996 book, *Bombing to Win: Airpower and Coercion in Warfare*, Pape, a civilian scholar at the University of Chicago, identifies two major types of coercive air operations: strategic bombing and interdiction. The former, defined as air attacks against fixed military, industrial, or civilian targets in and near political and economic centers, he further categorizes into missions that seek punishment, denial, or decapitation. A punishment strategy inflicts punishment on civilians, seeking to raise the societal costs of continued resistance to the point that the resistor concedes to the coercer's demands. It is this form of strategic bombing that best captures Douhet's thinking and, in Pape's view, has dominated perspectives on military coercion. A denial strategy seeks to deny the resistor the military ability to achieve its political or territorial objectives. An ideal strategic-bombing denial strategy, which Pape also refers to as strategic interdiction, would involve targeting things like weapons plants and critical raw materials used in war production. Unlike punishment, denial measures require the "pin-point accuracy" of weapons. Finally, "decapitation" is a new form of strategic bombing, demanding and enabled by the increased precision of weapons. The logic behind decapitation is that key leadership facilities and communications networks in the opponent's political centers, as well as key nodes in a nation's economic infrastructure, like oil refineries, are "a modern state's Achilles heel ... if [these targets] are knocked out, the whole house of cards comes down."[14]

In contrast to strategic bombing, interdiction involves only denial. Such missions target the opponent's military ability to achieve its political or territorial objectives by focusing on the battlefield and on lines of supply to the battlefield. Ideal targets of airpower in this regard (again requiring pin-point accuracy) would include an enemy's fielded forces; theater-level command, communications, and logistics; and lines of supply between military production sites and the combat theater. These sorts of air interdiction tasks—which Pape also calls operational interdiction missions—technically take place behind enemy lines and comprise one of two forms of theater air attack, the other being the close air support of front-line troops. Theater air attack, either (operational) interdiction or in support of front-line forces, had its origins in World War One; it is these activities that Douhet dismissed as irrelevant and that Mitchell continued to view as valuable in the conduct of war.

The core of Pape's argument is that strategic bombing in its punishment and decapitation forms is ineffectual and "doesn't matter."[15] At the same time, airpower can be useful in theater air attack, both close air support and operational interdiction, while strategic interdiction (strategic bombing denial) can matter under some circumstances. Another way of capturing his argument is that of the coercive air *strategies*—punishment, denial, and decapitation—only denial strategies can make a positive contribution from the coercer's perspective. This is true of both types of coercive air *operations*, strategic bombing and (operational) interdiction, but especially true of the latter.

When it comes to punishment strategies, Pape's argument echoes conclusions drawn decades earlier from Germany's World War Two bombing of Britain. "The supposed causal chain [of punishment]—civilian hardship produces public anger which forms political opposition against the government—does not stand up"; in fact such punishment generates more public anger against the coercer than the government. Nor do decapitation strategies work, because of the difficulty of locating individual leaders—decapitation is primarily a problem of intelligence, not combat effectiveness. Governments are still hard to overthrow, and, even if overthrown, may be replaced with a still less palatable leadership (from the coercer's perspective).

Coercive airpower operations that focus on denial strategies can make a difference to the outcome of a war. Yet Pape avoids describing such operations as actually being "effective," only allowing that they can "matter" or be a contributing element, and even then he is careful to add limits. Strategic-bombing denial strategies are helpful only in the case of a protracted war of attrition that is decided by overall economic and material superiority, not in a short war using existing stocks of war supplies. That is to say, if strategic interdiction is to be useful it requires simultaneous operational interdiction. And even if these two conditions are met, "strategic airpower cannot be decisive. *The most it can do is to reduce the costs that friendly land and theatre air forces have to pay to defeat enemy forces on the battlefield*" (emphasis added).[16]

Pape is more positive about the value of airpower when it comes to the theater-level denial strategy of operational interdiction, and the close air support of troops. "The coercive strategy that benefits most from the PGM [precision-guided munitions] revolution is theatre air attack," he argues, "[t]his is because many of the most important theatre interdiction targets, as well as ground support targets, are point targets requiring direct hits." Such targets include things like tanks, armored personnel carriers, self-propelled artillery howitzers, communications bunkers, and bridges, all of which are easier to destroy from the air with PGMs than without—although, Pape notes prophetically, given the Kosovo experience later in the decade, that the task is still difficult (see below). The increased effectiveness of tactical airpower does not mean that it has replaced landpower as the penultimate coercer; rather, it means that airpower at this level "*can do most of the work, leaving ground forces to mop up*" (emphasis added).[17]

An important caveat is theater airpower's applicability, or lack thereof, to non-conventional war. Whereas conventional forces use large mechanized platforms, operate along fairly defined front lines, and seek to destroy enemy military forces, unconventional forces (whether state or non-state) operate in small units dispersed over large areas, have no defined front lines, and seek to gain control of the population. The character of unconventional war is such that there are no or minimal supply lines to target, and the fielded forces themselves, being mixed in with the population, are extremely difficult to identify and therefore target. Anticipating debates that arose in subsequent years, Pape concludes that, in general, denial air strategies are more likely to succeed against conventional forces than against guerrillas.

Benjamin Lambeth

Building on Pape's analysis, long-time airpower specialist Benjamin Lambeth of the RAND Corporation presents a perspective that accords in many ways with that of

Pape but is distinguished by its "glass half-full" assessment, as against Pape's "glass half-empty" characterization. Originally a specialist in Soviet airpower, during the first post-Cold War decade Lambeth centers his analysis of airpower on the 1991 Gulf War, stating his views in a number of articles and ultimately in a 2000 book, *The Transformation of American Airpower*. The most ineffectual ways of employing airpower—strategic bombing for decapitation or punishment—are found to be, in essence, straw-man goals that were pursued either marginally or not at all during that conflict.

Much of the airpower debate after the Gulf War centered on whether striking "center of gravity" targets, defined as leadership and infrastructure targets located in and around Bagdad, made a difference to the war's outcome. But Lambeth notes that this goal, what Pape calls decapitation, was by no means a central one for Coalition leaders. Center of gravity targets accounted for less than 10 percent of the allied sorties flown throughout the war. Meanwhile, the discussion over the efficacy of punishment attacks is a moot one, rendered obsolete by the growing precision of weapons. Far from seeking punishing attacks against large numbers of civilians, post-Cold War Western militaries strive for ever greater precision and as few civilian casualties as possible. Douhet's model of inflicting high costs on civilians as the first step in a logic leading to enemy surrender, Lambeth notes, is "scarcely likely" to be the approach adopted by any present-day allied joint force. "Douhet was driven by that logic because airpower had no capability at the time he wrote to do anything *but* cause indiscriminate destruction of civilian targets."[18] In the post-Cold War era, with advanced precision technology, there are far different options.

Where Lambeth and Pape agree is in the areas of emphasis noted above—that airpower can reduce the costs of warfare to ground forces, and that it can do much of the battlefield work, prior to introducing ground forces. For Lambeth, the Gulf War demonstrated that airpower could enable a commander to hold off ordering a land force frontal assault against enemy forces until such time as the potential costs of a ground-based offensive in terms of friendly lives had been substantially reduced. "[A]irpower now has the potential to carry a lion's share of the burden for shaping and determining war outcomes, thereby enabling other force elements to achieve their goals with a minimum of pain, effort, and cost."[19] This suggested, in turn, that "the principal role of land power in high-intensity conflict may now be merely to secure a win rather than achieve it."[20]

Lambeth neatly characterizes the core of the airpower debate unleashed by the 1991 Gulf War as being one between land-warfare specialists, who argued that there is still a requirement for "boots on the ground" to conclude a win in warfare, and airpower proponents, who argue that the ability of modern airpower to affect land warfare had "crossed a threshold in which its effects are fundamentally greater than before."[21] He sees value in both perspectives, and is careful to factor the role of landpower into his airpower strategic thinking. Airpower alone cannot win wars, and the issue is not whether airpower can "do it alone." Rather, the core of Lambeth's argument is that advances in technology have dramatically increased the combat potential of airpower *in comparison to* that of other force elements. "What is distinctive about contemporary American air power … is that it has pulled well ahead of surface forces, both land and maritime, in its *relative* capacity … to achieve the effects of massing forces without having to mass."[22]

For Lambeth, the Gulf War demonstrated that advances in airpower had enabled a number of capabilities previously unavailable to commanders, including power projection, stand-off precision strike, and increased situational awareness. Power projection refers simply to the ability to move military forces to distances far away from the US homeland and to sustain them there. This can be achieved using ships and, in the case of the United States, carrier battle groups, but in the 1990s it also became possible using new strategic lift aircraft capable of transporting very large loads great distances without refueling. The unique aspect of air force power projection, noted the US Air Force's vision statement of the time, *Global Engagement: A Vision for the 21st Century Air Force*, was that power projection could be done rapidly, in terms of days or even hours, rather than weeks and months. The air force thus identified one if its core competencies to be "Global Attack," or the ability to attack rapidly anywhere on the globe at any time.

A second capability brought on by airpower advances was stand-off precision strike. This had been enabled by the dramatically increased precision of weapons—precision-guided munitions or PGMs—which during the Gulf War were guided by laser but now are far more commonly guided by satellite. The advent of GPS-guided PGMs has meant that virtually any target that can be identified can be destroyed—although target identification itself remains problematic. In Lambeth's view, an equally, if not more, important advance in military aviation was the introduction of low observable or stealth technology. This allowed aircraft to fly undetected to enemy areas to drop their bombs, thus approaching for the first time, and until stealth countermeasures are developed, the Douhetian promise of aircraft operating in complete freedom of flight.

Finally, a critical aspect of airpower as identified by Lambeth in the 1990s is its positive impact on "situational awareness," or the ability to see what is happening on the battlefield. This was enabled by the introduction of unmanned aerial vehicles and specialized manned aircraft, along with earth-observation satellites. Not only was increased situational awareness bringing about almost complete knowledge of an operational situation, but denying the same information to enemy forces was enabling "information superiority," also identified as a US Air Force core competency.

The increased and unfettered use of airpower was made possible because US airpower had achieved a quintessentially Douhetian attribute—command of the air or what Lambeth called "air dominance." "The real essence of American air power's new-found leverage," argued Lambeth, is "its ability to seize prompt control of the air and then to proceed, using that dominance, to destroy … an enemy's diverse sources of military power [on the ground]."[23] In the Gulf War it was learned that residual heat from daytime exposure to sunlight made tanks highly visible at night to infrared sensors in jet targeting pods, enabling coalition fighters to target Iraqi tanks buried in the desert sand by the multiple hundreds with laser-guided bombs. During this time period, the US Air Force identified one of its core competencies as being Air and Space Superiority, defined to mean "control over what moves through air and space," thereby allowing "freedom *from* attack and freedom *to* attack"[24]—words that strongly echoed a Douhetian perspective. Because command of the air was enjoyed by default, with no enemy nation approaching US airpower capabilities, there is even less discussion of combat in the air than there was in Douhet's time. Ironically, also, during the 1991 Gulf War the US-led Coalition destroyed the Iraqi air force on the ground, just as Douhet would have had it.

For Lambeth, the combination of increased precision, better battlefield information and therefore situational awareness, stealth technology, and overall air dominance, meant that airpower had matured to the point that its use could now produce strategic effects in warfare. That is to say, airpower could have impacts that were game changing in nature, achieving national/political objectives directly, not just tactical/battlefield objectives like defeating enemy forces. This idea, along with others related to the role and value of airpower, was debated with renewed vigor at the end of the decade and in the aftermath of 9/11.

The second post-Cold War decade

NATO's air campaign in and around Kosovo in the spring of 1999, the war in Afghanistan in 2001–2, and the Iraq War of 2003 sparked significant theorizing about conventional airpower, some of which centered on ideas that had been raised in the first post-Cold War decade, such as the ability of airpower to achieve strategic effects, the utility of punishment, the military effectiveness of operational interdiction, and the value of decapitation; and others that were essentially new or had not been fully examined in the past, notably the use of airpower in combination with indigenous forces and with Western surface forces (i.e. jointness). Both the further examination of previous ideas and the exploration of essentially new areas of inquiry served to push forward the boundaries of existing airpower theory.

Strategic effects?

In his work on the Gulf War, Lambeth was careful to set himself apart from the more ardent airpower proponents. "It is not [my intent] to suggest that air power can win wars all by itself ... success in major theatre wars will, as before, continue to require the involvement of all force elements in appropriately integrated fashion."[25] No sooner was the ink dry on that clarification than a war came along that seemed to suggest, at first glance, that it was after all possible for airpower to win a war all by itself. In the wake of Operation Allied Force, which comprised 78 days of air strikes against Serbian targets but no NATO ground force deployment, some scholars and practitioners saw the conflict as a watershed in the history of airpower, approaching Douhet's view that wars could be won with airpower alone.

Yet, although there were some voices lauding the apparent effectiveness of airpower in Kosovo, in fact the second post-Cold War decade featured far more views that qualified—in some cases significantly—the ability of airpower to achieve political goals. Lambeth concurs with the statement that Operation Allied Force was the most precise application of airpower in history in terms of non-combatant casualties, and notes that Kosovo was indeed the first time in which airpower coerced an enemy leader to yield with no friendly land combat whatsoever. But, as he points out, it hardly follows that the conflict demonstrated that airpower could now win wars on its own. Airpower was the only military instrument utilized; however, several non-combat factors were also identified as being critical to Milosevic's capitulation, among them the threat of NATO ground force deployment, economic and diplomatic pressure on Serbian elites, and the political isolation of Serbia. Overall, most airpower theorists would likely support the assessment of two scholars not long after the conflict, that "[T]he Kosovo experience does little to vindicate the general argument that air attacks alone can compel enemy states to yield on key interests."[26]

Utility of punishment

One aspect of the airpower debate that was at least partially supported by the Kosovo experience was the effectiveness of strategic bombing against commercial and industrial targets. Whereas Douhet argued in favor of this as a means of crushing the material resistance of the enemy, Pape had raised and discounted a punishment strategy of attacking civilian sectors of the economy. And yet, ironically, Lambeth notes in an in-depth assessment of the Kosovo campaign, "in contrast to the coalition's ultimately unsuccessful efforts to coerce Saddam Hussein into submission [in 1991], punishment *did* seem to work against Milosevic."[27] As concisely summed up by Stephen Biddle, "Whereas Serbia's military survived nearly intact, its power grid and transportation network took heavy damage … It was the threat to this critical economic foundation that changed minds in Belgrade."[28] Some have concluded that striking strategic targets, including infrastructure, can make a contribution to the success of coercion.

Airpower's impact on the morale of the targeted population, a topic featured prominently in Douhet's strategic thought, was mixed. The NATO attacks both inflamed Serbian nationalist sentiment and negatively impacted on the population's support for Milosevic, to the degree that he had to take account of this in his calculations. Scholars revisiting the 1991 Gulf War a decade later found a similarly indeterminate picture. Airpower affected Iraqi morale and contributed to the collapse of the front-line infantry, but "even after five weeks of bombing, the best Iraqi units … were willing to … fight. Air attacks did not neutralize the Iraqi force by crippling their morale."[29]

Utility of interdiction

Meanwhile, airpower's effectiveness in operational interdiction traveled along a varying yet slightly positive trajectory post-9/11, after decidedly mixed results in the Gulf War and Kosovo. In *Bombing to Win*, as noted above, Pape identified, yet qualified, this as an area where airpower could make a tangible contribution, while Lambeth has noted that airpower had a hard time finding and destroying Serbian tanks hiding under trees in ones and twos in the Kosovo campaign. Biddle, working from the Pentagon's own post-war assessments, further calculated that between one and four thousand Iraqi tanks and armored vehicles survived the war. "By contrast," he notes, "the entire German army in Normandy had fewer than 500 tanks in July 1944."[30] Revisiting the Gulf War a decade after its conclusion, one academic elaborated that such a high survival rate can be explained by the fact that "seeing" targets, even in the relatively easy (in situational-awareness terms) operational environment of the desert, requires a heat signature, and therefore movement. For this reason, a static, defensively oriented force is "maddeningly difficult" to detect.[31] Moreover, it is very easy to create decoys that are indistinguishable from real targets, a lesson that was learned to even greater degree in Kosovo, where most Serbian tanks remained unscathed by NATO airpower. Adversaries operating in mountainous, forested terrain, such as Kosovo, can easily camouflage their movements, while the effectiveness of airpower against light infantry, by definition operating without heavy mechanized equipment, is limited in almost any environment.

Operation Enduring Freedom in Afghanistan in 2001–2 revealed significant advances in two airpower capabilities originally identified by Lambeth in the first post-Cold War decade: situational awareness and stand-off strike. Almost any target that can be identified can be destroyed with precision munitions; the difficulty lies in detection. In Kosovo, much of the situational-awareness picture was filled out by pilots who, confined by force vulnerability concerns, could not operate below 10,000 feet. Perhaps in response to such constraints, subsequent years saw dramatic advances in the capabilities of Unmanned Aerials Vehicles (UAVs) and other situational-awareness assets.

The war in Afghanistan "was conducted under an overarching intelligence, surveillance, and reconnaissance umbrella that stared down relentlessly in search of enemy activity," notes Lambeth. "That umbrella was formed by a constellation of overlapping multispectral sensor platforms."[32] Significantly, advances in individual platforms were married with a new ability to synthesize information into a single picture, creating a clearer view of the battlefield than ever before. The overall effect of these developments was the emergence of a new airpower concept called "persistent surveillance."[33] In the years since the 2001–2 Afghan war this concept has in itself persisted as a continually developing one. With the post-2003 shift to counterinsurgency missions, for example, a significant degree of emphasis has been placed on ensuring the persistent surveillance of roadways to warn against improvised explosive devices. The 2001–2 war in Afghanistan also revealed enhanced denial/interdiction capabilities as a result of new developments in stand-off precision strike. Persistent surveillance assets were armed with precision-strike capabilities to debut a new airpower concept of unmanned combat. Since then, this form of warfare has been used extensively, not only by the US military but also by the Central Intelligence Agency.

Decapitation

Theorists and practitioners revisited the strategic airpower concept of decapitation in the second post-Cold War decade. Notwithstanding admonishments from scholars like Robert Pape, based on the 1991 Gulf War, that decapitation is ineffectual and "doesn't matter," the concept proved enticing enough to be attempted again in the opening stages of the 2003 Iraq War. With dramatically improved precision in weapons, US President George W. Bush moved forward the invasion date by one day in an attempt to strike Saddam Hussein directly and thereby "decapitate" the Iraqi regime. The strategy was billed as "shock and awe" (see Chapter 4) and a key component—familiar in airpower theory terms—was the belief that the removal of Saddam would deliver a big enough psychological blow to make his regime collapse. The Pentagon's plan was to overwhelm the country's leadership and military command infrastructure by using highly lethal precision munitions to strike strategically important targets, while at the same time avoiding wholesale destruction and civilian casualties.

But numerous strikes against command and control targets in the war's opening stages failed to kill or topple Saddam. Based on this, and also on unsuccessful attempts to target Taliban leaders in the early stages of Operation Enduring Freedom, Robert Pape argued in a 2004 re-examination that decapitation as an effective strategic airpower concept remained as elusive as ever. Such strikes are heavily dependent on accurate and timely military intelligence, and even a successful hit may not translate into coercive success, since "no current theory can predict whether air power alone can force regimes to change or assure they will change in the right direction."[34] In fact, the impressive win in Iraq in 2003 took place only after the use of airpower was shifted to battlefield targets in support of ground forces. While aircraft prepared the scene for the ground campaign, it was the Coalition ground forces that eventually toppled the regime.

New theoretical boundaries

The use and value of airpower working in combination with surface force elements marked a notable and in some respects new area of discussion about airpower in the

second post-Cold War decade. During the 2001–2 war in Afghanistan US special operations forces (SOFs) operating on horseback used laser rangefinders and GPS devices to
call in extremely precise air strikes, accurate to within a few meters. During the 2003
Iraq War airpower also worked very closely with friendly ground forces, helping them to
defeat enemy forces more efficiently. Although "jointness" had been part of the military
dialogue for over a decade by this point, its practical application reached a qualitatively
new level in the wars of the new millennium. Theorists have stressed that the revolutionary impact of advances in airpower technology, including precision strike and surveillance capabilities, has been to multiply the effectiveness of using air- and landpower
together. "Most analyses have focused on [airpower's] ability to destroy ground targets
directly," Biddle predicted in a seminal study from the previous decade, "Yet its *indirect*
role in increasing Coalition *ground* force effectiveness … may [be] just as important"
(emphasis in original).[35]

Airpower also worked in tandem with indigenous ground forces in Afghanistan and
Iraq, giving rise to a new theoretical framework for examining the use and value of
airpower. According to the Afghan model of warfare, local forces (vice American
conventional ground forces) combined with US special operations forces and precision
airpower to carry out battlefield objectives. In Afghanistan American SOFs and airpower worked in conjunction with some 15,000 Northern Alliance fighters to defeat the
Taliban and al Qaeda, while in Iraq American SOFs and airpower worked with
Kurdish fighters to defeat northern Iraqi forces. Along similar lines, NATO airpower
operated in support of rebel forces in Libya in 2011 (see Box 3.1).

Box 3.1 The NATO operation in Libya

- Bloodshed broke out in Libya after forces loyal to the regime of Libyan leader
  Muammar Qaddafi fought back against an uprising by rebel forces.
- In March 2011 the UN Security Council passed a resolution authorizing "all
  necessary measures" to protect Libyan civilians and civilian-populated areas
  against Qaddafi's forces, and to enforce compliance with a ban on flights over
  Libyan airspace.
- NATO established Operation Unified Protector to implement the military
  aspects of the resolution. Unstated but apparent from the beginning was the
  broader military and political goal of assisting rebel forces in overthrowing
  the Qaddafi regime.
- NATO's targeting progressively expanded, first confined to implementing the
  no-fly zone; then including precision strikes against government forces on the
  ground, including tanks, artillery, and loyalist soldiers; and finally moving
  beyond dispersed strikes against tactical activities to include strategic strikes
  against palaces, headquarters, and communications centers.
- These strikes had some impact on the rebels' ability to overcome Qaddafi's
  better-equipped forces. But the balance was not fully tilted until Britain,
  France, and other nations deployed special operations forces on the ground
  inside Libya to help train and arm the rebels.
- The coordination of NATO precision airpower in close air support of
  increasingly proficient indigenous ground forces ultimately served to remove
  the Qaddafi regime, providing further validation of the Afghan model of warfare.

The advent of the Afghan model gave rise to a scholarly debate as to its true and future value. Some scholars note that Coalition airpower transformed Afghanistan's Northern Alliance into a lethal fighting force, and that it enabled an inferior force to act decisively in northern Iraq. From this perspective, despite its shortcomings, the model is a valuable option because it minimizes US casualties and can bring legitimacy to a post-conflict situation. Other scholars have criticized the approach, pointing out that although the model was highly effective in many areas of Afghanistan, the reliance on Pakistani forces and Afghan militias in Tora Bora allowed Osama bin Laden to escape. Several theorists warn against the danger of over-reliance on indigenous allies to conduct the ground force operation because such forces do not always have the necessary skill and motivation to accomplish the mission assigned to them. This is particularly because opponents, such as the Taliban, will quickly adjust to such tactics. "The Taliban did not just passively suffer under American attack," argues Biddle in an assessment of the model; "they adapted their methods … and as they did the war changed character."[36]

Airpower and counterinsurgency

A final area of elaboration in airpower theory in the second post-Cold War decade lay in its role and value in conducting missions against insurgents and guerrillas. Strategic thought in this aspect of airpower theory was driven by real-life events on the ground, as apparent Western wins in Afghanistan and Iraq turned into protracted insurgencies and stabilization and reconstruction missions. The irregular conflicts that followed in these regions, as well as the 2006 Israeli war against Hezbollah in Lebanon, demonstrated the enduring difficulty of using airpower to root out guerrillas and insurgents. Insurgents meld themselves into the population, making it all but impossible for airpower to strike them without also killing civilians. Moreover, insurgencies, by their nature, provide few lucrative targets to strike with airpower. Notes airpower theorist James Corum: "Virtually all of the decisive targets favoured by the best known airpower theorists," such as industrial nodes, national command centers, and large conventional armies, "do not exist in wars against guerrillas or insurgents. Indeed, the air campaigns that are designed to shock and awe and demoralize a conventional enemy … are basically irrelevant to small wars."[37]

That said, in their 2003 book, *Airpower in Small Wars*, Corum and Wray Johnson find that there is still an important role for airpower in countering insurgents and terrorists. The increased situational awareness provided by airborne assets like Unmanned Aerial Vehicles (UAVs) is critical to any mission, low or high intensity alike, while precision airpower has proven very effective in some irregular warfare circumstances, such as against Taliban targets in Afghanistan. Indeed, along the Afghan-Pakistan border US strikes against terrorist suspects became increasingly accurate over time. Moreover, lightly armed friendly forces operating without the necessary precision artillery can be highly dependent on the ability of precision airpower to inflict losses on the enemy. Overall, the theorists conclude that "[w]hile high-tech weaponry is not the whole answer to fighting terrorists and insurgents it certainly makes for an effective force multiplier." Consistent with other theorists of this period, they also find that "[airpower] is most effective when it is carefully coordinated with ground forces."[38]

Conclusion

Airpower's seeming and unexpected battlefield success in the 1991 Gulf War sparked a more significant degree of theorizing about conventional airpower than had taken place since the pre-atomic era. The scholarship was abundant and included works by Robert Pape, Stephen Biddle, and Benjamin Lambeth, among others. Douhetian themes provided some of the analytical boundaries, such as the value of applying airpower against strategic targets, but much was new, notably the themes of jointness and operational interdiction, ignored by Douhet and now placed center stage by advances in situational awareness and precision technology. Subsequent conflicts in Kosovo, Afghanistan, and Iraq sparked an elaboration and refinement of earlier themes by Pape and Lambeth, but also prompted an assessment of new areas of inquiry, such as the use of airpower in counterinsurgency and the value of combining Western airpower with indigenous allies, by scholars such as Biddle, James Corum, and others.

Taken together, post-Cold War strategic thought reveals a theory of airpower that might include the following tenets: precision airpower can approach but not entirely achieve strategic effects in war; precision airpower can make a very significant contribution to the outcome of war when applied in conjunction with friendly ground forces; airpower can rarely be used effectively in a strategic-bombing "decapitation" strategy, dependent as it is on highly accurate and timely intelligence information; strategic-bombing punishment strategies against population centers belong to a pre-precision era; strategic-bombing punishment strategies against economic and other critical nodes can, under some circumstances, contribute to achieving strategic effects in war; the use of airpower can impact on but not cripple the morale of targeted forces; airpower's effectiveness in working with indigenous forces is mixed and its greatest value lies in reducing friendly casualties; the utility of airpower in counterinsurgency missions is inversely related to the proximity of insurgents to civilian population centers; and airpower's contribution to situational awareness is critical across all forms of warfare, from conventional to counterinsurgency.

Unstated in all of this is that the use of airpower in any of these roles and circumstances is made feasible only by America's continuing command of the air, i.e. the lack of threat to its airborne assets. This situation emerged with the demise of the Soviet Union and has remained a unique aspect of the international security environment throughout the post-Cold War decades. The increasingly effective marriage of land maneuver forces with precision power rests on the almost unquestioned assumption of US air supremacy. The boundaries of airpower theory will be tested and pushed forward again if and when there emerges a peer competitor to the United States.

Notes

1 For a detailed discussion of Douhet's background see Phillip S. Meilinger, "Douhet and Modern War," *Comparative Strategy* 12 (1993): 321–38. For an early examination of Douhet's thoughts, see Edward Warner, "Douhet, Mitchell, Seversky: Theories of Air Warfare," in Edward Mead Earle, *Makers of Modern Strategy: Military Thought from Machiavelli to Hitler* (Princeton, NJ: Princeton University Press, 1943).
2 Guilio Douhet, *The Command of the Air*, trans. Dino Ferrari, ed. Joseph Patrick Harahan and Richard H. Kohn (Tuscaloosa, AL: University Of Alabama Press, 1942), 9.
3 Meilinger, "Douhet and Modern War," 328.
4 Ibid., 325.
5 Douhet, *The Command of the Air*, 24.
6 Ibid., 23.
7 Meilinger, "Douhet and Modern War," 327.
8 William Mitchell, *Winged Defense* (Port Washington, NY: Kennikat Press, 1925), 126–27.
9 Douhet, *The Command of the Air*, 28.

10 Ibid., 99.
11 Ibid., 94, 100.
12 See Andrew L. Stigler, "A Clear Victory for Air Power: NATO's Empty Threat to Invade Kosovo," *International Security* 27, no. 3 (Winter 2002/03): 124–57.
13 John Warden, *The Air Campaign: Planning for Combat* (Washington, DC: Brassey's, 1989), 88–89. First published by the National Defense University Press, 1988.
14 Robert A. Pape, "The Limits of Precision-guided Air Power," *Security Studies* 7, no. 2 (Winter 1997/98), 97.
15 Robert A. Pape, *Bombing to Win: Airpower and Coercion in War* (Ithaca, NY: Cornell University Press, 1996), 316.
16 Ibid., 317.
17 Ibid., 325, 326.
18 Benjamin S. Lambeth, "Bounding the Air Power Debate," *Strategic Review* (Fall 1997), 49.
19 Ibid., 53.
20 Benjamin S. Lambeth, "The Technology Revolution in Air Warfare," *Survival* 39, no. 1 (Spring 1997), 66.
21 Ibid., 65–66.
22 Benjamin S. Lambeth, *The Transformation of American Air Power* (Ithaca, NY: Cornell University Press, 2000), 8, 274.
23 Ibid., 266.
24 US Air Force, *Global Engagement: A Vision for the 21st Century Air Force* (Washington, DC: Department of the Air Force, 1996).
25 Benjamin S. Lambeth, "Air Power, Space Power and Geography," *Journal of Strategic Studies* 22, no. 2 (1999), 64.
26 Daniel L. Byman and Matthew C. Waxman, "Kosovo and the Great Airpower Debate," *International Security* 24, no. 4 (Spring 2000), 6.
27 Benjamin S. Lambeth, *NATO's Air War for Kosovo: A Strategic and Operational Assessment* (Santa Monica, CA: RAND Corporation, 2001), 224.
28 Stephen Biddle, "New Way of War? Debating the Kosovo Model," *Foreign Affairs* 81, no. 3 (May/June 2002), 140.
29 Daryl G. Press, "The Myth of Air Power in the Persian Gulf War and the Future of Warfare," *International Security* 26, no. 2 (Fall 2001), 37.
30 Stephen Biddle, "Victory Misunderstood: What the Gulf War Tells Us about the Future of Conflict," *International Security* 21, no. 2 (Fall 1996), 152.
31 Press, "The Myth of Air Power," 41, 43.
32 Benjamin S. Lambeth, *Air Power against Terror: America's Conduct of Operation Enduring Freedom* (Santa Monica, CA: RAND Corporation, 2005), 253.
33 Michael O'Hanlon, "A Flawed Masterpiece," *Foreign Affairs* 81, no. 3 (May/June 2002), 59.
34 Robert Pape, "The True Worth of Air Power," *Foreign Affairs* 83, no. 2 (March/April 2004), 118.
35 Biddle, "Victory Misunderstood," 162.
36 Stephen Biddle, "Afghanistan and the Future of Warfare," *Foreign Affairs* 82, no. 2 (March/April 2003), 35.
37 James S. Corum, "The Air Campaign of the Present and Future—Using Airpower Against Insurgents and Terrorists," in Allan D. English, *Air Campaigns in the New World Order* (Winnipeg, MB: University of Manitoba Centre for Defence and Security Studies, 2005), 26.
38 James S. Corum and Wray R. Johnson, *Airpower in Small Wars: Fighting Terrorists and Insurgents* (Lawrence, KS: University Press of Kansas, 2003), 430–31, 433.

Further reading

Corum, James S. and Wray R. Johnson. *Airpower in Small Wars: Fighting Terrorists and Insurgents* (Lawrence, KS: University Press of Kansas, 2003).
Douhet, Guilio. *The Command of the Air*, trans. Dino Ferrari, ed. Joseph Patrick Harahan and Richard H. Kohn (Tuscaloosa, AL: University Of Alabama Press, 1942).
Gray, Colin. *Airpower for Strategic Effect* (New York: Columbia University Press, 2011).

Lambeth, Benjamin S. *Air Power against Terror: America's Conduct of Operation Enduring Freedom* (Santa Monica, CA: RAND Corporation, 2005).

——. *The Transformation of American Air Power* (Ithaca, NY: Cornell University Press, 2000).

Mitchell, William. *Winged Defense* (Port Washington, NY: Kennikat Press, 1925).

Pape, Robert A. *Bombing to Win: Airpower and Coercion in War* (Ithaca, NY: Cornell University Press, 1996).

United States Air Force. *Global Engagement: A Vision for the 21st Century Air Force* (Washington, DC: Department of the Air Force, 1996).

Warden, John. *The Air Campaign: Planning for Combat* (Washington, DC: Brassey's, 1989).

4 Joint theory and military transformation

A glance back at the historical record reveals that the idea of sea, land, and more recently air forces operating "jointly" on the battlefield is not a new one. Europeans began thinking about cooperation between sea and land forces as early as the seventeenth century, although this was generally limited to landing ground forces some distance from the homeland and then resupplying them by sea. The American Civil War saw the first joint operations, with seaborne attacks on ground targets and the landing of naval troops. The value and importance of joint warfare became most apparent in World War One when the Dardanelles campaign failed largely because of a lack of cooperation between the British army and navy. By the latter part of the war both sides were operating jointly, using aircraft to support ground forces. Two decades later Germany's lightning war, or blitzkrieg, tactics in the opening days of World War Two fully revealed the power and potential of integrating air- and landpower. The United States subsequently conducted joint operations in the Pacific, while the Normandy invasion represented the most complex joint operation of the war.

Yet military services have historically been far more likely to resist cooperation, and this reality has been reflected in the content of strategic thought. Although Jomini discussed amphibious warfare, and Corbett spent some time detailing the linkages between naval power and landpower, Clausewitz famously ignored naval warfare, Mahan gave only passing attention to the employment of naval forces against the land (and when he did so advised that it should be avoided), while Douhet argued strenuously that airpower should operate independently of other dimensions of war. Even the tactical brilliance of blitzkrieg was not followed by any appreciable body of thought on joint warfare. For Williamson Murray, inter-service cooperation in the late stages of World War Two represented the peak of jointness, with such cooperation not to be seen again until the 1991 Gulf War.[1]

Truly joint warfare is arguably a late twentieth-century, if not twenty-first-century, phenomenon. As advances in civilian information technologies in the 1970s spilled over into the military-technological realm it became increasingly possible and desirable for sea, land and air forces to be integrated into what is often described as a "seamless" three-dimensional battlefield. Contemporary strategic thought on joint warfare began with the US Army's seminal AirLand Battle, first enunciated in the early 1980s and officially adopted in the closing days of the Cold War (see Chapter 2). But the furtherance of jointness in practice, at least in America's case, required legislation. The 1986 Goldwater-Nichols Act was specifically designed to promote cooperation and reduce inter-service rivalry. Joint ideas were later picked up and pushed forward as part of 1990s thinking about a Revolution in Military Affairs (RMA), later called Military

Transformation, while the actual conduct of genuinely joint warfare first took place in Afghanistan in 2001–2 and Iraq in 2003.

This chapter examines strategic thought on joint warfare in the post-Cold War period. It begins by highlighting the origins and content of, and thinkers involved in, the so-called Revolution in Military Affairs, later known as Military Transformation. They include former Secretary of Defense William Perry, Army Lieutenant Colonel (retired) Andrew Krepinevich, Andrew Marshall, long-standing Director of the Pentagon's Office of Net Assessment, scholar Eliot Cohen, the futurists Alvin and Heidi Toffler, Admiral (retired) William Owens, and Army General (retired) John Shalikashvili. The chapter then turns to more detailed concepts that emerged from the overall RMA/ Transformation construct, including Network Centric Warfare, Effects Based Operations, and Rapid Decisive Operations or "shock and awe." These concepts cross environmental boundaries and cannot be neatly categorized into the sea, land or air dimensions of warfare, and are therefore considered as representing strategic thought on joint warfare. Notable theorists here include Vice Admiral Arthur Cebrowski, Air Force Lieutenant General David Deptula, and US Joint Forces Command. The ideas of Air Force Colonel John Warden, analyst Harlan Ullman, and Marine Corps General James Mattis are also relevant. The chapter concludes with some thoughts on the elements of contemporary joint theory.

The Revolution in Military Affairs

Strategic thinking about a contemporary Revolution in Military Affairs can be traced to the late 1970s when Soviet military officers began to write about a military technical revolution (MTR). At the time, the conventional military advantage of the Soviet Union and its satellites over that of the United States and its allies was significant in absolute numbers—at least three to one—and so large that NATO had always retained the nuclear trump card, refusing to rule out the first use of nuclear weapons. But fledgling advances in military technologies such as the military application of computers, satellite surveillance, and long-range missiles were already of a degree that Soviet writers were concerned that the balance in conventional force capability would shift significantly in the Western favor. By the mid-1980s interest in a MTR had risen to the highest levels in the Soviet military, with the Chief of the Soviet General Staff, Nicolai Ogarkov, writing extensively on the need for the Soviet Union to reorient his country's defense budget towards the sorts of electronic investment that could be seen in the United States.

William Perry

The collapse of the Soviet Union rendered mute Ogarkov's case, but the trends he and other Soviet writers had identified were accurate. In the late 1970s the United States had launched an "offset strategy," which involved using the US technological edge to offset the Soviet Union's advantage in numbers. A notable thinker behind this strategy was William Perry, the Pentagon's Undersecretary of Defense for Research and Engineering in the Carter administration and later Secretary of Defense in the first Clinton administration. As Perry describes in a 1991 *Foreign Affairs* article, "high technology" was explicitly pursued as a means of addressing the Soviet threat.[2] The idea was not to build better ships, tanks and aircraft—since no matter how advanced the platform, they would still be outnumbered—but rather to develop new technologies that could support each individual platform in a manner that it multiplied the platform's combat effectiveness. The goal, in short, was to strengthen the US military through the use of technological *synergy*. Notable technological advances that could further this goal could be found in communications, computers, command, control and intelligence processing (C4I); stealth or low-observability; precision guidance; and intelligence gathering, surveillance and reconnaissance (ISR).

The impact of these technologies was apparent in the Gulf War. The combination of advanced C4I and ISR, including for the first time using satellite systems to support field commanders, dramatically increased what Perry called "situation awareness," that is, a knowledge of where friendly and opposing forces were located, thereby according commanders a degree of understanding about what was going on in the field that had not been achieved in any previous operation. Meanwhile, incorporating stealth technology into fighter aircraft and arming them with significantly more precise weapons than had historically been the case gave Coalition forces "air dominance" by enabling them to quickly suppress enemy air-defense systems. In later writings Perry would stress the demonstrated synergy and enhanced war-fighting capability created by combining stealth, advances in precision strike, new levels of situation or battlespace awareness, and "focused logistics" (applying advanced technologies to logistics efforts).[3]

Marshall, Krepinevich and the Office of Net Assessment

Whether this enhanced war-fighting capability could be considered revolutionary was debated extensively in military circles throughout much of the decade. The intellectual charge was led by the Pentagon's Office of Net Assessment (ONA), particularly Andrew Marshall and Andrew Krepinevich. In probably the first US assessment of what was then still called the MTR, Krepinevich argued in a 1992 ONA paper that a military revolution occurred when technological change combined with operational (or doctrinal) innovation and organizational adaptation in such a way as to fundamentally alter the character and conduct of war.[4] This became the essence of the ONA's "official" definition of a RMA during the 1990s. Krepinenich later elaborated that the new circumstances could be considered revolutionary if they produced a dramatic change by "an order of magnitude" in the combat potential and military effectiveness of a military force. By this criterion, he argued, there had been as many as ten revolutions in military affairs since the fourteenth century (see Box 4.1).[5]

Box 4.1 Military revolutions

In 1993 the Pentagon's Office of Net Assessment defined a RMA as "a major change in the nature of warfare brought about by the innovative application of technologies which, combined with dramatic changes in military doctrine and operational and organizational concepts, fundamentally alters the character and conduct of military operations." By this definition, it is possible to identify at least ten military revolutions since the fourteenth century:

- The *Infantry Revolution*, where longbow technology and accompanying tactical innovations enabled infantry to displace cavalry as the dominant force on the battlefield;

- The *Artillery Revolution*, in which longer gun barrels, metallurgical break-throughs, and changes in the form of gunpowder made artillery more powerful and cheaper, and accompanying organization changes in siege warfare forced defenders to abandon their castles;
- The *Revolution of Sail and Shot*, in which ships moved from oar-driven to sail-propelled power, enabling them to mount heavy cannons and transforming warships from floating garrisons of soldiers to artillery platforms;
- The *Fortress Revolution*, involving lower, thicker walls that rendered artillery less effective and moved the advantage to the defense;
- The *Gunpowder Revolution*, in which the technological innovation of musket fire was combined with a doctrinal change to linear (*vice* square) tactics;
- The *Napoleonic Revolution*, where the industrial revolution and the mass production of weapons enabled the *levée en masse*, that is, the quantum leap in the size of field armies;
- The *Land Warfare Revolution*, in which new civilian technologies like the railway and telegraph greatly enhanced strategic mobility, enabling military commanders to sustain large armies in the field and coordinate widely dispersed operations;
- The *Naval Revolution*, wherein sail gave way to steam power, and ships moved from being wooden to iron clad, leading to heavier and bigger battleships and guns, and new tactics away from broadside artillery mounts;
- The *Interwar Revolutions in Mechanization, Aviation and Information*, prompted by technological advances in mechanization and radio that ultimately enabled Germany's blitzkrieg tactics of joint operations involving aviation and mechanized forces; and
- The *Nuclear Revolution* of nuclear weapons, which prompted significant doctrinal theorizing and, once coupled with ballistic missiles, also led to the creation of new organizations within the militaries of the superpowers.

See Andrew F. Krepinevich, "Cavalry to Computer: The Pattern of Military Revolutions," *National Interest* (Fall 1994).

Other analysts were more specific in their meaning of "fundamentally alter." Thinkers at the Center for Strategic and International Studies identified a MTR as a "fundamental advance in technology, doctrine or organization that renders existing methods of conducting warfare obsolete,"[6] while RAND Corporation similarly stressed that a RMA involved a paradigm shift in the nature and conduct of military operations that "render[ed] obsolete or irrelevant one or more core competencies of a dominant player."[7] Krepinevich himself argued in his initial MTR assessment that change would be revolutionary if at some point the cumulative effects of technological advances and military innovation "invalidated former conceptual frameworks."[8] If, for example, advances in stand-off precision strike were to invalidate or render obsolete the former military advantage in having massive formations of even the best tanks, then this could be considered revolutionary. Or, historically, one could point to the Artillery Revolution, when the development of artillery rendered obsolete the former protection afforded by thick castle walls.

Members of the ONA were careful to emphasize that advanced military technologies did not constitute a revolution; rather, the full realization of a RMA required the three prongs of technological innovation, doctrinal or operational innovation, and organizational innovation. The Office replaced the term MTR with that of RMA specifically to highlight the imperative of going beyond technology. And in one of his few publicly available writings Andrew Marshall underlined that the critical factor in past RMAs (for example blitzkrieg) was "not technological surprise but the adoption of innovative operational concepts and organizations to exploit commonly available systems."[9] A "true RMA," one US Army War College scholar echoed, "transcends technology, engendering changes in organization, doctrine and strategy."[10]

In such a framework one could identify contemporary RMA technologies as those specified by Perry, namely C4I, ISR and precision guidance. Doctrinal changes then made possible or facilitated by these new technologies included stand-off precision strike from naval and air platforms against land targets; ground forces that were both more expeditionary in the sense of getting to a theater of operations quickly, and more agile and maneuverable on the battlefield, operating nonlinearly and in dispersed locations; and, significantly, an overall increased jointness among services. Organizational changes centered on creating agile, maneuverable forces, which in turn translated into units that were smaller than in the past and more tailorable to a particular task at hand.

Despite the "not just technology" statements of many RMA thinkers, critics took to task the technological orientation. Colin Gray, author of numerous works on military strategy, for example, argued that Krepinevich's "requirement that an RMA functions, inter alia, with the application of new technologies" represented a "fatal flaw." Stating a RMA to be a "discontinuous increase in military capability and effectiveness," Gray stressed that, above all, it was "vital not to require by definition that RMAs be triggered by new technology." But while RMAs should not be taken to be *triggered* by new technology, it is difficult to dispute that they will normally include new technology. Of the ten revolutions identified by Krepinevich all but one, the Fortress Revolution, involved important technological advances, while one, the Nuclear Revolution, was almost entirely technological in nature. "Occasionally," Gray later admits, "there is a discontinuity in military affairs in which the cutting edge for change truly is, or certainly includes, technological innovation."[11]

Eliot Cohen and the Tofflers

In fact, it was difficult for RMA proponents to escape the RMA's technological origins. Eliot Cohen, a scholar noted for his historical perspective, pointed out in 1996 that the contemporary revolution in military affairs, like many before it, had its origins in the civilian technological world and in the rise of information technologies.[12] Indeed, this was the very argument put forward by futurists Alvin and Heidi Toffler in their 1993 book, *War and Anti-War*. In their view, "the way we make war reflects the way we make wealth."[13] Over the course of human history how people make wealth had gone through two "waves" and was by then well into a third. During the first wave most people made their livelihood toiling by hand, whether by hunting or through agriculture; the means of warfare was hand-to-hand combat. In the second wave, launched with the Industrial Revolution, people made their living through mass production in factories; warfare, too, was waged en masse, beginning with Napoleon's *levée en masse*, progressing through the American Civil War and the two World Wars, and reaching its epitome with the development of the atomic bomb. In the 1970s a third wave began. The development of information technologies led to "de-massified," precision, smart economies (rooms of computers replaced with personal computers and then handheld devices, products tailored to individuals, knowledge workers), and these changes were, by the late 1980s, starting to be mirrored in warfare.

The Tofflers identified a number of distinct aspects of third-wave warfare, including smaller units, greater autonomy at lower levels, and more highly educated and technically expert troops. But they also pointed to the increased importance of "systems integration," a precursor to an accelerating tendency toward jointness that was being facilitated by technological advances, particularly advanced C4I that better enabled individual services to "talk" to one another. As Eliot Cohen highlighted, a key military impact of the integration of civilian information technologies into military affairs was that

> the new military would be an increasingly joint force ... In militaries around the world the traditional division into armies, navies and air forces ... has begun to break down. Not only have air operations become inseparable from almost any action on the ground, but naval forces increasingly deliver fire against a wide range of ground targets.[14]

William Owens and the system of systems

Increased jointness among services facilitated by technology was a central aspect of conceptual discussions surrounding the RMA in the 1990s. One of the first strategic thinkers to fully articulate a vision of resulting changes in the conduct of war was US Admiral (now retired) William Owens. Considered along with William Perry, Andrew Marshall and former Chairman of the Joint Chiefs of Staff General (retired) John Shalikashvili as among the RMA's founding fathers,[15] Owens arrived in the Pentagon in 1994 to take up his position as Vice Chairman of the Joint Chiefs of Staff. He soon became the most vocal military advocate of harnessing and accelerating the military-technological advances that had taken place over the previous decade or more.

Owens is one of the few, if not the only post-Cold War strategic thinker on joint warfare who has a significant body of literature to which one can point. In various articles from the mid-1990s onward he expressed his views on jointness and the RMA, bringing them together in his 2000 book, *Lifting the Fog of War*. The title refers to the vast array of satellites, unmanned aerial vehicles, reconnaissance aircraft, and even special operations forces that were giving the US military an unprecedented ability to know the location of friendly and enemy forces on the battlefield, by day or night, in any kind of weather—harnessing at new levels the age-old requirement for commanders to "see over the next hill." Historically, the lack of clear information about the enemy's and one's own military forces had hindered the effectiveness of military operations. But new technological advances were promising to "lift the fog of war," giving commanders the ability to see and understand everything on the battlefield.

A second area of Owens' strategic thinking centered on Clausewitz's other well-known admonishment, the friction of war. Advanced military systems, Owens argued, existed in three different areas: those designed "to see" (ISR); "to tell" (C4I); and "to act" (precision force). The problem, however, was that these systems were "stovepiped" in their own categories and unable to "talk" to one another. The challenge was to get these three broad circles of competencies to overlap and interact. If systems designed to gather surveillance information could transfer it in near-real time to those making the decisions, the result would be dominant battlespace knowledge or awareness; if commanders could relay their decisions in near-real time to systems designed to unleash precision force, the outcome would be near-perfect mission assignment; and if ISR systems could relay their information directly back to those that had "acted," the result would be immediate and complete battle assessment.[16] The idea of bringing three circles of systems together in this manner yielded the term "system of systems" and represented the "synergy" first identified by Perry several years earlier.

For Owens, the system of systems, and the RMA's technological advances in general, were quintessentially linked to jointness in the conduct of war. "As this broad concept [the system of systems] emerges over the next decade," Owens argued in the mid-1990s, "it will carry with it the revolution in military affairs (RMA) and a new appreciation of joint military operations, for this revolution depends ultimately on contributions from all the services."[17] The RMA, he later underlined, would "remain only a promise unless the Pentagon correctly rewrites combat doctrine to force truly joint operations."[18]

John Shalikashvili and Joint Vision 2010

For strategic thinking about implementing joint operations in practice we can point to *Joint Vision 2010*, produced under the guidance of General John Shalikashvili. Much of the vision contains ideas that are particularly relevant to land forces, such as mobility, dispersion, de-massification, and non-linearity in warfare. As a result, Chapter 2 on Landpower included a discussion of the US military's *Joint Vision 2010* of 1996 and its follow-on document, *Joint Vision 2020*, released in 2000. But the overall conceptual emphasis of the these vision statements is on joint capability and the need to achieve a seamless integration of service capabilities, if only to retain effectiveness with less redundancy in an era of constrained resources.

Of the new operational concepts introduced by *Joint Vision 2010*, including precision engagement, full dimensional protection, focused logistics, and dominant maneuver, it is the latter that most significantly pushed forward conceptual thinking on joint theory. The idea behind "dominant maneuver" was to use sea, land, air, and space forces in synchronized fashion, operating with speed and agility from many areas of the battlefield, thereby achieving significant military advantage over an opponent. *Joint Vision 2010* specifically envisioned forces operating "cross-dimensionally," such as air or naval forces against ground targets, or ground and naval forces against air defenses.[19] It also clearly reflected ideas put forward by Owens, particularly those of a "systems of systems" and dominant battlespace awareness.

Critiques

The notion that advanced military technologies could reduce the fog and friction of war was a controversial one and invited criticism. The claims were seen as disconnected from historical experience, and from what adversaries may think, want, and do—a perfect example of what Clausewitz called the war on paper as opposed to war as it really is. "As long as war involves human beings," pointed out one scholar, "no technology can completely eliminate friction, ambiguity, and uncertainty."[20] Against the optimistic talks of technological advances reducing the fog and friction of war, Major General Robert Scales (see Chapter 2) warned in a 1997 article that warfare remained "an inherently uncertain enterprise in which chance, friction, and the limitations of the human mind under stress profoundly limit our ability to predict outcomes."[21] To be fair, Owens in his writings and Shalikashvili in *Joint Vision 2010* in some ways pre-empted these critiques. New technologies would not fully dissipate the fog and friction of war, they argued; rather they would mitigate their impact, introducing a disparity significant enough to render the United States dominance in warfare.[22] Nonetheless, not long after the release of *Joint Vision 2010* one could sense a palatable swing away from the earlier revolutionary rhetoric.

Military transformation

By the late 1990s the notion of a RMA was starting to be seen as too dramatic, as promising too much. Moreover, the term itself seemed to indicate a definitive end-state, a point at which the revolution would have finished its course, and yet most foresaw several decades of continuous change. In its place started to seep the term Military Transfor-mation, or simply Transformation. In fact, the designation was not so new. Early on, Marshall referred to the RMA as a "process of transformation,"[23] and others, such as Colin Gray and even Owens, simply equated RMAs to "transformations of war."[24] The change in emphasis, which ironically was not promoted by any particular war or international event (as is arguably more often the case), was first given prominent visi-bility with the release of a report by the bipartisan National Defense Panel at the end of 1997, entitled *Transforming Defense*. The trend continued over the next several years, and by the early years of the Bush administration the term RMA had all but disappeared in the United States, replaced with that of transformation.

Arthur Cebrowski, NCW and military transformation

While the terms and timeframe had changed, the substantive content had not. If anything, the war in Afghanistan in late 2001/early 2002, and later the 2003 Iraq War, seemingly vindicated the promises made by mid-1990s RMA proponents. Highly mobile, dis-persed army special operations forces called in precision air strikes from air force and navy platforms. Advanced command and control, surveillance, and precision guidance systems were used extensively, and jointly, throughout the war. Thus, although Secretary of Defense Donald Rumsfeld spoke and wrote in early 2002 of "Transforming the Mili-tary," his expressed ideas echoed earlier discussions of the RMA—smaller, more mobile forces; precision engagement; increased battlespace awareness; and, above all, the imperative of jointness.[25]

Into these changed yet not-so-changed circumstances stepped Arthur Cebrowski, a revolutionary-minded thinker who had first put forward the concept of network-centric warfare (NCW) in 1998. As noted in Chapter 1, the idea behind NCW was to focus more on the combat capability achieved when different platforms are linked together, than on the attributes of an individual platform. "We are in the midst of a revolution in military affairs (RMA) unlike any seen since the Napoleonic Age ... [and the] levee en masse," Cebrowksi and John J. Garstka argued in a seminal *U.S. Naval Institute Proceedings* article, " ... a fundamental shift from what we call platform-centric warfare to something we call network-centric warfare."[26] Eliot Cohen put the revolutionary nature of this shift into perspective:

> From the middle of the nineteenth century until very recently, platforms dominated warfare: the newest ship, plane, or tank outclassed its rivals and in most cases

speedily rendered them obsolete … The wheel has now turned again. The platform has become less important, while the quality of what it carries—sensors, munitions, and electronics of all kinds—has become critical.[27]

In promoting the potential of networked warfare, Cebrowski and Gartska took their cue from the civilian commercial world where, they observed, the power of the personal computer grew exponentially once it was part of a network. "It is not so much about the computer as it is about the computer in the networked condition,"[28] they pointed out. In their view, network-centric warfare—"with all apologies to Clausewitz"—was a new theory of war, in that it identified new sources of power, showed how those new sources pointed to new structures and organizations, and pointed to new political and military strategies.[29]

The earliest formulation of NCW was associated with the US Navy, both conceptually and in practice. Technological advances in C4I proceeded most rapidly in the US Navy and, prompted by requirements to be technologically interoperable with their American counterpart, within other NATO navies. But the notion of NCW as conceived by Cebrowksi is relevant to all services. In a land force environment, for example, it points to linking together the combat power of tanks, armored personnel carriers, and artillery howitzers; in an air environment it might link unmanned aerial vehicle (UAV) sensor information with the combat potential of a fighter jet. Most notably, truly revolutionary change could not arrive until NCW made the transition to the joint world. The requirement was for sea, land, and air platforms to be able to transfer information amongst one another—for example, for reconnaissance vehicles on the ground to be able to receive images from fighter-jet targeting pods or UAVs. This was a formidable military transformation challenge, and one that Rumsfeld tapped Cebrowski to address.

In 2001, shortly before the 9/11 attacks, Rumsfeld appointed Cebrowksi as director of a newly created Office of Force Transformation in the Pentagon. With a mandate to promote the transformation of the US military services, the office issued a *Transformation Planning Guidance*, designed to facilitate the service's efforts to frame their transformation roadmaps, as well as a broader statement of America's strategic approach to military transformation. Transformation was defined as "a process that shapes the changing nature of competition and cooperation through new combinations of concepts, capabilities, people and organizations that exploit our nation's advantages and protect against our asymmetric vulnerabilities."[30] The common theme pervading both documents, which did not appear until 2003, was the imperative of pursuing and implementing technologies and doctrines that would facilitate and ultimately bring to fruition a situation of true jointness in operations. Interoperability—the ability to transfer information—was the first key step, and a difficult one, considering that early communications systems were developed along service lines, with little or no common architecture. Once technological interoperability was achieved, a military could be "networked," but for Cebrowksi, as expressed by the Office of Force Transformation, NCW demanded additional steps. "NCW," it argued, "is the military expression of the information age … [it] refers to the combination of emerging tactics, techniques, and technologies that a networked force employs to create decisive warfighting advantage."[31] Protocols and common means of acting in certain situations still had to be established, i.e. joint doctrine; as a result, the services were also asked to develop joint operating concepts. Jointness enabled by interoperable technology and joint doctrine would ultimately allow for new attributes in the conduct of war that were originally associated with the RMA, things like dispersed and de-massed forces.

Cebrowski, as stated in an eloquent post-mortem discussion of his career and strategic thought, was convinced that the American military "stood on the threshold of an explosion of information, knowledge and understanding of warfare, as well as, most importantly, greater precision in waging it."[32] In his view, advances in military technologies had a moral quality about them because greater precision could enable the achievement of objectives with less loss of life. Others were less sanguine. Colleagues agreed that advanced technologies were useful in warfare, but they were not so convinced of an effective trade-off between military mass and networked forces. Nonetheless, a number of concepts linked to NCW, the earlier system of systems, and indeed the whole RMA dialogue and the characteristics of war it encompassed—particularly the nonlinear, synchronized nature of war—flourished in the early 2000s.

Effects-based operations and related concepts

By the turn of the millennium, strategic thinking related to joint theory was beginning to involve more refined concepts under the overall NCW umbrella, including that of effects-based operations (EBO) and rapid decisive operations (RDO). But whereas NCW had its intellectual home in the US Navy, EBO, and RDO were more comfortably located in the US Air Force. The fact that NWC, EBO, and RDO must be examined together, and yet originated in different services, indicates their underlying "joint" nature. So too does the reality that extensive discussions and promulgations of EBO and RDO—and later refutations of these concepts' validity—came from US Joint Forces Command.

John Warden

The roots of EBO lie in the strategic thought of John Warden. The retired US Air Force Colonel is best known for drawing up the 1991 Gulf War air campaign and for enunciating a Five Rings Model of enemy centers of gravity—command and leadership, critical war industry, infrastructure, population, and fielded military—that should be subject to a "parallel warfare" strategy of simultaneous (*vice* serial) precision strikes (see Chapter 3). But Warden's strategic thought also went beyond the use of force. A strong proponent of psychological effects in war, the "indirect" approach of Sun Tzu and Liddell Hart, Warden advocated that planners focus less on destroying and killing and more on how to create chaos, confusion, and paralysis. In addition, he emphasized the importance of integrating military instruments with those in the economic and political dimensions.

David Deptula

David Deptula, Warden's subordinate during the Gulf War and now Lieutenant General, elaborated on the ideas originally planted by Warden, framing them in terms of the EBO concept. "The construct of warfare employed during the Gulf War air campaign has become known as *parallel warfare*," he noted in a 2001 monograph, "and was based upon achieving specific effects, not absolute destruction of targets lists."[33] He stressed the distinction between destruction-based and effects-based warfare, arguing that the objective of striking the specific centers of gravity identified by Warden was not to annihilate the enemy or wear him out through attrition, but rather to have a desired effect on adversary behavior.

Deptula's vision of EBO took as its starting-point the view that rendering the enemy force useless is just as effective as eliminating that enemy force, and that a viable alternative to a destruction concept of war is one based on controlling the enemy's ability to operate. Whereas early airpower theorists advocated the destruction of industrial and population centers, EBO went further, "aiming not just to impede the means of the enemy to conduct war or the will of the people to continue war, but the very ability of the enemy to control its vital functions."[34] He gave as an example the targeting of Iraqi power plants in the opening stages of the Gulf War, where the effect was to induce other power plant managers to shut down their plants in advance to avoid being targeted— an example of the achievement of warfare objectives without the destructive use of force. In this sense Deptula, and Warden before him, shared with Cebrowski the desire to achieve a more bloodless form of war. The logical end-game of EBO, Deptula later stressed, was to attain security objectives without resorting to destruction or visible disruption.[35] An advocate of Sun Tzu's perspective that the acme of skill in warfare is to subdue the enemy without battle, he highlighted EBO as a springboard for better linking military, economic, and diplomatic instruments of national power.

Deptula also placed EBO squarely in a joint force framework. In the old attrition or annihilation way of thinking about war, he argued, ground forces were at the center of the "universe," with air and maritime forces orbiting around land forces in support; by contrast, in the new, effects-based war-planning approach, the Joint Force Commander stood at the center of the universe, with joint land, air, and maritime forces all making contributions. Finally, he linked EBO to another term in the defense lexicon, RDO, arguing that such operations seek to achieve an effects-based result with greater rapidity and less mass.

Harlan Ullman and "shock and awe"

The RDO concept originated with Harlan Ullman, a former US naval officer and a scholar with the Center for Strategic and International Studies. In a slim volume published in 1996, *Shock and Awe: Achieving Rapid Dominance*, Ullman and his colleague argued that the aim of Rapid Dominance was "to affect the will, perception, and understanding of the adversary … [by] imposing a regime of Shock and Awe." In the term Rapid Dominance, "rapid" meant the ability to move quickly before the enemy could react, while "dominance" referred to affecting and dominating the enemy's will, both physically and psychologically. The strategy would be effective, Ullman argued, if, by acting on a sufficiently timely basis, friendly forces could so overload an adversary's perceptions and understanding of events that they rendered him incapable of resistance at the tactical and strategic levels, paralyzing his will to carry on.[36]

US Joint Forces Command

RDO, shock and awe, and even EBO originated as airpower concepts but were subsequently stretched to fill a joint box. A clear indication of this trend was the substantial amount of strategic thinking about EBO and RDO carried out by US Joint Forces Command. In a 2001 doctrine document it defined EBO as a "philosophy that focuses on obtaining a desired strategic outcome or 'effect' on the enemy, through the application of a full range of military and non-military capabilities."[37] The "effect," in turn, could be either a physical or psychological/behavioral outcome. The command stressed the concept's applicability or added value to joint operations, arguing that EBO was a joint command and staff thinking process designed to improve unified action. Moreover, its object (echoing Warden's original observation) was to harmonize and synchronize military actions with those of other instruments of national power, including political and economic, so as to achieve unity of effort in joint operations planning and execution. The command further linked EBO to the earlier NCW concept, arguing that joint operations of the future would be knowledge centric, effects based, and networked. EBO was seen by other US military joint organizations as a supporting concept to NCW, and a focus on the *effects* of military operations came to be defined as the nature of the objective of NCW.[38] But, "[a]t its core," the Joint Warfighting Center argued in 2007, "an effects-based approach [remains] a refinement of how we think about joint operations."[39]

Joint Forces Command defined RDO as one that integrates knowledge, command and control, and EBO to achieve the desired political/military effect. While EBO refers more to the purpose of an operation (to achieve an effect), RDO referred more to how operations were conducted, i.e. a concept of operations, much like NCW. The command characterized current operations as sequential, progressive, linear, attrition based, and demanding "de-conflicted" service operations, as compared to RDO, which would be simultaneous, parallel, distributed, effects based, and have fully "integrated" (joint) service capabilities. In this latter regard, RDO would require the integrated application of dominant maneuver (a predominantly landpower concept) and precision engagement (a predominantly airpower concept), as called for in *Joint Vision 2010*. In military parlance, the idea behind RDO was to get inside the enemy's decision cycle so as to cause the opposing forces to lose coherence. For Joint Forces Command, in the early 2000s, RDO constituted the essence of military transformation whereby the US and its allies would assault the adversary from directions and in dimensions against which he had no counter, creating confusion, loss of coherence, and ultimately a change in behavior such that the adversary was no longer acting counter to US interests.[40]

In the years leading up to the 2003 Iraq War "shock and awe" came to be seen as requiring a series of unrelenting waves of strikes across many targets, combining sea, air, land and space forces. The idea was to rely on precision force and agile units—two components of the original RMA concept—to defeat opposing forces, while avoiding wholesale destruction and civilian casualties. The war itself was a concrete manifestation of the strategy; precision strikes were conducted on hundreds of targets in parallel with the deployment of maneuver forces on the ground. While some interpreted Operation Iraqi Freedom as vindicating "shock and awe," others saw a degree of failure. An unrealized component of the strategy was to decapitate the Iraqi leadership in the opening stages of the war, with the aim of creating a psychological blow that would paralyze the Iraqi war effort from the outset.

In any case, the humbling experience of the years of Iraqi insurgency that followed had an impact on future strategic thinking. By the second half of the 2000s Joint Forces Command had dropped the RDO construct, perhaps because no convincing explanation could be found as to why it would necessarily always be better for operations to be rapid. As some critics pointed out, the political leadership may find a graduated response desirable or necessary for any number of reasons, such as to avoid escalation to the use of nuclear weapons, or to keep allies on board. EBO lasted somewhat longer than RDO as a concept in vogue, but it, too, invited many critiques which, by the decade's end, had almost buried it.

Critiques of effects-based operations

At its core, EBO was a planning tool that encouraged identifying the desired strategic outcome or objective in a campaign and then deriving the means required to achieve the objective. This was presented as a change from a historical tendency to focus in the first instance on the means, which in turn were usually destructive. Do you want to destroy a bridge, or do you want to cut off the flow of enemy supplies across it? Do you want to cut off the supplies, or do you want to prevent enemy resupply altogether?[41] But critics argued that this new way of thinking was not so new, and that planners had always thought in terms of strategic outcomes and objectives.

More troubling was the concern, expressed by General James Mattis, Commander of Joint Forces Command in the latter part of the 2000s, and several others that the effects-based approach could lead to a dangerous self-delusion about the capacity to control outcomes. EBO was premised on the assumption that one can predict how an enemy will react to a given situation. The concept laid claim not just to first-order effects, but also to second- and even third-order effects. Its tenets implied that war was a science rather than an art and a science, and that war and strategic outcomes could somehow be controlled. Like NCW before it, EBO was criticized as being contrary to all historical experience, and certainly to the Clausewitzian dictum that war, more than any other human activity, most closely resembles a game of cards.

By 2008 General Mattis found it necessary to issue his own guidance on EBO. "I am convinced that the various interpretations of EBO have caused confusion throughout the joint force," he stated. "EBO has been misapplied and overextended to the point that it actually hinders rather than helps joint operations."[42] Specific concerns from the US Army and Marine Corps and other observers included that EBO assumed a level of unachievable predictability; called for an unobtainable level of knowledge of the enemy; was too prescriptive and over-engineered; and discounted the human dimension in war. EBO was seen as setting up an intellectual "Maginot Line" around which the enemy could maneuver, and as overemphasizing precision air strikes to the detriment of ground force operations. But EBO did not disappear entirely. From its various tenets, Mattis and Joint Forces Command retained as useful the attention the concept gave to the interaction of military and non-military instruments, promoting unity of action, and conducting periodic assessments of operations to determine progress toward achieving objectives.

Conclusion

Strategic thought pertaining to joint theory in the first two decades following the end of the Cold War was closely linked to overarching conceptions of the changing nature of warfare. Ultimately sparked or enabled by the civilian world's information revolution, these broad conceptions progressively included the MTR, the RMA, and military transformation. The attributes included as part of each of these phenomena varied by thinker, and there was inevitably a significant degree of overlap; in some cases only the title changed, not the content. Certain warfare characteristics pervaded and recurred in the discussions, whether the subject was MTR, RMA, parallel war, system of systems, NCW, military transformation, EBO, or RDO and shock and awe—attributes like "dispersed," "nonlinear," "simultaneous," an emphasis on speed, and the requirement for a concentration of effects, *vice* mass. But the most consistently stated objective—sometimes achieved and sometimes only an aspiration—was "jointness" in warfare.

The elaboration of joint theory has involved advancements and retrenchments. Early ideas on the RMA and the associated systems of systems and NCW concepts were at first embraced by many but later deemed out of touch with historical experience, only to be followed a few years later by RDO and EBO as the centerpiece of military transformation. Initially boosted by RMA/Transformation-validating wars in Afghanistan and Iraq, these newer concepts were in their own turn later found to be historically wanting. But while the utility or relevance of various conceptions of the conduct of war that emerged in the 1990s and 2000s has at times been questioned, the imperative of jointness that flows through each of them has not. Much as Joint Forces Command has retained those aspects of EBO that are helpful while discarding the rest, so too is it important to identify the essential elements of joint theory.

Separating the wheat from the chaff, post-Cold War strategic thought relevant to joint theory reveals a theory of joint warfare that might include the following tenets: contemporary military operations are such that navy, army, air, and space forces must be fully interoperable in practical and technological terms; that is to say, services must have compatible doctrines and concepts of operations and compatible technologies for receiving and transmitting information; the traditional assigning of a military operation to a single service is a thing of the past; operations demand and are more effective if they involve contributions from two or more services; the integration of service capabilities into a joint framework enhances friendly force battlespace awareness and response time; missions must be assigned not according to service but according to the requirement, regardless of which service fulfills it; and contemporary operations must go beyond joint to include non-military (governmental and non-governmental) instruments. This latter element is particularly relevant to strategic thought from the mid-2000s onward. Prompted by circumstances in Iraq and Afghanistan, new thinking has centered on counterinsurgency and irregular warfare. It is to these strategic theorists that we now turn.

Notes

1 Williamson Murray, "The Evolution of Joint Warfare," *Joint Forces Quarterly* (Summer 2002), 35.
2 William J. Perry, "Desert Storm and Deterrence," *Foreign Affairs* 70, no. 4 (Fall 1991), 69.
3 William J. Perry, "Defense in an Age of Hope," *Foreign Affairs* 75, no. 6 (November/ December 1996), 77.
4 Andrew F. Krepinevich, *The Military Technical Revolution: A Preliminary Assessment* (Washington, DC: Center for Strategic and Budgetary Assessments, 2002) (originally written in 1992 for the Office of Net Assessment).
5 Andrew F. Krepinevich, "Cavalry to Computer: The Pattern of Military Revolutions," *National Interest* (Fall 1994), 31.
6 Michael J. Mazarr, *The Military Technical Revolution: A Structural Framework* (Washington, DC: Center for Strategic and International Studies, March 1993), 16.
7 Richard O. Hundley, *Past Revolutions, Future Transformations* (Santa Monica, CA: RAND Corporation, 1999), 9.
8 Krepinevich, *The Military Technical Revolution*, 3.
9 Andrew W. Marshall, "The 1995 RMA Essay Contest: A Postscript," *Joint Forces Quarterly* (Winter 1995–96), 81.
10 Stephen J. Blank, "Preparing for the Next War: Reflections on the Revolution in Military Affairs," *Strategic Review* (Spring 1996), 17.

11 Colin S. Gray, *Strategy for Chaos: Revolutions in Military Affairs and the Evidence of History* (London: Frank Cass, 2002), 4–5, 45.
12 Eliot A. Cohen, "A Revolution in Warfare," *Foreign Affairs* 75, no. 2 (March/April 1996), 42.
13 Alvin Toffler and Heidi Toffler, *War and Anti-war* (New York: Warner Books, 1993), 2.
14 Cohen, "A Revolution in Warfare," 47.
15 James Blaker, *Understanding the Revolution in Military Affairs* (Washington, DC: Progressive Policy Institute, January 1997), 5.
16 William A. Owens, *Lifting the Fog of War* (New York: Farrar, Straus and Giroux, 2000), 99.
17 William A. Owens, "The Emerging System of Systems," *Military Review* (May–June 1995), 17.
18 Owens, *Lifting the Fog of War*, 97.
19 US Joint Chiefs of Staff, "Joint Vision 2010: America's Military Preparing for Tomorrow," *Joint Force Quarterly* (Summer 1996), 42; US Joint Chiefs of Staff, *Joint Vision 2020* (Washington, DC: Joint Chiefs of Staff, 2000), 20.
20 Mackubin Thomas Owens, "Technology, the RMA, and Future War," *Strategic Review* (Spring 1998), 67.
21 Paul van Riper and Robert H. Scales, Jr., "Preparing for War in the 21st Century," *Parameters* (Autumn 1997).
22 William A. Owens, "The American Revolution in Military Affairs," *Joint Forces Quarterly* (Winter 1995–96), 38; US Joint Chiefs of Staff, "Joint Vision 2010," 41.
23 A. W. Marshall, "Some Thoughts in Military Revolutions," Office of Net Assessment Memorandum, July 27, 1993.
24 Gray, *Strategy for Chaos*, 9; William A. Owens, "The Once and Future Revolution in Military Affairs," *Joint Forces Quarterly* (Summer 2002), 55.
25 See Donald H. Rumsfeld, "Transforming the Military," *Foreign Affairs* 81, no. 3 (May/June 2002).
26 Arthur K. Cebrowski and John J. Garstka, "Network-centric Warfare: Its Origins and Future," *U.S. Naval Institute Proceedings* 124, no. 1 (January 1998).
27 Cohen, "A Revolution in Warfare,"45.
28 Cebrowski and Garstka, "Network-centric Warfare."
29 James Blaker, "Arthur K. Cebrowski: A Retrospective," *Naval War College Review* 59, no. 2 (Spring 2006), 138, 140.
30 US Office of Force Transformation, *Transformation Planning Guidance* (Washington, DC: Office of Force Transformation, April 2003), 3.
31 US Office of Force Transformation, *Military Transformation: A Strategic Approach* (Washington, DC: Office of Force Transformation, Fall 2003), 13.
32 Blaker, "Arthur K. Cebrowski," 135. Cebrowski died of cancer in November 2005.
33 David Deptula, *Effects-based Operations: Change in the Nature of Warfare* (Arlington, VA: Aerospace Education Foundaton, 2001), 3.
34 Ibid., 8.
35 David Deptula, "Effects-based Operations: A U.S. Commander's Perspective," *Journal of the Singapore Armed Forces* 31, no. 2 (2005).
36 Harlan K. Ullman and James P. Wade, *Shock and Awe: Achieving Rapid Dominance* (Washington, DC: National Defense University Press, 1996), 14–15.
37 US Joint Forces Command, *A Concept for Rapid Decisive Operations* (RDO White Paper Version 2.0), August 9, 2001.
38 Erik J. Dahl, "Network Centric Warfare and the Death of Operational Art," *Defence Studies* 2, no. 1 (Spring 2002), 5, 15.
39 US Joint Warfighting Center, "An Effects-based Approach: Refining how We Think about Joint Operations," *Joint Forces Quarterly* 44, no. 1 (1st quarter 2007), 3.
40 U.S. Joint Forces Command, Joint Forces Command Glossary, as quoted in Ian Roxborough, "From Revolution to Transformation: The State of the Field," *Joint Forces Quarterly* (Autumn 2002), 72.
41 Dahl, "Network Centric Warfare," 15.
42 James N. Mattis, "USJFCOM Commander's Guidance for Effects-based Operations," *Joint Forces Quarterly* 51 (4th quarter 2008), 105.

Further reading

Cebrowski, Arthur K. and John J. Garstka. "Network-centric Warfare: Its Origins and Future," *U.S. Naval Institute Proceedings* 124, no. 1 (January 1998).

Cohen, Eliot A. "A Revolution in Warfare," *Foreign Affairs* 75, no. 2 (March/April 1996).

Gray, Colin S. *Strategy for Chaos: Revolutions in Military Affairs and the Evidence of History* (London: Frank Cass, 2002).

Krepinevich, Andrew F. "Cavalry to Computer: The Pattern of Military Revolutions," *National Interest* (Fall 1994).

——. *The Military Technical Revolution: A Preliminary Assessment* (Washington, DC: Center for Strategic and Budgetary Asssessments, 2002).

Mazarr, Michael J. *The Military Technical Revolution: A Structural Framework* (Washington, DC: Center for Strategic and International Studies, March 1993).

Owens, William A. *Lifting the Fog of War* (New York: Farrar, Straus and Giroux, 2000).

——. "The Emerging System of Systems," *Military Review* (May–June 1995).

Toffler, Alvin and Heidi Toffler. *War and Anti-war* (New York: Warner Books, 1993).

United States Joint Chiefs of Staff. *Joint Vision 2010* (Washington, DC: Department of Defense, 1996).

——. *Joint Vision 2020* (Washington, DC: Department of Defense, 2000).

5 Irregular war

Insurgency, counterinsurgency and New War

In the decades since the fall of the Berlin Wall there has been a substantial amount of strategic thinking about irregular war. Broadly defined by what it is not—irregular war is *not* conventional or regular war between two organized militaries of opposing states—this form of war includes at least one non-state entity. America's 2006 Quadrennial Defense Review counted terrorism, insurgency, and guerrilla warfare as part of irregular warfare. Guerrilla warfare refers to the tactics of hit and run, of enemies who avoid direct battles by hiding in the countryside or urban areas, of opponents who, in the words of C. E. Callwell at the turn of the twentieth century, refuse "to meet [regular forces] in the open field."[1] Terrorism eludes a commonly accepted definition, but generally includes attacks on civilians or non-combatants, the seemingly random use of violence, and the purposeful creation of fear or panic to intimidate a population or compel a government to do or not do something. Like guerrilla war, terrorism, notes contemporary strategic thinker David Kilcullen, "is in the tactical repertoire of virtually every insurgency."[2]

In contrast to the tactical nature of guerrilla warfare and terrorism, insurgency, or what was at one time referred to as revolutionary war, is explicitly tied to an overall goal. "Revolutionary war," argued scholars during the Cold War, "refers to the seizure of political power by the use of armed force ... Revolutionary wars occur *within* states, and have as their objective the seizure of state power" (emphasis in original).[3] More recent US joint doctrine has placed the objective in broader terms, defining insurgency as an organized movement aimed at weakening the control and legitimacy of an established government or occupying power, with the aim of getting the people to accept the insurgents' authority as legitimate.[4] Kilcullen has expanded the goal still further to accommodate a global insurgency aspiring well beyond the control of a state or government apparatus. Insurgency, he argues, is a popular movement that seeks to overthrow *the status quo* (emphasis added) through—in addition to terrorism—subversion, political activity, insurrection, and armed conflict.

This chapter examines strategic thought on irregular warfare and specifically on insurgency, counterinsurgency (COIN), and New War. Apart from Sun Tzu, who was arguably the first to formulate the principles of revolutionary war—attack weakness, avoid strength, and be patient (see Chapter 2)—strategic thinking about irregular and revolutionary warfare is relatively new. Jomini advised states to avoid involvement in what today would be called counterinsurgency operations, while Clausewitz, notes military historian Martin Van Creveld, "ultimately ... presented war as something made by [national] armies."[5] Insurgencies are as old as warfare itself, but revolutionary warfare as a fully defined concept is relatively new because it is linked to two phenomena of more recent times: industrialization and imperialism. This chapter begins by briefly highlighting the strategic thought of early and mid-twentieth-century revolutionary warfare theorists and practitioners, including Callwell, T. E. Lawrence, Mao Tse Tung, David Galula, and Robert Thompson. It then goes on to examine in more detail the substantial and accelerating amount of strategic thought on insurgency, counter-insurgency, and New War from the mid-1980s onward. Notable thinkers include Thomas Hammes, Mary Kaldor, Kilcullen, Andrew Krepinevich, William Lind, Rupert Smith, David Petraeus, and Van Creveld. The chapter concludes with some thoughts on the conduct of contemporary irregular warfare.

Revolutionary war in the early and mid-twentieth century

Callwell on counterinsurgency

Described by some as the Clausewitz of colonial warfare, British army Colonel C. E. Callwell fought in Afghanistan, Crete, and South Africa in the 1880s and 1890s. His experiences led him to conclude that the conditions and mode of fighting in small wars were so distinct from those of conventional warfare that irregular warfare had to be carried out on the basis of totally different methods. In his *Small Wars: Their Principles and Practice* (3rd edition 1906), Callwell therefore sought to sketch out broad rules that governed the conduct of operations in conflicts against adversaries unaccounted for in the works of Clausewitz and Jomini. Small wars he defined by exclusion as all those where opposing forces were not both regular forces, and he makes the useful point that the term "small war" in fact had no relation to the scale of the conflict, merely to the types of entities participating.[6]

Covering a great range of detail, from the overall causes and objectives of small wars, to innumerable tactical elements of military operations, to problems of supply and intelligence, many of Callwell's broad dictums survived the test of time. He notes, for example, the difficulty of determining population support for an insurrection, the mobility and strategic advantage enjoyed by the insurgent, operating as he is on his home territory, and the need to set clear goals in the conduct of an operation. Yet others, like the requirement to seek enemy collapse as soon as possible, would seem unrealistic, and it is inevitable that the relevance of tactical elements, such as how best to employ camels and cavalry in flank attacks, would be washed away by time. But a more notable overall weakness was the entirely military focus of Callwell's strategic thought, on measures to kinetically eliminate the insurgent. In later years counterinsurgency would shift dramatically to focus on non-kinetic measures and securing the population.

Callwell sets out from the beginning to discuss his subject from the point of view of the regular troops seeking to quell the insurgency, that is, the counterinsurgent perspective. The unintended effect was that by the time World War One was underway *Small Wars* seemed obsolete. This was not because the primary war of the era was state to state but rather because, as T. E. Lawrence argued, the advantage had shifted to the insurgent. The new perspective of interest was from that of the irregular forces.

Lawrence on insurgency

T. E. Lawrence, the British army officer who traveled with and advised the Arab Bedouin during the Arab revolt against Ottoman Turk rule in 1916–18, wrote extensively. In a 1917 article he listed and elaborated 27 articles or practices that outsiders like the

British should follow to win over the trust of a specific people, the Bedouin. But his more general thoughts on guerrilla warfare are best gathered from a chapter in the autobiographical account of his role in the revolt, *Seven Pillars of Wisdom*, first published in 1926. Confined to a tent, due to illness, he reflected on the nature and conduct of the war of which he was a part, setting down his "shadowy principles" for what would later be called insurgency. From his contemplations he concluded that a successful rebellion by what he referred to as "irregulars" had to have: "an unassailable base, guarded not just from attack, but from the fear of attack"; a friendly population of which only 2 percent had to be active, and the rest quietly sympathetic so that movements were not betrayed; a technologically sophisticated enemy dependent on modes of communications and supply that were therefore vulnerable to disruption; and an enemy that was too weak in numbers as compared to the size of territory to effectively control it by means of interlocking fortified posts. The rebels themselves had to have "the virtues of secrecy and self-control, and the qualities of speed, endurance and independence" from lines of supply; as well as the technical equipment necessary to paralyze the enemy's communications.

A notable aspect of Lawrence's strategic thought is that he focused on the support of the people, not the elimination of the enemy. "A province would be won," he argued, "when we had taught the civilians in it to die for our ideal of freedom. *The presence of the enemy was secondary*" (emphasis added). Lawrence singled out the importance of individual members of the insurgency, contrasting them to the regular forces fighting on the battlefields of Europe: "Governments saw men only in mass; but our men, being irregulars, were not formations, but individuals. An individual death, like a pebble dropped in water, might make but a brief hole; yet rings of sorrow widen out therefrom. We could not afford casualties." Tactically, he said, the mode of conduct should be "tip and run," using the smallest force in the quickest time at the farthest place. He likened the character of operations to that of naval war in mobility, ubiquity, and independence of bases, rendering the rebel free, as are naval forces in command of the sea, "to take as much or as little of the war as he will."[7] But while the tactics were rapid, the overall battle would be long and protracted. Granted time, mobility, security, and doctrine, the insurgent would prevail, not by destroying the enemy but by wearing him out through exhaustion.

In discussing the principles that emerged from his experience during the Arab revolt, Lawrence developed a theoretical base that would have general application to future irregular wars. Many of his insights have endured. But they collectively comprised just a few pages in hundreds of historical recounting, and in this regard were not fully developed. It is with Mao Tse-Tung that we first see the clear fusion of theory and practice in irregular war.

Mao on insurgency

Like many strategic thinkers of this volume, the leader of the Chinese Communist Party and later founder of the People's Republic of China was a prodigious writer but is best known for a particular work. Mao Tse-Tung's *On Guerrilla Warfare*, first penned during the Long March of 1935 and considered the basic text for revolutionary war, set out a strategy that he successfully implemented during and after World War Two, first against the Nationalists, then the Japanese, and later the Nationalists again. Looking at the Marxist, proletarian revolution of Russia, Mao quickly realized that the methods of revolutionary war in an industrial society did not readily apply to the largely agrarian population of China. He therefore adapted his tactics and techniques to a peasant-based guerrilla war, his term for what we would today call insurgency because it went beyond tactics to include a specific revolutionary goal.

For Mao, guerrilla warfare was a weapon that a nation inferior in arms and military equipment could employ against a more powerful aggressor nation, and its pursuit in the Chinese context had as its goal the complete emancipation of the Chinese people. The core of his strategic thought is that successful insurgency involves seven fundamental steps: arousing and organizing the people; achieving internal unification politically; establishing bases; equipping forces; recovering national strength; destroying the enemy's strength; and regaining lost territories.[8] These seven steps were later intellectually organized into three "phases," with the result that it has become common to speak of phases of revolutionary warfare. The first comprises consolidating base areas in isolated terrain and persuading inhabitants to support the movement, which gradually acquires the quality of "mass"; the second involves direct yet limited action against the enemy, including the use of terrorism and sabotage to procure arms and supplies and thereby equip the masses; and the third entails transforming guerrilla forces into a more orthodox establishment capable of engaging the enemy in a conventional battle.[9]

Like Callwell and Lawrence before him, Mao recognized that the general features of revolutionary war differ fundamentally from regular operations. Of overwhelming importance is the support of the people. Guerrilla warfare is revolutionary in nature, he argued, because if it is not to fail it must necessarily involve achieving political objectives that coincide with the aspirations of the people. Assistance, cooperation, or at a minimum sympathy, are critical: "guerrilla warfare derives from the masses and is supported by them [and] it can neither exist nor flourish if it separates itself from their sympathies." In his well-quoted phrase, the people are the water and the troops are the fish, and the fish cannot live outside the water. Mao put forward three rules and eight remarks designed to achieve the support, or at least not to engender the hostility, of the people, including such things as being courteous, not stealing or breaking things, and paying for anything damaged.[10]

As for actual operations, Mao argued that basic guerrilla strategy must be based on alertness, mobility, and attack. Conducting their activity in the enemy's rear areas, guerrillas were to exterminate small enemy forces, harass large enemy forces, attack enemy lines of communications, and force the enemy to disperse his strength. The influence of Sun Tzu is apparent in Mao's thought: guerrillas are advised to withdraw when the enemy advances; harass him when he stops; strike him when he is weary; pursue him when he withdraws. Moreover, the revolutionary must be willing to carry out such activities over a period of years, if not decades, prolonging the struggle and making it into a protracted war. "There is in guerrilla warfare," Mao stresses, "no such thing as a decisive battle.[11]

Galula on counterinsurgency

Whereas Lawrence and Mao provide the principles and rules of revolutionary war from the revolutionary's perspective, David Galula, a French military officer who fought during the Algerian War in the late 1950s, presents a counter-revolutionary or, in his words, counterinsurgent, approach. "Counterrevolutionary," he argues, has a certain reactionary connotation, and thus he establishes "revolutionary war" as the overall phenomenon, with insurgency and counterinsurgency two, yet very different, aspects of the same war. This is similarly the approach adopted in America's 2006 counterinsurgency doctrine.[12] In his book, *Counterinsurgency Warfare: Theory and Practice* (1964), Galula notes that up until that time there had been numerous analyses of revolutionary war from the insurgent's perspective, but few studies from the "other side." After surveying the tenets of successful insurgency, he sets out to fill the counterinsurgent vacuum by defining the laws of such warfare, deducing from them its principles, and suggesting concrete courses of action.

The first law Galula determines is that the support of the population is as necessary for the counterinsurgent as it is for the insurgent. "What is the crux of the problem for the counterinsurgent?" Galula asks and then answers. It is not to "clear" a sector of insurgents, for this can always be done; the counterinsurgent is, after all, the asymmetrically more powerful participant in military terms. Rather, the challenge is to keep it clean, and this cannot be done without the support of the population. This, he argues, is where the fight must be conducted—hence the now well-worn phrase of fighting for the "hearts and minds" of the people—despite the fact, and recognizing, that the insurgent has a head start in this area of some years or even decades. Victory, for the counterinsurgent, does not involve the destruction of an insurgent's forces because he will readily set up shop elsewhere; rather, it entails the permanent isolation of the insurgent from the population, enforced by the population. A large part of this, Galula implies, must be to address porous borders. "The border areas are a permanent source of weakness for the counterinsurgent," he notes, and conversely "an advantage that is usually exploited by the insurgent."[13]

Galula's second law centers on how to gain the population's support—on how not only to obtain its sympathy and approval, but also its active participation in the fight against the insurgent. In a variation of Lawrence's view that only 2 percent of the population need actively to support the rebellion as long as the rest are passively supportive, Galula observes that in most cases a revolutionary war will have an active minority for the cause, a neutral majority, *and* an active minority against the cause. The challenge for the counterinsurgent lies in eliminating the minority for the cause, while empowering the minority against it to rally the neutral majority. Galula offers no specific advice on how to do this, except to say that every operation, whether political, economic, military, or social in nature, must be geared to this end. He further points to the conditionality of the population's support as a third law, noting that successful military and police operations against insurgents and their political organizations must take place in order to lift the threat of reprisals against the population. However desirable political, social, and economic reforms, measures to ensure the population's security must come first. These measures and operations, a fourth law, are necessarily intensive and long in duration. They must successively be applied area by area, not over the whole country at once, a method that in recent years has become known as the "oil spot" approach. Galula sets out eight concrete steps of action that a counterinsurgent should follow within a selected area, including such things as concentrating force to destroy the main body of insurgents, cutting off population links with the guerrillas, and winning over or suppressing insurgent remnants.[14]

Thompson on counterinsurgency

Drawing on his experience in Malaya in the 1950s and also in Vietnam in the early years before the American "surge" of 1965, British air force officer Sir Robert Thompson offered principles of counterinsurgency that echo or complement those of Galula. In his *Defeating Communist Insurgency* (1966), Thompson makes the useful argument that an insurgency cannot be treated in isolation from broader factors. It must be addressed in the context of an overall plan that covers, in addition to security measures, all political, social, and economic aspects that bear on the insurgency—an approach not unlike that of today's "whole of government" or comprehensive approach. To do otherwise, he points out, would not bring long-term stability but only invite a return to insurgency.

Thompson also stresses the necessity that the counterinsurgent function in accordance with the law, however tempting it may be to treat guerrilla action outside the normal safeguards of domestic law. To do otherwise, he argues, would undermine the long-term legitimacy of the government that is trying to re-establish control. Like Galula, Thompson identifies the population, not the insurgent, as the primary target, in his case (because he is dealing with communism) recommending that the subversive political organization be broken up and eliminated, so as to separate the fish from the water. Finally, he lends credence to Galula's emphasis on securing specific base areas first, rather than all areas at once, working methodically outward. Thompson recommends that the focus of this (oil spot) approach be first on urban and developed localities, where there is the greatest population, communications, and economic activity, even if that means, at least in the short term, conceding remoter areas to the insurgent.[15]

Post Cold War

Andrew Krepinevich on insurgency and counterinsurgency

It is perhaps not surprising that much of early strategic thought on revolutionary war was conducted by British and French practitioners, as the notable European colonial powers of the early to mid-twentieth century. US thinkers on insurgency were slow to emerge, despite or perhaps because of America's experience in Vietnam. One of the first was Andrew Krepinevich, a retired Lieutenant Colonel in the US Army and now Director of the Center for Strategic and Budgetary Assessments, whose ideas figured extensively in the RMA literature of the 1990s (see Chapter 4), but whose strategic thought both before and since that time has included insurgency and counterinsurgency.

In his book *The Army and Vietnam* (1986), Krepinevich was one of the first to squarely face the US military's failure to grasp the nature of the conflict in which it was involved. Krepinevich draws attention to the protracted nature of an insurgency conducted methodically over years and decades; the three phases of insurgency popularized by Mao; and the fact that insurgency focuses on gaining the support of the population, either through willing cooperation or as a result of threats, i.e. capturing the minds, if not the hearts, of the population. Counterinsurgency, in turn, requires winning the hearts and minds of this same population; addressing the conditionality of population support by ensuring long-term security; securing the government's base areas; separating the guerrilla forces from the population; and eliminating insurgent infrastructure. Counterinsurgency, Krepinevich points out, involves coordination among many government organizations, of which the military is only one.[16]

Most, if not all, of these themes were recognizable to anyone familiar with the earlier revolutionary warfare literature. Krepinevich's contribution at this time was not so much to add new strategic thinking on revolutionary war as to highlight the fact that insurgency and counterinsurgency represent major departures from conventional war; that the United States Army in the 1970s, still strongly influenced by World Wars One and Two and the Korean War, was neither trained nor organized to fight effectively in an insurgency conflict environment; and to make the case that low-intensity warfare and counterinsurgency represented the most likely arena of future conflict for the US Army—a commonplace perspective in the second decade of the twenty-first century, but no less than a radical argument in 1986.

In later work Krepinevich recasts important ideas into new language, for added emphasis. He notes that the center of gravity in counterinsurgency warfare is the target nation's population, but goes further to point out that in the case where an external power provides a major portion of the counterinsurgent forces the population of that external power, too, becomes a center of gravity in the conflict. His reference is to the United States, but it could equally have been to France and the Algerian insurgency that was Galula's topic. On the central theme of population security, Krepinevich highlights the wrongheadedness of focusing exclusively or prevalently on hunting down and killing insurgents. "Should counterinsurgent forces ... focus their principal efforts on destroying insurgent forces, as is more typical of conventional warfare, and accord population security a lower priority, they will play into insurgents' hands."[17] So, too, would they do if they were to display a lack of patience, since insurgents can make a powerful argument to the population that, while foreign troops will someday depart, the insurgents will remain, and therefore must be accommodated. Finally, looking to the specific case study of Iraq in the mid-2000s, and echoing the perspective of Galula and Thompson before him, Krepinevich argues it was not possible to guarantee security to all of Iraq simultaneously. Rather, the approach should be one of an expanding oil spot that focuses at first on key (likely urban) areas, and gradually yet inexorably expands outward over time.

Martin van Creveld on non-trinitarian war

Military historian Martin van Creveld places insurgent and counterinsurgent activity, what he calls low-intensity warfare, into broad historical context. Writing in the waning days of the Cold War, van Creveld, an Israeli scholar at the University of Jerusalem, notes that for much of human history war was waged by non-state social entities. "Trinitarian" warfare, a reference to Clausewitz's observation that war as a total phenomenon reflects the interaction of a trinity of forces—the people, the army, and the government—is a comparatively recent phenomenon, having dominated the international scene only since after the 1648 Peace of Westphalia.

Van Creveld argued that the trinitarian, Clausewitzian universe, resting as it does "on the assumption that war is made predominantly by states or, to be exact, by governments," was coming to an end, to be replaced by "non-trinitarian" or "post-Clausewitzian" warfare.[18] Where there are no states, he notes, the threefold division into government, army, and people does not exist. And the future global landscape, he argued, was likely to feature an increasing number of war-making organizations of a non-state variety. Low-intensity conflicts were increasing, a product of the decolonization trend of the post-World War Two period that then took root, once decolonization ended, in other areas of the world. State-to-state warfare had already become comparatively rare, primarily as a result of the spread of nuclear weapons. In van Creveld's view, states were set to lose their monopoly over armed violence. Indeed, they already had—it was just that "the military establishments of developed countries clung to Trinitarian war because it was a game with which they had long been familiar and they liked to play."[19] But future war would not be waged by states and armies. Rather, it would be waged by non-state actors, like terrorists and guerrillas.

Lind on fourth-generation warfare

Van Creveld's non-trinitarian view of the world is fundamental to fourth-generation warfare (4GW), a concept that is traced to a seminal 1989 *Military Review* article by William S. Lind and four US military officers. In it Lind, at the time at the Washington-based conservative think-tank the Free Congress Foundation, argued that over the course of modern history, developments in warfare had gone through three distinct "generations" of military development, defined by watersheds that had been dialectically qualitative, and was set to move into a fourth generation. The first three generations concerned armies and states and thus could be located in the trinitarian universe of Clausewitz (although Lind himself did not use this term). They included the first-generation tactics of infantry lines and columns; the second-generation move to indirect fire, where massed firepower from artillery replaced massed manpower, but where tactics remained essentially linear; and the nonlinear, maneuver warfare of the third generation, displayed most notably during World War Two.

These generations do not replace but overlap one another. Lind argued, for example, that second-generation warfare remained the US Army's modus operandi until the 1980s, long after Germany had introduced third-generation warfare in the form of *blitzkrieg*. Moreover, numerous features of third-generation warfare could be expected to carry over into the fourth: greater dispersion on the battlefield; increased speed and tempo of operations; decreased dependence on centralized logistics; more emphasis on maneuver and less on mass; smaller, more agile forces; nonlinear warfare with no definable battle lines or fronts; and an increasing dependence on joint operations. Most, if not all, of these features were later bundled into a package known as the Revolution in Military Affairs (RMA) (see Chapter 4). Indeed, Lind's first vision for fourth-generation warfare, a potential technology-driven fourth generation, aligns closely with 1990s perspectives on the RMA: "Technologically ... very few soldiers could have the same battlefield effect as a current [1989] brigade"; "highly mobile elements, composed of very intelligent soldiers armed with high-technology, may range over wide areas"; "units will combine reconnaissance and strike functions"; "Remote, 'smart' assets ... may play a key role."[20]

The strategic thought for which Lind is remembered, and continues to be quoted, is his second vision of future war, a potential idea-driven fourth generation. Conducted by non-state entities such as terrorists, fourth-generation warfare can be distinguished by at least two important signposts, both of which first emerged in second-generation warfare and were present in the third but are pushed to a qualitatively greater degree in fourth-generation warfare. The first is a shift in focus from the enemy's front to his rear. "Terrorism," Lind argues, "takes this [pre-existing trend] a major step further. It attempts to bypass the enemy's military entirely and strike directly at his homeland—at civilian targets. Ideally the enemy's military is simply irrelevant to the terrorist." The second signpost centers on the aspect of using the enemy's strength against him. "Terrorists use a free society's freedom and openness, its greatest strengths against it. They can move freely within our society, while actively working to subvert it."[21]

Lind also identifies additional possible elements of fourth-generation warfare. Such an attacker might: not work within a nation-state (i.e. trinitarian) framework but rather have a non-national or transnational base, such as an ideology or religion; conduct direct attacks on the enemy's culture, bypassing not only its military, but also the state itself, in the manner, for example, that drug trafficking directly targets US citizens; and use highly sophisticated psychological warfare directly against the people, especially through the manipulation of television news media. All these things in combination, Lind and his colleagues argued, could constitute at least the beginnings of a fourth generation of warfare. "[T]he progressive weakening of the state and the rise of alternative, non-state primary loyalties," he later argued, "constitutes the heart of my definition of Fourth Generation war."[22]

Hammes

The highly prescient content of Lind's potential idea-driven fourth generation of warfare—which in many ways anticipated the rise of al Qaeda a decade later—is the starting-point of strategic thought on 4GW in the early post-9/11 period. The most notable theorist in this regard is Thomas X. Hammes, a Colonel in the United States Marines Corps, who has presented his strategic thought on fourth-generation warfare in a number of articles and in his 2004 book, *The Sling and the Stone: On War in the 21st Century*. For Hammes, 4GW is "an evolved form of insurgency." Mao was the originator of this form of war, but whereas Mao initially set out a three-phase plan that would arouse and unite the Chinese people against the outside power, Japan, 4GW skips the population altogether, directly targeting the mind of the enemy decision maker.

The phenomenon of direct attacks against the far enemy is not new. It dates to Ho Chi Minh and Vo Nguyen Giap, the North Vietnamese president and military commander respectively, who during the Vietnam War followed a refined Maoist model by combining the three-phase approach with an aggressive, direct attack on the national will of the outside power, first France and then the United States.[23] The distinction here is that 4GW has largely dropped the population aspect altogether, while the internet and globalized communications have made the direct approach, previously dependent on television coverage, exponentially more potent. Hammes also points out that contemporary insurgents are no longer the unified, hierarchical organizations that the Chinese and later the Vietnamese developed in the early and mid-twentieth century. Rather, there has been a worldwide shift from hierarchical to networked organizations. In some cases they are based on traditional linkages between and among people, simple real-world networks, including criminal networks. But in most they operate in cyberspace, ultimately connected through the internet.

Fourth-generation warfare, like all insurgencies, does not attempt to win by defeating the enemy's military forces. For Hammes, it is a form of war that "uses all available networks—political, economic, social and military—to convince the enemy's political decision makers that their strategic goals are either unachievable or too costly for the perceived benefit."[24] He equates 4GW to "netwar," a term originated by RAND scholars John Arquilla and David Ronfeldt in the early 1990s. In their conception, netwar pertains to conflicts short of war, involves actors who may or may not be military, and is distinguished by the fact that at least one of the protagonists, usually a non-state, paramilitary, or other irregular force, organizes as a network rather than a hierarchy. "An archetypal netwar actor consists of a web (or network) of dispersed, interconnected 'nodes' ... The design is both acephalous (headless) and polycephalous (hydra-headed)."[25] For Arquilla and Ronfeldt, netwar involves "trying to disrupt, damage, or modify what a target population knows or thinks it knows about itself and the world around it."[26] The concept both reflects, and is tied to, the information revolution.

Targeting the minds of enemy decision makers is the organizing principle that governs 4GW activities at each of the strategic, operational, and tactical levels. Strategically, 4GW practitioners will undertake a communications plan using such things as insurgent websites and the global communications media in general. Operationally, 4GW opponents "will examine our entire society to find vulnerabilities" and then attempt to strike them. The quintessential example is the 9/11 attacks, but other scenarios can be envisioned. Tactically, 4GW takes place in the complex environment of low-intensity conflict—here is the connection of 4GW to actual insurgent activity on the ground. The more dramatic and bloody the image, the stronger the message. These high-impact messages will probably come through visual media and they will be part of, indeed the substance of, "the strategic communications plan designed to shift their enemy's view of the world."[27] Once the outside power is driven out, Hammes argues, there will ensue a traditional 2GW civil war (i.e. war amongst the people)—or perhaps, although he does not say this, a "traditional" insurgency along Maoist lines.

The concept of 4GW has been criticized on at least three broad fronts. The first is the degree to which terrorists and insurgents are effective against countries and militaries stuck in the second or third generation of warfare. Based on an examination of history, argues one scholar, "it is probably a bit hasty to conclude that non-traditional forms of warfare will always best traditional forces."[28] A second and related critique is the degree to which the focus on insurgency and 4GW is appropriate, or whether it is a luxury afforded only by the fact that at the beginning of the twenty-first century there is an "unusual and temporary absence of Great Power conflictuality."[29]

But the strongest critique is whether Hammes has actually identified something novel or new. This is an unresolved question in Hammes' own strategic thought, which argues at the same time that 4GW: has been around for seven decades; has been the dominant form of warfare for 50 years; and is a "new form of war." Fourth-generation warfare, at least at the strategic level, is different from the indigenous population-centric insurgency of Mao. The notion of operational-level attacks against the enemy's society at home is also a new element, as is the shift from hierarchical to networked insurgent "leadership." But, with the exception of advancements in communications technology, it is difficult to distinguish the core of Hammes' 4GW conception—directly targeting the minds of enemy decision makers—from the North Vietnamese approach, which after the defeat at Tet in 1968 shifted from targeting US military forces in Vietnam to directly weakening US political will at home. In this regard, a large part of the 4GW concept arguably comes down to the relatively new and pervasive power of the internet. Perhaps this is the true "potential technology-driven fourth generation of warfare" alluded to by Lind at the close of the Cold War.

New Wars scholars

The strategic thought of William Lind and Thomas Hammes has been characterized as a popular form of "New Wars" thinking.[30] This is a term that first emerged in the 1990s, largely in response to the civil war in former Yugoslavia, but also elsewhere, and the difficulty faced by the international (state-based) community in addressing such conflicts. One of the best-known New Wars scholars is Mary Kaldor, whose 1999 volume *New and Old Wars* argued that in the 1990s a type of organized violence emerged in Africa and Eastern Europe that was "new" in terms of its goals and methods of warfare. Echoing van Creveld, she argues that these new wars arose in the context of the erosion of the autonomy of the state and, in some cases, the complete disintegration of the state. In place of the geopolitical or ideological goals of the Cold War, new wars were about "identity politics," or the claim to power on the basis of having a particular national, clan, religious, or linguistic identity.[31] In its prosecution, she argues, new warfare borrows from revolutionary warfare the strategy of controlling territory through political control rather than capturing territory from enemy forces, a task that is somewhat easier in the case of new wars, since the central authority is weak or nonexistent. But whereas "traditional" guerrilla warfare and counterinsurgency is, at least in theory, aimed at political control of the population through winning "hearts and minds," the new warfare aimed at controlling it by getting rid of everyone of a different identity, through such means as population expulsion, forcible resettlement, and mass killing. The phenomenon was captured at the time in the well-used phrase "ethnic cleansing."

In *The New Wars*, Herfried Munkler similarly argues that in such wars force is mainly directed not against the enemy's armed force but against the civilian population. Fighting may flare up anywhere; there is no distinction between front, rear, and homeland, no decisive battle of the sort that characterizes inter-state war. In new wars the conduct of war involves direct attacks using terrorist tactics, an "offensive form of the strategic asymmetrization of force,"[32] rather than the more traditional indirect targeting of guerrilla warfare. The aim of fighting is either to drive a population from a certain area through ethnic cleansing, or to force it to supply and support certain groups. This latter phenomenon draws in the economic dimension, wherein a large aspect of new wars involves war as a way of life. The boundaries between working life and war become blurred, players are driven more by economic motives than political ones, and they essentially make a living out of war, in some cases amassing fortunes. For Munkler, the two main features that differentiate the new wars from the inter-state wars of the past are their commercialization and their growing asymmetry.

Britain's Rupert Smith, Deputy Supreme Allied Commander Europe during NATO's (1999) Operation Allied Force in Kosovo, does not use the "New War" terminology in his 2005 book *The Utility of Force*, but he does draw out changes in the conduct of war that echo the New War literature. Smith argues that a paradigm shift has taken place in war, from inter-state industrial war of comparable, largely symmetric forces waging war on a battlefield, to a paradigm of "war amongst the people [that] reflects the hard fact that there is no secluded battlefield upon which armies engage, nor are there necessarily armies, definitely not on all sides." War amongst the people, he argues, "is the reality in which the people in the streets and houses and fields—all the people, anywhere—are the battlefield. Military engagements can take place anywhere: in the presence of civilians, against civilians, in defence of civilians," and they are between sides that are mostly non-state.[33]

Scholar Richard Shultz goes still further than Kaldor and Smith, identifying a specific set of questions that can give an "operational level assessment of how internal warfare is conducted by modern warriors."[34] Questions within the framework center on the non-state armed groups' concept of warfare, organization and command and control, area of operations, types and targets of operations, and constraints and limitations, like the laws of armed conflict. A final category is the role of outside actors. Many argue that inter-communal strife is nothing new—it existed in the early twentieth century and before. Rather, what has been new in the post-Cold War era has been stepped-up efforts on the part of the international community to intervene in or address the strife, often played out in the global media. The character of New War accordingly forms the backdrop against which Smith presents his strategic thought on trends that make up the paradigm of war amongst the people *from the perspective of the* (state-based) *intervener*. Among the trends he identifies is the fact that the interveners, no less so than the parties themselves, fight amongst the people and not on the battlefield. Because the enemy is hiding in and amongst the people, the challenge faced by the intervening force is "to differentiate between the enemy and the people and to win the latter over to you." In addition, and significantly, the ends for which organizations like NATO fight "are changing from the hard objectives that decide a political outcome to those establishing conditions in which the outcome may be decided." The objective of intervention is not to take or hold territory but to create a condition in which humanitarian activity can take place and a political outcome can be negotiated. "Overall," Smith argues, "if decisive victory was the hallmark of interstate war, establishing a condition may be deemed the hallmark of the new paradigm of war against the people."[35]

How best to create such a condition was then, and remains now, an unanswered question. Kaldor argues that approaches like peace keeping and peace enforcement, attempted by the international community during the 1990s, are not appropriate because they still treat the new wars "as Clausewitzian wars in which the warring parties are states, or if not states, groups with a claim to statehood." She argues instead for "a new form of cosmopolitan political mobilization, which embraces both the so-called international community and local populations, and which is capable of countering … particularism," and calls on the international community to engage in an ambitious agenda of enforcing cosmopolitan norms, including international humanitarian and human rights law.[36] Smith is more practical in his approach, arguing that in planning an intervention with military force the international community must start by giving coherent answers to two sets of questions. The first set (of about 20 questions) centers on defining "the outcome and the effort to be set to achieving it," while the second set (of about a half dozen questions) focuses on making the intervention credible in the eyes of the people and the opponent that is hiding in and amongst the people.[37] Determining what objectives can be achieved by military force, and the limitations on the use of force beyond them, forms the overarching strategic starting-point—a reality that Smith applies not just to the new wars of the 1990s but also to the counterinsurgent efforts in Iraq in the period after the 2003 Iraq War.

Kilcullen on insurgency and counterinsurgency

In his strategic thought David Kilcullen goes somewhat further than Hammes in pinpointing the new character of insurgency. A Lieutenant Colonel in the Australian Army who later advised the Pentagon on counterinsurgency, Kilcullen identifies the key distinguishing aspect of post-Cold War insurgency as lying not in the method but in the goal of revolutionary or insurgent activity. The global jihad being waged by al Qaeda, he argued in a 2005 article that caught the Pentagon's attention, is clearly an insurgency—that is, a popular movement that seeks to change the status quo through violence and subversion: so far, much the same as a classical Maoist insurgency. But, he goes on, "whereas traditional insurgencies sought to overthrow established governments or social orders in one state or district, this insurgency seeks to transform the entire Islamic world and remake its relationship with the rest of the globe."[38] Classical theory, he elaborates in later work, treats insurgency as something that occurs within one country, between a non-state actor and a single government, with the goal being to gain control of the state. But many contemporary insurgents may be simply trying to destroy the state, not seize control of the reins of power. "The insurgents seek to expel foreigners, but have little to say about what might replace the national government."[39] Moreover, in al Qaeda-linked insurgencies, the insurgent may not be seeking to achieve any practical real-world objective, but rather to gain God's favor.

Kilcullen notes that in the modern era some classical insurgencies do exist, such as in Colombia and Thailand, where insurgents seek to challenge the status quo, a functioning political body. But others follow state failure, and the battle is over an ungoverned space, a situation that may be better described in New War terms as a "war amongst the people" than as an insurgency. Still more are sparked by an outside intervening power, against which the insurgents react. The invading coalition is, in a sense, more revolutionary than the insurgent, who is fighting to repel an occupier or to preserve the status quo of ungoverned spaces. Tied to this phenomenon is an entire cycle of activity, sparked by the initial presence of al Qaeda or an associated movement, that leads to the creation of "accidental" guerrillas. In his book *The Accidental Guerrilla*, Kilcullen argues that such guerrillas are the product of a four-stage process that is not unlike a disease. Transnational extremists first "infect" an ungoverned area; the "contagion," initially resisted by the local people, who see them as alien outsiders, spreads via co-option and intimidation throughout the country and region; outside powers eventually intervene, taking action against the extremist presence using a range of tools from humanitarian aid to military force; finally, the local population lashes out in an immune "rejection" response, closing ranks with the original alien outsiders against the new external threat. Local people fight alongside extremist forces, in the process becoming accidental guerrillas.

It is not difficult to see that at this stage the insurgency, despite having its origins in the existence of extremists with no real-world goals, begins to look like traditional counterinsurgency. As Kilcullen notes, at the operational level counterinsurgency remains a competition among sides, each seeking to mobilize the population. "The people remain the prize."[40] Tactically, whereas classical insurgents generally hid amongst the people in rural environments, modern insurgents are at least as likely to be found amongst the people in urban environments.

Other features echo those identified by Hammes. Modern communications, Kilcullen argues, has had the effect of compressing the operational level, such that tactical events have strategic effect once spread through the internet, i.e. they become part of the strategic communications plan. Kilcullen also approaches Hammes' view that all insurgent activity is aimed at the minds of enemy decision makers when he notes that the pervasive and near-instantaneous character of modern media, the "globalization effect" of an instantaneous worldwide audience, is such that revolutionary war is almost 100 percent political, with little or no focus on the military aspect at the local level. And although he argues that the notion of organizational networks and nodes is a bit too organized, Kilcullen comes close to Hammes' perspective when he notes that modern insurgencies discard hierarchy in favor of a "self-synchronizing swarm of independent but cooperating cells."[41]

A notable aspect of Kilcullen's strategic thought lies in his elaboration of this organizational aspect of modern insurgency. The essence of jihadist "operational art"—the existence of such a thing in itself being controversial—he argues, lies in its ability to aggregate numerous tactical actions into one common movement. This is done through a "nested series of links" across theaters and including groups with common ideologies, cultures, languages, and, above all, the shared Islamic faith.

Kilcullen's analysis has important repercussions for counterinsurgency. In its classical form, as put forward, for example, by Galula and Thompson, counterinsurgency is optimized to defeat insurgency in one country. But traditional concepts are problematic when applied to countering a global insurgency. Here the approach must first be on severing the links and communications between al Qaeda's core leadership and local and regional players, isolating theater-level actors from their global sponsors. The idea behind this strategy, what Kilcullen calls "disaggregation," is not to resolve a specific conflict situation but rather to ensure that the insurgent activity is isolated from that in other theaters. "The pathology of [contemporary] insurgency," one scholar has argued, "suggests that we [must] isolate the guerrillas physically, cybernetically and psychologically from their base of support and from the media."[42] If it subsequently becomes necessary to address the local insurgency itself (and Kilcullen advises to avoid this if at all possible), then at least eight counterinsurgent "best practices" come into play, the most notable of which are to adopt a comprehensive (whole of government) approach that integrates civil and military efforts; ensure population security; build local security forces; conduct combat strikes against insurgents when necessary; and effect a region-wide approach that controls borders and disrupts insurgent safe havens.[43]

Petraeus and counterinsurgency

"Best practices" is perhaps the best way to characterize US counterinsurgency doctrine as expressed in the 2006 US Army and Marine Corps Counterinsurgency Field Manual (FM 3–24), produced under the guidance of US Army General David Petraeus. Notwithstanding substantial discussion during this period, by Hammes and Kilcullen and others, of the transnational, globalized nature of modern insurgency, and of the need to sever links and networks operating across boundaries, FM 3–24 is strongly imbued with a classical, Maoist perspective. This is reflected in its characterization of insurgencies as "normally seeking to achieve one of two goals: to overthrow the existing social order and reallocate power within a single state, or to break away from state control and form an autonomous entity."[44] Its counterinsurgency doctrine is accordingly "state-centric," reflecting Galula's rejoinder to Maoist doctrine and focused on what Kilcullen would call the operational (*vice* strategic) level of counterinsurgency.

FM 3–24 puts forward a number of principles, imperatives, and paradoxes pertaining to counterinsurgency operations that together form the core of Petraeus' strategic thinking (see Box 5.1). Upon FM 3–24's publication it was the paradoxes that drew the most attention. This may have been because at a time when kinetic approaches were largely and ineffectually dominating American counterinsurgency responses, they emphasized the strength of non-kinetic responses (while still underscoring that killing clearly will often be necessary).

Box 5.1 The US Army–Marine Corps Counterinsurgency Field Manual

The core of official US strategic thought on counterinsurgency lies in the 2006 US Army–Marine Corps Counterinsurgency Field Manual, which identifies several historical principles for COIN, contemporary imperatives for COIN, and paradoxes of COIN operations.

Historical principles:

- *Legitimacy is the main objective.* Any COIN operation must seek to establish an effective, legitimate government.
- *Unity of effort is essential.* Outside military, diplomatic, governmental, and non-governmental organizations must coordinate their COIN efforts.
- *Political factors are primary.* Military commanders must consider at all times how operations will impact on host-nation legitimacy.
- *Counterinsurgents must understand the environment.* Soldiers and Marines must understand the society and culture within which they are conducting operations.
- *Intelligence drives operations.* As with all military operations, intelligence is imperative; however, COIN missions are unique in that counterinsurgents' own actions are a key generator of intelligence. A cycle develops wherein operations create intelligence that defines subsequent operations.
- *Insurgents must be isolated from their cause and support.* Killing every insurgent is not possible; a better approach is to redress the social, political, and economic grievances that fuel the insurgency, and to cut off physical and financial support—all extremely difficult tasks.
- *Security under the law is essential.* Security of the population is essential and involves establishing a legal system in line with local culture and practices to deal with insurgents.
- *Counterinsurgents should prepare for a long-term commitment.* The populace must have confidence in the long-term will and staying power of the counterinsurgents and host-nation government.

Contemporary imperatives:

- *Manage information and expectations.* The populace must be given a realistic set of expectations so that the lack of immediate results is not interpreted as counterinsurgent or host-nation deception.
- *Use the appropriate level of force.* Commanders must apply appropriate and measured levels of force precisely so as to minimize loss of life and any potential backlash.
- *Learn and adapt.* Insurgents constantly exchange information about counterinsurgent vulnerabilities, so counterinsurgents must be able to adapt their best practices just as fast.
- *Empower the lowest levels.* Higher commanders should empower subordinates to make decisions within the commander's intent because in COIN local commanders have the best grasp of the situation.
- *Support the host nation.* While it may be easier for counterinsurgents to conduct operations themselves, it is better to work to strengthen host-nation capabilities, since the long-term goal is to leave a government able to stand by itself.

Paradoxes of counterinsurgency operations:

- *Sometimes the more you protect your force, the less secure you may be.* Keeping military forces safe in their compounds rather than out amongst the people reduces access to the intelligence needed to drive successful operations.
- *Sometimes the more force is used, the less effective it is.* The greater the use of force, the greater the chance of collateral damage and mistakes and the greater the opportunity for insurgent propaganda.
- *The more successful the counterinsurgency is, the less force can be used and the more risk must be accepted.* As counterinsurgent efforts progress, more reliance is placed on police work and troops will have to adhere to more stringent rules of engagement that may involve greater risk to the counterinsurgent.
- *Sometimes doing nothing is the best reaction.* Sometimes insurgents attempt to incite a counterinsurgent reaction that would create a propaganda opportunity.
- *Some of the best weapons for counterinsurgents do not shoot.* Legitimacy and public support for the host nation's government can be achieved at times with activities that do not involve killing insurgents.
- *The host nation doing something tolerably is normally better than the counter-insurgent doing it well.* "Tolerable" host-nation activity promotes the creation of a government able to stand by itself, but if the host nation cannot perform tolerably. counterinsurgents may have to act.
- *If a tactic works this week, it might not work next week; if it works in this province, it might not work in the next.* Insurgents quickly adjust to successful COIN practices, so counterinsurgents need to continually adapt.
- *Tactical success guarantees nothing.* Military action cannot achieve success in COIN but must be linked to host-nation political goals.
- *Many important decisions are not made by generals.* Successful COIN requires competence and judgment at all levels, since even tactical decisions can have strategic consequences.

Perhaps the most useful strategic direction for operational-level activities is found in the manual's summary of successful counterinsurgency practices, which advises the occupying power, amongst other things, to focus on the population, its needs and its security; establish and expand secure areas; and secure host-nation borders. Indeed, "secure the population" has been identified by Petraeus as the central lesson of counterinsurgency.[45] The doctrine later elaborates that COIN efforts should begin by controlling key areas and that security and influence should then spread out from secured areas. But considering its importance, this "oil spot" strategy, which was advised by counterinsurgency theorists from Galula to Thompson to Krepinevich, receives surprisingly little attention. The latter two theorists stressed especially the importance of first securing the populous urban areas, an approach that was adopted in practice when it came to implementing the doctrine's tenets in Iraq.

Despite FM 3–24's predominantly classical COIN approach, the manual does touch on elements familiar from Hammes' and Kilcullen's strategic thought. "Today's operational environment," it notes, "includes a new kind of insurgency, one that seeks to impose revolutionary change worldwide ... Defeating such enemies requires a global, strategic response [that] addresses the array of linked resources and conflicts that sustain these movements."[46] But the manual is short on what measures might be taken to effect such "disaggregation." It includes an extensive discussion of tools to map an insurgent organization's social network, noting that "such knowledge helps commanders understand what the network looks like, how it is connected, and how best to defeat it," such as whether one should target enemy forces or enemy leaders.[47] But, as with Kilcullen's strategic thought, there are no further details on how, in this globalized, interconnected, real-time world, it is actually possible to sever links and isolate insurgents. This may be by design. The COIN manual agrees that networked organizations are difficult to destroy, but goes on to argue that networks in any case have a limited ability to attain strategic success because they cannot easily muster and focus power. Meanwhile, commanders on the ground have expressed the view that thinking of the enemy as a network has had the effect of understating the critical and enduring importance of geography and controlling key terrain as a first step in spreading stability outward—perhaps a case of classical theory trumping the new-wave thinking of the information age.

Conclusion

Revolutionary war, including insurgency and counterinsurgency, is relatively new as a fully developed concept. T. E. Lawrence's recollections, from the early interwar period, were the first to include principles of successful insurgency activity, but it is to Mao and his World War Two-era writings that we attribute the beginnings of comprehensive strategic thought on the insurgency component of revolutionary war. The conventional nature of that war, as well as the Korean War that followed, meant that counter-insurgency doctrine did not immediately appear. Only in the mid-1960s, after a decade or more of conflicts associated with decolonization, was there substantial strategic thinking on counterinsurgency, notably by Galula but also by Thompson.

The strategic thought of Krepinevich in the 1980s, and especially of Petraeus in the 2000s, is important because, even more so than that of Galula, it integrates both the insurgent and counterinsurgent perspectives. But they are consciously housed in the concepts and ideas of earlier strategic thinkers—secure the population, isolate insurgents, address porous borders and safe havens, integrate military and civilian approaches, etc.—and therefore do not so much offer new strategic thinking as highlight and remind us (again) of the need to pay attention to this enduring form of war. That the classics remain relevant is indicated by the fact that it was possible to read, in 2010, of Lawrence of Arabia's ideas guiding the US Army in Iraq and Afghanistan; of the "new" approach adopted by the former commander of forces in Afghanistan, General Stanley McChrystal, being to consolidate the populous urban areas as a means of establishing and then spreading stability; and of a key barrier to winning in Afghanistan being its porous borders, where insurgents seek safe haven.

Van Creveld provides a convincing case as to why insurgency and counterinsurgency will continue to command the world's attention, even as his assertion, shared by Lind, that the state's place as the predominant international actor is waning has proven to be, at a minimum, premature. New War scholarship takes the erosion of the state as a starting-point and contrasts player objectives with those of guerrilla warfare and counterinsurgency. Even if it arguably does not actually identify a new phenomenon, New War thinking deepens our understanding of civil war and draws our attention to the difficulties faced by state-based actors in responding. Hammes and Kilcullen bring revolutionary doctrine into the modern, globalized, information age, drawing out a number of critical new factors: some contemporary insurgencies are "global" in that they are not focused, as was the case in the past, on a single country or region; some are even "beyond global," in that they do not have any definable, real-world, political objectives; facilitated by globalization, these actors may seek to strike enemy territory directly, bypassing regional military operations altogether; others focus on home but are merely reacting against the activities and presence of an external power; in most cases the insurgent leadership does not exist in a traditional hierarchical sense but is highly networked; and today's insurgencies are even more political than in the past, taking full advantage of the instantaneous and pervasive nature of modern media.

Yet although the information era has added a new dimension to insurgency and counterinsurgency, at its core it remains essentially unchanged. Drawing on the views of classical and post-Cold War strategic theorists, a contemporary theory of counter-insurgency might include a number of key tenets. Counterinsurgents should: focus in the first instance on securing the population using non-kinetic means; balance this with highly discriminate, direct combat strikes against the small minority that will always be in favor of the insurgency; adopt a strategy of securing the population in large urban areas first, spreading security and stability outward from these consolidated areas; where security has been established, integrate economic, political, and social measures at the earliest opportunity, i.e. adopt a comprehensive, whole of government approach; address porous borders; seal off safe havens; conduct counterinsurgent activity in accordance with the law to promote legitimacy; implement a strategic communications plan at home, preparing the population for a lengthy engagement with friendly casualties; examine and strive to devise measures to sever linkages between insurgent theaters; and balance commitment to the counterinsurgent effort abroad with home-land security measures to defend against the operational level of 4GW.

By the end of the first decade of the twenty-first century most or all of these princi-ples had been relearned and fully absorbed by the political and military leadership addressing modern insurgencies. But NATO officials estimate it takes on average 13 years for outside powers to win a counterinsurgency campaign, far longer than most democracies find it possible to make a commitment. The challenge, as ever, lies in finding the patience and political will to sustain in practice, over time, the enduring elements of counterinsurgency theory.

Notes

1 C. E. Callwell, *Small Wars: Their Principles and Practice*, 3rd edition (Lincoln, NE: University of Nebraska Press, 1996, first published 1906), 21.
2 David J. Kilcullen, "Countering Global Insurgency," *Journal of Strategic Studies* 28, no. 4 (August 2005), 603.
3 John Shy and Thomas W. Collier, "Revolutionary War," in Peter Paret, ed., *Makers of Modern Strategy from Machiavelli to the Nuclear Age* (Princeton, NJ: Princeton University Press, 1986), 817.
4 Department of the Army, *The U.S. Army – Marine Corps Counterinsurgency Field Manual* (Chicago, IL: University of Chicago Press, 2007) (hereafter known as FM 3–24), 2.
5 Martin van Creveld, *The Transformation of War* (New York: The Free Press, 1991), 42.
6 Callwell, *Small Wars*, 21.
7 T. E. Lawrence, *Seven Pillars of Wisdom: A Triumph* (London: Jonathan Cape, 1940), 199, 202, 345–46.

8 Mao Tse-Tung, *On Guerrilla Warfare*, trans. Samuel B. Griffith (New York: Praeger Publishers, 1961), 42–43.
9 Griffith, introduction to *On Guerrilla Warfare*, 20–22.
10 Mao Tse-Tung, *On Guerrilla Warfare*, 44, 92–93.
11 Ibid., 46, 52–53, 98.
12 FM 3–24, 2.
13 David Galula, *Counterinsurgency Warfare: Theory and Practice* (New York: Praeger Publishers, 1964), 35.
14 The full list is: (1) concentrate enough armed forces to destroy or expel the main body of armed insurgents; (2) detach for the area sufficient troops to oppose an insurgent's comeback in strength; (3) establish contact with the population and control its movements to cut off its links with the guerrillas; (4) destroy the local insurgent political organization; (5) set up new provisional local authorities using elections; (6) test the authorities by assigning tasks, replace incompetents, and organize self-defence units; (7) educate the leaders; (8) win over or suppress the last insurgent remnants. See Galula, *Counterinsurgency Warfare*, 80.
15 Robert Thompson, *Defeating Communist Insurgency* (New York: Praeger Publishers, 1966), 50–57.
16 Andrew F. Krepinevich, *The Army and Vietnam* (Baltimore, MD: Johns Hopkins University Press, 1986), 7–15.
17 Andrew F. Krepinevich, *The War in Iraq: The Nature of Insurgency Warfare* (Washington, DC: Center for Strategic and Budgetary Analysis, 2 June 2004), 1, 3 and 6.
18 van Creveld, *The Transformation of War*, 49.
19 Ibid., 59.
20 William S. Lind, Keith M. Nightengale, John Schmitt, Joseph W. Sutton and G. I. Wilson, "The Changing Face of War: Into the Fourth Generation," *Military Review* (October 1989), 6.
21 Ibid., 8–9.
22 William S. Lind, "Parting Thoughts, for Now," December 15, 2009, http://original.antiwar.com, accessed June 2010.
23 Thomas X. Hammes, "War Evolves into the Fourth Generation," *Contemporary Security Policy* 26, no. 2 (August 2005), 198.
24 Thomas X. Hammes, *The Sling and the Stone: On War in the 21st Century* (St. Paul, MN: Zenith Press, 2004), 2.
25 John Arquilla and David Ronfeldt, *The Advent of Netwar* (Santa Monica, CA: RAND Corporation, 1996), 1, 3, 6, 9 and 21.
26 John Arquilla and David Ronfeldt, "Cyberwar is Coming!" *Comparative Strategy* 12 (1993), 144–45.
27 Hammes, "War Evolves into the Fourth Generation," 15.
28 James J. Wirtz, "Politics with Guns: A Response to T. X. Hammes," *Contemporary Security Policy* 26, no. 2 (August 2005), 224.
29 Edward N. Luttwak, "A Brief Note on 'Fourth-generation Warfare'," *Contemporary Security Policy* 26, no. 2 (August 2005), 227.
30 Bart Schuurman, "Clausewitz and the 'New Wars' Scholars," *Parameters* (Spring 2010), 90.
31 Mary Kaldor, *New and Old Wars: Organized Violence in a Global Era* (Stanford, CA: Stanford University Press, 1999), 76.
32 Herfried Munkler, *The New Wars* (Malden, MA: Polity Press, 2002), 29.
33 Rupert Smith, *The Utility of Force: The Art of War in the Modern World* (London: Allen Lane, 2005), 3.
34 Richard H. Shultz, Jr. and Andrea J. Dew, *Insurgents, Terrorists and Militias: The Warriors of Contemporary Combat* (New York: Columbia University Press, 2006), 37.
35 Smith, *The Utility of Force*, 269–70, 397.
36 Kaldor, *New and Old Wars*, 113–14, 124–25.
37 Smith, *The Utility of Force*, 384–85.
38 David J. Kilcullen, "Countering Global Insurgency," *Journal of Strategic Studies* 28, no. 4 (August 2005), 604.
39 David Kilcullen, "Counter-insurgency *Redux*," *Survival* 48, no. 4 (Winter 2006–7), 115–16.
40 David Kilcullen, *The Accidental Guerrilla: Fighting Small Wars in the Midst of a Big One* (New York: Oxford University Press, 2009), 35–38.

41 Kilcullen, "Counter-insurgency *Redux*," 117.
42 James J. Schneider, "T. E. Lawrence and the Mind of an Insurgent," *Army* (July 2005), 36.
43 Kilcullen, *The Accidental Guerrilla*, 264–69.
44 FM 3–24, 3.
45 Fareed Zakaria, "The General: An Interview with David Petraeus," *Newsweek*, January 4, 2009.
46 FM 3–24, 8.
47 Ibid., 111 and 328.

Further reading

Arquilla, John and David Ronfeldt. *The Advent of Netwar* (Santa Monica, CA: RAND Corporation, 1996).
Callwell, C. E. *Small Wars: Their Principles and Practice*, 3rd edition (Lincoln, NE: University of Nebraska Press, 1996).
Galula, David. *Counterinsurgency Warfare: Theory and Practice* (New York: Praeger Publishers, 1964).
Hammes, Thomas X. *The Sling and the Stone: On War in the 21st Century* (St. Paul, MN: Zenith Press, 2004).
Kaldor, Mary. *New and Old Wars: Organized Violence in a Global Era* (Stanford, CA: Stanford University Press, 1999).
Kilcullen, David. *The Accidental Guerrilla: Fighting Small Wars in the Midst of a Big One* (New York: Oxford University Press, 2009).
Krepinevich, Andrew F. *The Army and Vietnam* (Baltimore, MD: Johns Hopkins University Press, 1986).
Lawrence, T.E. *Seven Pillars of Wisdom: A Triumph* (London: Jonathan Cape, 1940).
Lind, William S. et al. "The Changing Face of War: Into the Fourth Generation," *Military Review* (October 1989).
Mao Tse-Tung. *On Guerrilla Warfare*, trans. Samuel B. Griffith (New York: Praeger Publishers, 1961).
Munkler, Herfried. *The New Wars* (Malden, MA: Polity Press, 2002).
Nagl, John A. *Learning to Eat Soup with a Knife: Counterinsurgency Lessons from Malaya and Vietnam* (Chicago, IL: University of Chicago Press, 2005).
Shultz, Richard H., Jr. and Andrea J. Dew. *Insurgents, Terrorists and Militias: The Warriors of Contemporary Combat* (New York: Columbia University Press, 2006).
Smith, Rupert. *The Utility of Force: The Art of War in the Modern World* (London: Allen Lane, 2005).
Thompson, Robert. *Defeating Communist Insurgency* (New York: Praeger Publishers, 1966).
United States Army. *The U.S. Army–Marine Corps Counterinsurgency Field Manual* (Chicago, IL: University of Chicago Press, 2007).
van Creveld, Martin. *The Transformation of War* (New York: The Free Press, 1991).

6   Cyberwar

Strategic thought on cyberwar is in its infancy. Like airpower in the 1910s, today ideas, principles, and doctrine on how best to use this potential weapon are at the early stages. And just as lingering questions about whether airpower could be usefully employed as an instrument of war were answered by the experience of World War One, so too did a real-life conflict point to a role for cyber attack in war, this time the Russia–Georgia conflict of 2008. Debates from the 1990s about whether offensive or only defensive information warfare is admissible have been replaced, in the post-9/11 and contemporary period, with explicit attempts to develop offensive capabilities and accompanying doctrine on cyberwar.

This chapter examines strategic thought on the conduct of war in the cyber dimension. One area where cyberwar breaks markedly from airpower, seapower, and landpower is in having natural boundaries with regard to the subject matter. The rough contours of what may be considered part of airpower, seapower, or landpower are readily identifiable, but what exactly do we mean by cyberwar? The confusion is implicitly alluded to above with the use of the term "information warfare," only one component of which is, in actual fact, cyberwar. As a result, we begin by defining the parameters of cyberwar for the purposes of this volume. Once these are established we see that strategic thinkers in this area form a small and eclectic group. They include Martin Libicki of the RAND Corporation, the Pentagon's military leadership, and the People's Liberation Army. The chapter goes on to examine the ideas of these strategic thinkers. Information is admittedly sparse, in part because strategic thought on cyberwar is relatively new, but also because the combination of military organizations as strategic thinkers, and the close link between cyberwar and intelligence assets, means that only limited information exists in the unclassified domain. What follows no doubt only scrapes the surface of the true depths of contemporary strategic thinking on cyberwar.

What is cyberwar?

Cyberwar, here, refers to hostile actions in cyberspace. Also called cyber attack or computer network attack (CNA), it can be defined as "the use of deliberate actions— perhaps over an extended period of time—to alter, disrupt, deceive, degrade or destroy adversary computer systems or networks and/or programs resident in or transiting these systems or networks."[1] Although the most straightforward means of executing a computer network attack is to physically destroy an adversary's computers, our concern here is the use of digital weapons, not kinetic attack. Cyberwar is an offensive cyber operation, as is another cyber operation, computer network exploitation (CNE). But

CNE is distinct from CNA in that those engaged in CNE do *not* want to disturb the normal functioning of a computer system; the idea is to obtain information, likely over an extended period of time. CNE is an espionage or intelligence-gathering activity and is not included here as part of cyberwar. (In practice, of course, it can be difficult for a state to determine if it is the target of CNA or CNE, because the two are closely linked from a technical point of view.)

Defining cyberwar as comprising the limited parameters of CNA is itself an evolution in strategic thinking about cyberwar, which has had several meanings, titles, loose references, and contexts in the period since the end of the Cold War. One of the earliest attempts to define cyberwar was made by two RAND researchers, John Arquilla and David Ronfeldt. In an influential 1993 journal article titled "Cyberwar is Coming!" they stated:

> cyberwar refers to knowledge related conflict at the military level ... [it] refers to conducting military operations according to information related principles ... It means disrupting and destroying information and communication systems ... It means trying to know everything about an adversary while keeping the adversary from knowing much about oneself.[2]

Two points emerge from this early discussion. First, Arquilla and Ronfeldt's conception of cyberwar largely echoed ideas that subsequently became associated with what was referred to in the 1990s as the Revolution in Military Affairs (RMA). The term "cyberwar," they note, was coined to discuss the military implications for warfare of the information revolution, including technological, doctrinal, and organizational changes, as well as the move from mass to information dominance and dispersing one's own fog of war as the source of a decisive advantage. These ideas, which were discussed with respect to the RMA in Chapter 4, are *not* the subject of this chapter. Thus, although Arquilla and Ronfeldt may have originated, and certainly popularized, the concept of cyberwar, they are not included here as cyberwar strategic thinkers. Their most important contribution to military strategic thought (and indeed their major area of focus) is in their companion idea of "netwar," which denotes an emerging mode of conflict involving non-state actors in which the protagonists use networked forms of organization, operating in small groups from dispersed but interconnected locations. In a highly prolific 1996 book, *Networks and Netwars*, they all but foretold the rise of al Qaeda and its mode of operation.

A second point is that Arquilla and Ronfeldt's discussion of cyberwar as involving the destruction of information and communications systems alluded to the broader concept of "information warfare." A catch-all phrase from the 1990s, the content of "information warfare" was first methodically dissected by Martin Libicki. In "What is Information Warfare?," a 1995 study for the National Defense University, Libicki identified seven forms of information warfare prevalent in the literature at the time that, taken together, would lead one to concur with Libicki that there was little that could not be considered information warfare. The forms included command and control warfare against the enemy's head and neck, whether through physical attack or CNA on military targets; intelligence-based warfare; electronic warfare; psychological warfare (PSYOPS); hacker warfare, that is, CNA on civilian targets; economic information warfare; and cyber warfare, described at the time as "a grab-bag of futuristic scenarios."[3] All of these things were considered different modes of information warfare or operations and their common element was that they were forms of warfare that somehow affected an enemy's information.

Some suggested modes of information warfare involved destroying information systems with weapons of pure information, such as computer viruses. But many components of what might be more appropriately termed the "grab-bag" of information warfare were not new and had nothing to do with the use of bits and bytes as instruments of war. PSYOPS, for example, is a form of warfare dating back decades, even centuries, and might involve such non-technological things as distributing leaflets and wristbands. Electronic warfare, involving the electromagnetic spectrum, has a long history and is familiar from such activities as the suppression of enemy air defenses. Command and control warfare includes the "antihead" action of the shipboard sniper that killed Admiral Nelson, and today more often than not refers to physical precision strikes against command centers, also described as "decapitation" in our discussion of airpower.

In the second half of the 1990s the Pentagon dropped the term information warfare in favor of information operations, to accommodate things such as propaganda that took place during peacetime. Today it is thus more current to locate cyberwar within a broader schema of "information operations," although the content of this term reads little differently from the original information warfare. The US military's joint publication *Information Operations* defines such operations as the integrated employment of electronic warfare, computer network operations, and psychological operations to influence, disrupt, and corrupt adversary information and information systems while defending one's own.[4] Parts of the US military also continue to include physical attack in the overall schema. The US Army's Training and Doctrine Command, for example, defines cyber attack to include CNA, electronic attack, and physical attack.[5] Confusingly, the Army also assigns the term "netwar" to the integrated use of CNA, electronic attack, and physical attack.[6]

Despite the organizing principle of somehow affecting adversary information, the various components of information operations arguably have little business being considered as a single category of operations. Most of the diverse aspects can stand on their own as a separate discipline. Moreover, as Libicki notes, "it is a daunting theoretical challenge to cover, in one treatment, computer hackers, electromagnetic wizards, drivers of airborne radar, leaflet droppers, bombers and sharpshooters."[7] Our concern here is altering, disrupting, deceiving, degrading, or destroying adversary computer systems or networks through the use of hostile digital attack. The parameters of what comprises cyberwar are necessarily limited to that of CNA so as to identify as coherent an area of inquiry as we do with respect to other warfare domains.

Permissibility

Although numerous types of operations have been included under the broader information warfare/information operations rubric, when debates were underway in the 1990s as to the permissibility of information warfare, they implicitly and invariably centered on one particular type of operation: computer strikes against computer systems. As late as 1998 "offensive information warfare"—meaning CNA—was considered taboo for public discussion. Critics charged that the Pentagon was legally prohibited from striking back against those seeking to access its computers and that it should stick to strictly defensive means such as blocking or slowing down information requests. "The debate on defensive hacker warfare concerns the appropriate role for the DoD [Department of Defense] in safeguarding non-military computers," Libicki noted in his 1995 National Defense University study. "The debate on offensive hacker warfare concerns whether it should take place at all."

Within a few years the ongoing deliberation was resolved in favor and the Pentagon was actively studying the use of cyber attacks to cripple or control adversary computer networks. In 1998 the Pentagon established the Joint Task Force–Computer Network Defense, with a mandate to protect the Pentagon's computer networks, and in 2000 the Task Force was also assigned an offensive mission. A few years later the organization was split into two, separating the offensive and defensive areas of focus. A 2002 presidential national security directive reportedly ordered the US government to develop guidance on launching cyber attacks against enemy computer systems, but the 2003 *National Strategy to Secure Cyberspace* focused only on the less controversial computer network defense.

Toward the end of the decade, however—and perhaps prompted by the cyber attacks against Estonia in 2007 (see Box 6.1) and Georgia in 2008—all pretext of a solely or predominantly defensive orientation was dropped. In 2010 US Cyber Command was created as a subcommand under US Strategic Command. The Command reunites the offensive and defensive cyber missions and is explicitly charged with authority not only to defend but also, should it be directed to do so by the president, to attack adversaries. To this end it will develop offensive cyber weapons, in addition to defensive capabilities. The Director of the National Security Agency (General Keith Alexander) has been double-hatted as Commander; his mandate is to conduct full-spectrum operations to defend American military networks and attack other countries' systems. Along these lines, for example, the US Air Force has been advised to develop an "integrated attack" capability, meaning the integration not only of air and space but also cyber capabilities into joint operations.[8] Possible US offensive cyberwar options could range from a "low-intensity" cyber intrusion such as listening in on the adversary's communications, to a "high-intensity" attack that cripples an enemy's air defense system to clear the way for a bomber attack. Despite the official mandate change, US officials remain hesitant to talk about offensive cyberwar, preferring to emphasize the need to defend computer networks, albeit in an ever more offensive manner (see below). When asked during confirmation hearings if the new US Cyber Command would develop significant offensive cyber weapons, General Alexander's response was classified.

Box 6.1 Cyber attack against Estonia

- The April 2007 decision by the government of Estonia to remove a Soviet war monument from the center of the capital, Tallinn, to a military cemetery, sparked rioting by several thousand protestors from Estonia's large ethic Russian population and a condemnation from Russia.

- At roughly the same time websites across Estonia came under cyber attack. Although the rioting soon ended, the internet attacks continued and intensi-fied until mid-May, targeting and making inaccessible the websites of banks, political parties, major companies, news organizations, and those of almost the entire government, parliament, and presidency.

- Although Estonia recovered quickly, the event was notable because it was the first known incidence of such an assault on a state. Estonia suspected the Russian government as the perpetrator, yet the nature of cyberwar is such that this cannot be conclusively determined.

- This action against a NATO member raised as-yet unresolved questions within the alliance about whether a cyber attack constitutes an armed attack under Article V of the North Atlantic Treaty.

Meanwhile NATO as an organization confines itself, at least officially, to a focus on computer network defense. Its 2010 strategic concept states that the cyber dimension of modern conflicts will figure in NATO doctrine but that it will do so in the form of improving capabilities to detect, assess, prevent, and recover in the case of a cyber attack. There is no mention of offensive cyber activity as a tool of warfare. In 2011 NATO's allied command transformation leadership confirmed NATO's defensive approach.[9] Consistent with this, a NATO Centre of Excellence set up after the 2007 attacks on Estonia to enhance the capability of NATO countries to address cyber threat focuses explicitly on defense activities, although some of its researchers have begun to examine offensive cyber warfare.[10]

In contrast to America's gradual shift in emphasis, and NATO's guarded stance, China appears to have taken the decision in the late 1990s to develop an offensive information warfare capability. The 1991 Gulf War demonstrated that it was not possible for a state to confront the United States directly on the conventional battlefield, while the 1996 Taiwan Crisis indicated to China the potential need to confront the United States in the future. To square this circle, China turned to focus on "asymmetric" approaches that would target US weaknesses and vulnerabilities—one of the first on the list being the dependence of America's technologically advanced military on computer systems and networks. US cyberwar experts have documented the explicit discussion by Chinese information operations theorists, including high-ranking generals, about offensive actions in cyberspace since about 1999 onward.[11] China's relative openness in this area contrasts with that of Russia, which has practiced cyberwar (notably in Georgia) but not published unclassified strategic thought in this area.

Strategic thought

It is against this backdrop that strategic thought on cyberwar has developed. If a contemporary Sun Tzu were to write a treatise on the conduct of war in the cyber dimension, what would it look like? The conduct of cyberwar flows naturally from the unique character and resulting goals of cyberwar.

Character of cyberwar

Perhaps the most notable distinguishing characteristic between the cyber dimension of warfare and that of other domains—sea, land, air, and space—is that there is not one definable expanse to be conquered. Cyberspace is a replicable construct and, being replicable, it exists in multiple locations at once. There is not *a* cyberspace that exists, with distinct parameters and perimeters within which conquest can take place. Rather, every system and every network can hold an unlimited number of spaces. Moreover, cyber-space is a vastly shifting landscape, as compared to the other domains. Portions of cyberspace continually change, evolving and expanding with technological innovation and the addition, removal, replacement, or reconfiguration of networks.

If we look conceptually at just one cyberspace in time, however, we see that even this is unique in nature because it is characterized by a complete lack of boundaries. Unlike kinetic weapons, a computer network attack can reach across the world at the speed of light, invisibly transiting many international borders en route to its target. "The lack of geopolitical boundaries," point out the US Joint Chiefs of Staff in the National Military Strategy for Cyberspace Operations, "allows cyberspace operations to occur rapidly nearly anywhere."[12] The instantaneous nature of cyberwar and the ability to attack the entire domain simultaneously are characteristics that make the cyber dimension of warfare particularly potentially dangerous.

The character of cyberwar is also distinguished by the fact that, unlike its kinetic brethren, an attack using cyber weapons has the potential to wreak widespread, massive damage. Although the immediate effects of cyber attack are unlikely to be comparable to those of weapons of mass destruction, a large-scale cyber attack could significantly affect the functioning of society, leading to many indirect casualties. Some have gone so far as to argue that cyberwar is potentially as destructive as nuclear war, a notion discounted by Libicki on the grounds that cyberwar is largely temporary and rapidly over.[13] A better characterization is that "Like chemical and biological weapons, cyber weapons can target large masses of people ... Unlike biological and chemical weapons they affect humans indirectly rather than directly. Cyber weapons thus ... occupy a completely new niche by their nature."[14]

Goal of cyberwar

The fact that cyberspace is a replicable construct means that the operational goal of cyberwar cannot be to destroy cyber capabilities, in the sense that a land force may seek to destroy an enemy's land forces. "While something akin to conquest can be defined for cyberspace, cyberspace itself cannot be conquered in any conventional sense."[15] Permanently damaging a system through CNA is not an option. As systems are attacked, vulnerabilities are revealed, repaired, and routed around. The systems themselves are hardened and are likely to become less, not more, vulnerable and less, not more, resistant to further coercion.

With destruction not an option (except in relatively rare cases when a cyber attack leads to physical damage), the cyber warrior looks to other objectives. The immediate goal may be to *blind* the opponent by creating so much noise around the signal that the useful information carried by it is lost in a sea of fuzz; to *disrupt* access to data; to *corrupt* information by adding false bits to existing ones, thereby *deceiving* the opponent and, related to this, to *confuse* or *disorient* the opponent by undermining the credibility of information; to *steal* information; and to *manipulate* opponent systems by making them do what their designers did not want them to do (see Box 6.2). A prevailing theme in the US literature is the goal of *denying* the enemy freedom of action. The US Joint Chiefs of Staff speak of "ensuring our freedom of action and denying the same to our adversaries" in order to secure "information superiority,"[16] and General Alexander, Commander of US Cyber Command, stresses that the principal effect of cyber warfare is to deny the enemy freedom of action in cyberspace.

Box 6.2 The Stuxnet virus

- A good example of cyberwar to manipulate opponent systems is the Stuxnet virus.
- In 2010 Iranian officials acknowledged that computers at one of their nuclear plants had been infected by a computer virus called Stuxnet.
- The malware worm was designed to lie in wait, searching for and targeting specific equipment that exists at Iran's uranium enrichment plant at Natanz.

The virus caused programmable logic computers made by the German electronics company Siemens, which are used at the plant to control gas centrifuges, to make the centrifuges spin out of control and break. Gas centrifuges can be used to produce highly enriched uranium and it is thought that Iran is pursuing a nuclear weapons program.

- The virus also covered its tracks by fooling operators into believing the equipment was working as usual. As a result, it was not discovered for over a year.
- There are confusing reports as to how many centrifuges were affected and how much damage was done. Iran has an interest in playing down the threat. But it is thought that the Stuxnet virus set back Iran's nuclear program by some years.
- The virus was so sophisticated that computer security experts suspect it was launched by the United States or Israel, but this has not been conclusively determined.
- The Stuxnet virus marked a watershed in warfare because it demonstrated that cyber activity can have kinetic, physical effects.

Ultimately, the strategic goal of offensive cyberwar may be to coerce the opponent, assert status or "teach other countries a lesson," disable an enemy capability, or support other service elements in prevailing in ongoing hostilities. US think-tanks have identified a possible end-goal of "strategic cyberwar," defined as state-on-state conflict carried out in cyberspace for the primary purpose of compelling the other side to accede.[17] It is possible for states to wage cyberwar for an extended period of time while refraining from physical violence. But unlike airpower, where there is some question as to whether it can "win" a war on its own, cyberwar is quintessentially a supporting form of warfare. "It is virtually impossible to take land by cyberwar," Libicki points out, "which is fine: Land has mostly gone out of fashion as a motive for conflict."[18] General Alexander has similarly implied that cyber weapons would be used mainly as an adjunct to conventional military operations.

The actors

Implicit in this discussion of the character of cyberwar is that it is only useful as a form of warfare against entities with fairly extensive computer networks. For this reason cyberwar is particularly amenable to state-on-state warfare, and even here there are examples—Serbia during the 1999 Kosovo conflict and even Iraq in 2003—of states possessing few high-value cyber targets during warfare. Cyberwar's requirement that an enemy have similar capabilities or vulnerabilities differentiates it from other forms of conflict. US air and space capabilities are, if anything, more dominant against adversaries with no such capabilities. By contrast, in cyberwar, adversaries must have a footprint—"no footprint, no impact."[19] Thus when we discuss the conduct of war in the cyber dimension the predominant focus of our analysis is the state actor.

Conduct of war

Martin Libicki. The character and possible goals of cyberwar form the backdrop against which there has been some strategic thinking on the conduct of war in this dimension. In his book *Cyberdeterrence and Cyberwar*, Martin Libicki draws out some notable principles in the conduct of cyberwar. He implies, for example, that cyberwar is *non-incremental* in nature. "At first glance cyberwar lends itself to an incremental approach because it presents such a broad range of options for contemplation ... At second glance, an incremental approach may be wrong."[20] This is because the relationship between cyber activities and their effect is nonlinear in nature. Tactical attacks can bring only mild annoyance for long periods of time and then suddenly cross a threshold into strategic effect. The notion, prevalent in other domains, of starting a conflict with a series of probes, and learning in the process one's own and one's adversary's weaknesses, does not hold up in the fifth domain. Because learning takes place so quickly on the part of the adversary and because cyberwar is ultimately non-incremental in nature, a better approach in this domain is that of *surprise*. "Cyberattacks are about *deception*, and the essence of deception is the difference between what you expect and what you get: surprise ... cyberwar is tailor made for surprise attack ... for a one-time *bolt from the blue*."[21]

The People's Liberation Army. As indicated above, strategic thought on cyberwar has also been underway for some time in the People's Liberation Army (PLA). Historically, China's warfare approach has been "active defense," meaning the country would not initiate an attack but would be ready to respond if attacked. In the information era this has changed to one of *active offense* in the conduct of war. The view is that the key to effective cyber operations is to take the initiative, launch cyber offensives and even act *pre-emptively*. The approach is closely linked to China's overall perspective on "informationized" warfare—the incorporation of advanced technologies into military operations—under which all activities now revolve around gaining information superiority on the battlefield.

China's military has developed a strategy called Integrated Network Electronic Warfare, designed to guide the combined employment of network warfare tools (bits) and electronic warfare weapons (waves) against an adversary's information systems. The strategy points to several possible principles of cyberwar. Cyber attack, it is argued, should be used in the *early or opening phases* of a conflict. The idea is to exploit a temporary period of adversary blindness with a series of traditional firepower attacks, i.e. physical strikes, on platforms and personnel. The cyber approach is also *targeted*, in that its integrated warfare method specifically identifies enemy C4ISR (command, control, communications, computers, intelligence, surveillance and reconnaissance) and logistics systems networks as the highest priority for information warfare attacks. "Attacks on an adversary's information systems are not meant to suppress all networks, transmissions, and sensors ... [but] only those nodes which the PLA's IW [information warfare] planners assess will most deeply affect enemy decision making, operations, and morale."[22]

The PLA's approach is thus qualitative and effects based in nature, organized around a determination of the operational *center of gravity* as represented by those nodes. In line with the goal of *denying* an opponent his freedom of action in cyberspace, China seeks information dominance or superiority by attacking an adversary's C4ISR infrastructure to prevent or disrupt the acquisition, processing, or transmission of information in support of combat operations. Finally, the PLA identifies the requirement for coordinated or *simultaneous* attacks on enemy networks and systems, and highlights the value of silent or *undetected* operations to either steal or manipulate information.

The US military community. The scholarly US literature on cyberwar indicates that at least 13 different doctrinal documents at the Office of the Secretary of Defense, Department of Defense, Navy, Army, Air Force and Strategic Command (STRATCOM) levels outline how America will fight a cyberwar. Despite this, however, information on America's conduct of war in the cyber domain is relatively limited—and for good reason. The quality of a CNA is derived from the ability to deceive, overcome, or circumvent defenses, while the quality of the defense is based on the ability to anticipate an enemy's offensive approaches. Once offensive or defensive techniques are known, in relatively short order corresponding enemy defenses and offensive approaches can be engineered.

That said, it is possible to identify in US strategic thinking some notable aspects of the conduct of war in the cyber dimension. A key theme in US military literature is the requirement to take the *offense*. Unlike in the other domains, where questions have historically arisen as to whether the offense or defense dominates, in the cyber domain the query is definitively answered in favor of the offense. "The offensive form of cyberspace operations," officials from US STRATCOM argue, "is far superior to the defensive form."[23] America's Deputy Secretary of Defense, William Lynn, has similarly stressed cyberwar's amenability to an offensive approach. "In cyberspace," he argues, "the offense has the upper hand" because the internet, designed to be rapidly expandable and without boundaries, creates an inherently "offense-dominant environment."[24] US allies have pointed out that cyberwar strongly favors the attacker over the defender.[25]

Although the dominance of the offense is a predominant theme in the US literature, that is not to say that the defense does not figure in strategic thinking about this warfare domain. The notion of defense is prevalent, but it is presented within an active rather than passive construct. General Alexander has stated that the United States needs to develop *dynamic* rather than passive defenses, meaning searching for adversaries on networks before they attack, rather than blocking attacks after they have been launched and detected.[26] To do otherwise is akin to letting a burglar stand outside your door trying successive keys until one unlocks the door—rather than actively seeking to locate and apprehend the burglar before he walks up the step. The Pentagon refers to this concept as *active defense*—hunting within the military's own networks. Along these lines, US defense analysts have stressed that computer network defense is more than building better firewalls and antivirus software.[27] It also involves seeing the threats before they come and perhaps allowing the US military to reach out into the adversary's cyber systems using CNA for cyber response. This is much different from the original perspective presented in the mid-1990s, that most of what US forces could usefully do in information warfare would be defensive, and that those defenses would be passive. (It is also distinct from China's former approach, noted above, which used the same term but was more passive in nature).

The US National Research Council concurs that passive defense is insufficient to ensure security and that it makes no sense to allow an adversary to pay no penalty for failed attacks until he or she succeeds or chooses to stop. They suggest taking measures to eliminate or degrade an adversary's ability to successfully prosecute an attack. Under this rubric, a CNA might be used for defensive purposes, to neutralize a cyber threat before it arrives at one's door. The Council, like China—and as practiced by Russia (see below)—also points to the use of cyber attack in the *early* or *opening phases* of a crises, before overt conflict begins.[28]

US military leaders stress the requirement for *speed* in the conduct of cyberwar. "The speed at which information moves in cyberspace approaches the speed of light," the Joint Chiefs of Staff have pointed out. "In war, operational speed is a source of combat power. When this speed is exploited, increased efficiency and productivity can result."[29] Part of this involves using the speed of information flow to gain and maintain the initiative, and to operate within the enemy's decision cycle. Beyond this, Lynn has stated that cyber warfare is like *maneuver* warfare in that speed and *agility* matter most, while US allies have drawn attention to speed, surprise, and economy of force as characteristics of war relevant to cyberwar.[30] Observers have cautioned that the speed with which electronic attacks can be conducted leaves "little time for cool headed reflection" and favors *pre-emptive* attack.[31] A prevailing theme is also a *silent* and *surreptitious* approach. One US cyber security firm has argued: "Hacking used to be about making noise. Now it's about staying silent."[32] The best approach to cyberwar, some argue, is to infiltrate the enemy's computers and networks, spy on them, and surreptitiously change pieces of their communications without them knowing it.[33]

Russia. One cannot point to a body of Russian strategic thought on cyberwar. Nonetheless, it is possible to draw out elements of its perspective on the conduct of war in the cyber dimension by looking at Russia's brief war with Georgia in August 2008, during which it allegedly launched cyber attacks against Georgia (this has not been definitively determined). Analysts note that the war was historic and unprecedented because it was the first time there had been a cyberspace domain attack coordinated with conventional warfare. The case drew out several potential principles for the future conduct of cyberwar, including the notion of *parallel* or *simultaneous* attacks by kinetic and cyber forces. At the operational and tactical level of war, alleged Russian cyberspace operations were closely *synchronized* with those in the land, sea, and air domains to achieve the desired effect.

Russia also undertook to identify the opponent's cyber *center of gravity*, in this case the Georgian government's ability to communicate with the outside world and put out its message. Russian patriotic hackers worked against Georgian systems in the weeks leading up to the actual shooting war, underscoring the value of *preparatory operations*—including reconnaissance activities and probing attacks—well in advance of any network attack conducted in actual support of a traditional military operation. The fact that Georgian hackers were targeted first reinforced as an important element in the conduct of cyberwar the idea of *pre-emption* to disrupt, degrade, and even remove retaliatory capability. Based on the Russia–Georgia war example, analysts argue that future patriotic hackers will be using the cyberspace equivalent of *fire* and *maneuver* operations directly in support of warfare in other domains.[34]

War questions

Thresholds

The advent of war in the cyber domain has raised a number of interrelated war questions. The first and most basic is whether cyberwar can be considered war. The definition of war as a conflict carried on by force of arms between nations or between parties within a nation is problematic when it comes to cyberwar. And yet, as one NATO official put it: "If a member state's communications centre is attacked with a missile, you call it an act of war. So what do you call it if the same installation is disabled with a cyber attack?"[35] The question of when offensive activities in cyberspace become an act of war is an important one because, under international law, article 51 of the UN Charter, the use of force in self-defense (cyber or kinetic) is allowable "if an armed attack occurs." Moreover, pre-emptive military activity, that is, anticipatory self-defense, is permitted if an armed attack is imminent but has not actually already occurred. American scholars have stressed that in assessing whether to respond to a cyber threat, the United States should not make a distinction between methods of attack, between cyber and kinetic tools, but should focus on effect.[36] The National Research Council concurs that notions related to "use of force" and "armed attack" should be judged primarily by the effects of an action, rather than its modality.[37]

Looking at effect, much of what is loosely called a cyber attack or cyberwar would not pass muster as an "attack" in the other domains. The intrusions are hacker, espionage, or criminal in nature and are better characterized as a network *irritant* than an act of war. Legal scholars have argued that we can begin to distinguish between a criminal act and an act of war in cyberspace if we define war in cyberspace as something that produces the equivalent effect to an armed attack. From this perspective, the thresholds for war or attack should not be very different from war in a kinetic environment. An action that did not directly cause substantial death or physical destruction (or was not imminently about to do so) would be unlikely to qualify as an armed attack.[38] Others have relaxed the terms slightly, arguing that cyber activities that could result in casualties or a regional power failure, such as planting logic bombs on the US electrical grid, might be considered warfare.[39]

Consequences

Current US doctrine is unclear on what the consequences would be for a state launching a cyber attack that is deemed to be an armed attack. Some have proposed a response using conventional armed forces. Others may recommend replying in kind through cyber means. Regardless, the commander of US Cyber Command and many others point out that a response would be conducted in accordance with long-standing rules and principles of war, including *proportionality*, *discrimination*, and *necessity*. The latter refers to anticipatory self-defense (noted above) and dates to the early 1800s; the former two are familiar from Just War Doctrine and date back centuries. Proportionality weighs the use of force, in this case CNA, against the minimum necessary to achieve the military goal, while discrimination weighs the use of force against the likelihood of collateral (i.e. civilian) damage. Lynn has pointed out the need for clear rules of engagement for responding to cyber attacks, based on a determination of "what action is necessary, appropriate, proportional and justified in each particular case based on the laws that govern action in times of war and peace."[40] The US National Research Council has gone into more detail, noting that limitations mandated by the laws of armed conflict regarding, among other things, the differentiation of targets, military necessity, and limiting collateral damage, would apply in cyberwar. "If it was legitimate to attack a target with kinetic weapons, it remains legitimate under the laws of armed conflict to attack it with cyberweapons."[41]

Imminence

This seemingly straightforward framework is complicated by additional factors, not least the fact that imminence, difficult to determine in any non-conventional war, is even more challenging when it comes to cyberwar. How do you determine that an attack is imminent? What degree of certainty is needed before authorizing a response? After the 9/11 terrorist attacks attempts were made at the multilateral level to adjust the concepts of necessity and imminence to the reality that an impending terrorist attack is far less visible than a traditional army massing on the border.[42] A similar effort, ideally encompassing some general benchmarks (such as the discovery of numerous logic bombs), will be required with respect to cyberwar.

Attribution

Even if it is deemed that an armed attack has taken place or imminently will take place, responding is complicated by the difficulty, in the cyber world, of assigning attribution. Today we still speak of the "alleged" Russian attacks on Estonia because the identity of the attackers remains unclear. Attribution is the major stumbling-block when it comes to adjusting the concept of deterrence to cyberwar. Without knowing the identity of the attacker, it is hard to threaten retaliation. The US military has set a goal of deterring adversaries from using offensive capabilities against US interests in cyberspace, and is improving its ability to locate the sources of electronic attack. Nonetheless, US officials believe deterrence by denial—making defenses effective enough to deny adversaries the benefit of an attack, despite the strength of offensive tools in cyberspace—will be more effective than deterrence by punishment or imposing costs of retaliation.[43]

Utility

Questions have also been raised about the utility of cyber attack as a tool of warfare. Cyber attack in its physical consequences is more like sabotage carried out by guerrillas or special operations forces, than like warfare in the sea, land, or air domains. Moreover, growing redundancies in the systems that control critical infrastructures mean that the degree to which they are vulnerable to an "electronic pearl harbor," a scenario presented in such books as Richard Clarke's 2010 *Cyber War*, may be overstated. The jury is out in this regard, and only time will tell the degree to which the cyber domain is a truly threatening one. Certainly the use of cyber attack in the Russia–Georgia war, and the Stuxnet virus, indicates cyberwar's potential as an offensive weapon of the future.

Unpredictability

Finally, even if the utility of cyberwar as an effective instrument of warfare can be determined, planners may be reluctant to wage cyberwar because of the unpredictable nature of the cyber instrument. Should a cruise missile be used to strike an adversary's command and control center we can know with certainty that some other facility around the corner or around the world will not also blow up as a result of that missile. But predicting the effects of a CNA on a complex set of computer systems can be far more difficult. A virus intended for another country's computer system could accidentally contaminate one's own or that of an ally. The effects of cyberspace weapons are global in nature and cannot necessarily be contained to a specific geographic theater. There is the potential for unintended collateral damage and unintended effects, making the use of cyber attack risky. Notes one senior US military official, when it comes to military weapons, one wants a predictable time and effect, something that is difficult to achieve in the cyber domain.[44] The Stuxnet virus gives a possible counter-example, targeting only a particular programmable logic controller made by Siemens that is prevalent in Iranian nuclear plants, and Clarke has gone so far as to describe the worm as a "precision guided munition."[45] Still, of the 100,000 hosts affected by the virus, 40,000 are outside of Iran, including some in the United States, indicating the potential for collateral or unintended damage.

Conclusion

Strategic thought on cyberwar, on hostile action in cyberspace, is in its infancy. Largely denied in the 1990s as an area of activity, since about the turn of the century offensive information warfare or CNA has been an area of growing—and since the latter half of the 2000s, accelerated—strategic focus. Driven by the desire to develop asymmetric offsets to American power, one of the earliest strategic thinkers in this area was the PLA. Martin Libicki of RAND has also produced several works in the area, as has the US military community writ large, including high-ranking military officers, civilian officials, and scholars. But strategic thought on the cyber dimension of war is relatively sparse as compared to that of other warfare domains. Cyber attack's close connection with intelligence gathering, and the fact that a CNA, once launched, is almost immediately susceptible to enemy counter-defenses and offensive approaches, means that many views on the conduct of war in this environment remain classified. That said, it is possible to identify some common themes with respect to cyberwar.

Taken together, post-Cold War strategic thought on cyberwar reveals a theory of cyberwar that might include the following tenets: cyberwar is quintessentially suited to offensive strategies, and even defensive approaches should, paradoxically, be pursued in an active or offensive manner; cyber strikes, rather than being broad brush in nature, should be targeted at specific high-value nodes deemed to be a center of gravity; speed, maneuver, and agility are important factors in cyberwar, which is best carried out in the opening phases of a conflict, or even pre-emptively; once conflict has started, cyber attacks should be conducted in parallel or simultaneously with conventional strikes, closely synchronized for maximum effect; cyberwar is non-incremental in nature; sharp learning curves on the part of the targeted party dictate that it is well suited to surprise and a one-time bolt from the blue; at the same time a silent, surreptitious, stealthy, and patient approach to cyberwar can be effective in manipulating information and achieving psychological effects.

These themes drawn from the unclassified literature no doubt only scratch the surface of the true depths of contemporary strategic thought on cyberwar. The particular nature of CNA is such that we are unlikely to see an official treatise any time soon on how best to carry out war in the cyber dimension. Future facets of cyberwar are more likely to be revealed in real-life experiences, such as the Russia–Georgia War, which ultimately provide the most instructive venue for understanding the conduct of war in the cyber domain.

Notes

1 National Research Council, *Technology, Policy, Law and Ethics Regarding U.S. Acquisition and Use of Cyberattack Capabilities* (Washington, DC: National Academies Press, 2009), 11.
2 John Arquilla and David Ronfeldt, "Cyberwar is Coming!," *Comparative Strategy* 12 (1993), 146.

3 See Martin Libicki, *What is Information Warfare?* (Washington, DC: National Defense University Institute for National Strategic Studies, ACIS Paper·3, August 1995) and Martin Libicki, *Conquest in Cyberspace: National Security and Information Warfare* (New York: Cambridge University Press, 2007), 16–17.
4 General Keith Alexander, "Warfighting in Cyberspace," *Joint Force Quarterly* 46, no.3 (4th quarter 2007), 59.
5 US Army Training and Doctrine Command, *Cyberspace Operations Concept Capability Plan 2016–2028* (Fort Monroe, VA: United States Army, February 2010), 21.
6 David M. Hollis, "USCYBERCOM: The Need for a Combatant Command versus a Subunified Command," *Joint Force Quarterly* 58, no. 3 (2010), fn 2.
7 Libicki, *Conquest in Cyberspace*, 17.
8 Richard Mesic et al., *Air Force Cyber Command (Provisional) Decision Support* (Santa Monica, CA: RAND Corporation, 2010), 16.
9 Author question to Polish General Mieczyslaw Bieniek, Deputy Commander NATO Supreme Allied Command Transformation, at the Ottawa Conference on Defence and Security, February 25, 2011.
10 See, for example, Kenneth Geers, *Sun Tzu and Cyber War* (Tallinn, Estonia: Cooperative Cyber Defence Centre of Excellence (CCD CoE) Publications, 2011), http://www.ccdcoe.org, accessed March 2011.
11 Timothy Thomas, "China's Electronic Long-range Reconnaissance," *Military Review* (November/December 2008).
12 Chairman of the US Joint Chiefs of Staff, *National Military Strategy for Cyberspace Operations* (Washington, DC: Department of Defense, December 2006), 4.
13 Libicki, *Conquest in Cyberspace*, 39.
14 William J. Bayles, "The Ethics of Computer Network Attack," *Parameters* (Spring 2001).
15 Libicki, *Conquest in Cyberspace*, 5.
16 Chairman of the US Joint Chiefs of Staff, *National Military Strategy for Cyberspace Operations*, 1.
17 Mesic et al., *Air Force Cyber Command*, 8.
18 Martin Libicki, *Cyberdeterrence and Cyberwar* (Santa Monica, CA: RAND Corporation, 2009), 121.
19 Ibid., 140.
20 Ibid., 127.
21 Ibid., 143 and 158.
22 Bryan Krekel, "Capability of the People's Republic of China to Conduct Cyber Warfare and Computer Network Exploitation," report prepared for the US–China Economic and Security Review Commission, October 9, 2009, 15.
23 Hollis, "USCYBERCOM," 51.
24 William J. Lynn III, "Defending a New Domain: The Pentagon's Cyberstrategy," *Foreign Affairs* 89, no. 5 (September/October 2010), 99.
25 Geers, *Sun Tzu and Cyber War*, http://www.ccdcoe.org.
26 William Matthews, "U.S. Faces Many Cyber Threats, Commander Warns," *Defense News*, September 27, 2010, 23.
27 Mesic et al., *Air Force Cyber Command*, 10.
28 National Research Council, *Technology, Policy, Law and Ethics*, 13, 161 and 166.
29 Chairman of the US Joint Chiefs of Staff, *National Military Strategy for Cyberspace Operations*, 4.
30 Geers, *Sun Tzu and Cyber War*, http://www.ccdcoe.org.
31 "Cyberwar," *Economist*, July 3, 2010, 11.
32 Greg Day of McAfee, as quoted in "War in the Fifth Domain," *Economist*, July 3, 2010, 26.
33 Bruce Schneier of Counterpane, as quoted in Rob Lever, "U.S. May Use Cyberhackers as War Weapon," *National Post*, February 17, 2003.
34 David Hollis, "Cyber War Case Study: Georgia 2008," *Small Wars Journal* (January 2011), 8.
35 NATO official as quoted in "A Cyber-riot: Estonia and Russia," *Economist*, May 12, 2007.
36 See James Adams, "Virtual Defense," *Foreign Affairs* 80, no. 3 (May/June 2001), 109.
37 National Research Council, *Technology, Policy, Law and Ethics*, 3 and 21.

38 James Lewis, *A Note on the Laws of War in Cyberspace* (Washington, DC: Center for Strategic and International Studies, April 2010), 2.
39 Senior US military source paraphrased in "War in the Fifth Domain," 28.
40 Lynn, "Defending a New Domain," 104.
41 National Research Council, *Technology, Policy, Law and Ethics*, 164.
42 See UN High-Level Panel on Threats Challenges and Change, *A More Secure World: Our Shared Responsibility* (New York: United Nations, 2004), 61–67.
43 Lynn, "Defending a New Domain," 99–100.
44 "War in the Fifth Domain," 28.
45 Ken Dilanian, "Iran's Nuclear Program and a New Era of Cyber War," *Los Angeles Times*, January 17, 2011.

Further reading

Alexander, Keith. "Warfighting in Cyberspace," *Joint Force Quarterly* 46, no. 3 (4th quarter 2007).

Arquilla, John and David Ronfeldt. "Cyberwar is Coming!" *Comparative Strategy* 12 (1993).

Hollis, David. "Cyber War Case Study: Georgia 2008," *Small Wars Journal* (January 2011).

Libicki, Martin. *Conquest in Cyberspace: National Security and Information Warfare* (New York: Cambridge University Press, 2007).

——. *Cyberdeterrence and Cyberwar* (Santa Monica, CA: RAND Corporation, 2009).

——. *What Is Information Warfare?* (Washington, DC: National Defense University Institute for National Strategic Studies, ACIS Paper 3, August 1995).

Lynn, William J. III. "Defending a New Domain: The Pentagon's Cyberstrategy," *Foreign Affairs* 89, no. 5 (September/October 2010).

United States Army Training and Doctrine Command. *Cyberspace Operations Concept Capability Plan 2016–2028* (Fort Monroe, VA: United States Army, February 2010).

United States Joint Chiefs of Staff. *National Military Strategy for Cyberspace Operations* (Washington, DC: Department of Defense, December 2006).

7   Nuclear power and deterrence

When we arrive at nuclear power we contemplate a qualitatively different dimension of warfare. Unlike seapower, landpower, airpower, and even cyberwar, where we can speak of the actual conduct of war, in the realm of nuclear power we are operating entirely in the abstract, theoretical sphere. As Lawrence Freedman so aptly put it in his 1986 assessment of Cold War nuclear strategists, the study of nuclear power and strategy is the study of the "non-use" of these weapons.[1]

Despite the fact that nuclear weapons were never used in the four and a half decades after the atomic bombs were dropped on Hiroshima and Nagasaki, the Cold War period was replete with policy and academic discussions of nuclear strategy—of whether and how to use nuclear means to achieve military and political ends. This well-known history begins with early post-war views that nuclear weapons were simply a more powerful tool of airpower, and continued on to Bernard Brodie's 1949 recognition that "thus far the chief purpose of our military establishment has been to win wars. From now on, its chief purpose must be to avert them";[2] to the Eisenhower adminis-tration's mid-1950s statement that it was prepared to massively retaliate with nuclear weapons against aggression anywhere; to a brief flirtation in the late 1950s with ideas about conducting limited nuclear war. It continued on with the Kennedy and Johnson administrations' mixing of conventional, tactical nuclear, and strategic nuclear threats into an escalating framework of flexible response; to the Carter administration's coun-tervailing strategy of meeting any Soviet escalation with an effective US response; and finally to the Reagan administration's emphasis on marrying offensive strategies with ballistic missile defenses. In the course of all this strategizing a whole new language emerged, including terms like first strike, second strike, counterforce, coun-tervalue, deterrence by punishment, deterrence by denial, and mutual assured des-truction. While the strategies are history, much (but not all) of the language remains relevant.

This chapter examines strategic thought on nuclear power and deterrence in the post-Cold War and post-9/11 period. Notable strategists include, among others, American scholar Keith Payne and British scholars Colin Gray and Freedman. Significant strategic thinking is also reflected in some key Pentagon documents, particularly the 2001 Nuclear Posture Review, the 2006 Deterrence Operations Joint Operating Concept, and, to a lesser extent, the 2010 Nuclear Posture Review. The organizing principle is the evolution of thinking about how to apply the deterrence concept to contemporary threats. Nuclear weapons figure prominently, of course, but perhaps the defining aspect of deterrence today, as compared to that of the Cold War period, is the degree to which non-nuclear capabilities and non-military elements now complete the deterrence menu.

Deterrence then

Because nuclear power is best put to the ends of averting war it is often discussed in the context of deterrence. Deterrence can be defined as the threat of force designed to convince an adversary, via a cost-benefit analysis on the part of the adversary, *not to take* an action of some kind. It is distinct from compellence, a more difficult-to-achieve goal, which involves getting an adversary *to take* an action of some kind, including reversing a previous activity.

The idea of threatening force to prevent conflict is as old as war itself. In historical accounts it can be traced back millennia and it figured, for example, in Thucydides' account of the Peloponnesian War. But it was during the nuclear era that the concept of deterrence first came to be examined with rigor. From the late 1950s onward US scholars spoke about "deterrence by punishment," under which an adversary is convinced not to take an action because the costs will be unacceptable; and "deterrence by denial," wherein the enemy is persuaded not to take an action because he cannot achieve his operational objectives. Although there were variations and nuances, during the Cold War deterrence by punishment and nuclear weapons dominated the analysis. The superpowers were deterred from military action by the threat the adversary's nuclear-armed international ballistic missiles posed to one's own population centers, otherwise referred to as "countervalue" targets. The strategic picture was stabilized by the fact that, after the Soviet Union achieved rough parity with the United States in nuclear capability in the mid-1960s, each side could absorb a "first strike"—a nuclear attack by the other side—and still have enough missiles and warheads survive the barrage to launch a devastating "second strike" or counterattack. To the extent that deterrence by denial played a role, it was when strategies moved toward nuclear war-fighting roles against military and leadership targets, also referred to as "counter-force."

All this led to a highly mathematical and capability-oriented means of achieving deterrence. The Cold War literature is vast on this topic and will not be discussed here. Suffice it to say that from the West's perspective there was one major adversary, the Soviet Union, which while seen as threatening and expansionist was also thought to be a rational actor, and a conservative one at that. Strategically, deterrence was achieved by maintaining a certain size of US nuclear arsenal that would guarantee a second strike against the Soviet Union. Requirements were debated almost exclusively in technical terms, i.e. the number and types of nuclear weapons necessary to maintain deterrence. Tactically, on the battlefields of Europe, deterrence was achieved by maintaining escalation dominance from conventional, to tactical nuclear, to strategic nuclear forces.

Deterrence is a unique concept in that, because it is judged by what does not happen, one can never be completely certain if it "worked." Nonetheless, because there was no military exchange between the superpowers during the Cold War it was deemed a success. As a result, the initial post-Cold War inclination was simply to apply the basic tenets of Cold War deterrence to post-Cold War circumstances, notably by continuing to focus on numbers of warheads and missiles held by the United States and Russia. Since these arsenals still exist the exercise has value, and the most recent Strategic Arms Reduction Treaty between the two countries entered into force in 2011. But much of the Cold War practice and perspective on nuclear policy and deterrence was rendered obsolete by the new threats and circumstances of the 1990s and 2000s.

Deterrence now

"We need a new model of deterrence theory, and we need it now," admonished the US Chairman of the Joint Chiefs of Staff, Admiral Michael Mullen, in 2008, "Terrorists *are* trying to obtain weapons of mass destruction. Some [rogue] states … *are* trying to build and/or improve their own nuclear weapons. The specter of state-on-state conflict, though diminished, has *not* disappeared" (emphasis in original).[3] In his view, not enough had been done to advance the Cold War theory of deterrence. "What is necessary," argued one US analyst, "is a reexamination of the underlying theory [of deterrence] and a determination of how to apply it to modern cases of concern, without the irrelevant attributes of Cold War deterrence."[4]

Despite these statements, the first two post-Cold War decades actually saw a fair bit of strategic thinking on nuclear power and deterrence, initially at the think-tank and scholarly level and later within official policy documents. Keith Payne's 1996 volume, *Deterrence in the Second Nuclear Age*, was one of the first significant studies to address the nature of the post-Cold War deterrence environment. Perhaps the most visible change was that the United States and its allies no longer had the luxury of being able to focus on just one large threat; rather, there would be several, smaller regional challengers like North Korea and, at that time, Iraq. Less visible were changes in how deterrence strategies would have to be carried out. In the post-Cold War era, the character of the US military threat, so central to how the deterrence concept was applied to the Soviet Union, was far less important than specific intelligence about the challenger and the particular context. "The initial step in identifying how we might be able to increase the reliability of deterrence policy is to harken back to Sun Tzu's fundamental admonition to 'know your enemy'," Payne emphasized, including "the challenger's character, motivation, determination and political context … the answers to these questions cannot be generalized."[5]

The idea of moving beyond the generalized assumptions of the Cold War to a practice of "tailoring" deterrence policies to a given opponent was one that emerged at this time. With the focus still on state actors, Payne argued the imperative of determining such basic things as: whether it is possible to actually communicate with the adversary in question, as there would be no "hot line" in place; what the enemy values most, i.e. his center of gravity; if the decision makers being targeted are actually in control of policy decisions; what sorts of threats the enemy would deem as credible; and whether there are cultural or idiosyncratic factors that have to be taken into account. In later work, Payne presents a deterrence framework designed to tailor deterrence policies to specific antagonists and contexts. Things like leadership characteristics, cost and risk tolerance, and beliefs about the credibility of US threats figure prominently and are followed by detailed US deterrence policy options. The idea, Payne notes, is to first "get inside" the decision-making process of the challenger to identify the particular factors that may be critical to the functioning of deterrence in a specific case, and then to determine the most appropriate approach. "There is no adequate alternative to the hard task of attempting to ascertain the particular opponent's modes of thought and core beliefs, assessing how they are likely to affect its [the opponent's] behavior, and formulating US deterrence policy in light of those findings."[6]

Not until the 2006 Quadrennial Defense Review did the term *tailored deterrence* appear in an official US policy document. The emphasis, however, was on capability approaches rather than on the background homework required in order to "know your enemy." "The Department is continuing its shift from a 'one size fits all' notion of deterrence toward more tailorable approaches," the report states. "The future force will provide a fully balanced, tailored capability to deter both state and non-state threats."[7] The Pentagon's *Deterrence Operations Joint Operating Concept* (JOC) released later that year, by contrast, is far more attuned to the subtleties of contemporary deterrence. It notes that US deterrence efforts must be tailored in character because the perceptions and resulting decision calculus of specific adversaries in specific circumstances are fundamentally different. It goes still further to make a distinction between the *direct means* of deterrence—the tailored capabilities—and the *enablers* that necessarily come first. A central enabler, indeed "the foundation of deterrence," is global situational awareness, a somewhat nebulous term that becomes more concrete when one looks at its components. These are two: the first, familiar from the Payne assessment, is to develop an underlying knowledge about adversary decision makers' values, culture, perceptions of benefits and costs, and risk propensity to the maximum extent possible; the second is to gain operational intelligence information about adversary assets, capabilities, and vulnerabilities.[8] In later work, Payne takes this theme still further, noting the requirement for "tailored intelligence" to understand the enemy as fully as possible. "Deterrence now," he states, "is first and foremost a matter of intelligence."[9]

The JOC makes an important contribution to strategic thought on deterrence because it goes beyond more narrowly conceived military capabilities to include broader, non-military elements that play in deterrence. Indeed, the US military has expanded the concept of strategic deterrence to include not only nuclear and conventional forces, as first spelled out in the New Triad (see below), but also diplomatic, economic, and informational tools. Thus the JOC mentions strategic communication, or "efforts to understand and engage key audiences in order to create, strengthen or preserve conditions favorable for the advancement of [US] interests" as a direct means of influencing the deterrence effort.[10] The effect is to take the idea of a tailored approach to a new level. Notes Payne, "in some cases, *non-military* approaches to deterrence may work best, in others *conventional force options* may be adequate and advantageous, in still other cases, *nuclear* threat options may be necessary to deter" (emphasis in original).[11]

Tailoring capabilities

This brief discussion of the evolution of strategic thinking on nuclear policy and deterrence reveals that the idea of tailored deterrence as it has emerged over the past two decades comprises two important facets: tailoring to specific actors and situations, and tailoring capabilities—the direct means versus enabler distinction made in the JOC. While Payne's strategic thought on deterrence in the first post-Cold War decade did much to address the former aspect, the earliest comprehensive attempt to address the changed capability requirements for deterrence dates to the Bush administration's 2001 Nuclear Posture Review (NPR). Released in December that year, but begun long before the 9/11 attacks, the NPR introduced a New Triad as the basis for America's nuclear posture. In place of the "old triad" of bombers, intercontinental ballistic missiles (ICBMs), and submarine-launched ballistic missiles (SLBMs) that formed the basis of strategic deterrence during the Cold War, the first leg of the New Triad includes all the offensive strike systems that were in the old triad (i.e. nuclear capabilities) *and* improved long-range conventional strike capabilities. In this way "strategic deterrence," previously a concept involving only intercontinental nuclear weapons, expanded to incorporate conventional forces. The other two legs of the New Triad are active and passive defenses, most notably missile defenses; and a "responsive infrastructure," meaning a research, development, and industrial infrastructure that is robust enough to maintain offensive and defensive forces.

The Bush administration's New Triad represented a long-overdue departure in strategic thinking about deterrence and the role and place of nuclear weapons in US deterrence policy. "As a result of [the NPR]," former Secretary of Defense Donald Rumsfeld stated in the foreword to the report, "the U.S. will no longer plan, size or sustain its forces as though Russia presented merely a smaller version of the threat posed by the former Soviet Union."[12] The NPR thus marked the official abandonment of mutual assured destruction as the core element of US nuclear policy. In place of an old triad of systems designed to pose a massive response to nuclear attack, the New Triad sought means of tailoring responses to particular circumstances and therefore to increase the credibility of deterrence—much as massive retaliation had been abandoned two generations earlier in favor of a more flexible approach. But the NPR also overwrote Flexible Response, revealing a belief that, rather than acting as the lower rung of an escalation ladder that culminated in a nuclear response, conventional forces themselves could act as a strategic deterrent. Finally, by including defense in its strategic doctrine, as well as potential counterforce capabilities, the NPR signaled a conceptual shift from a primarily "deterrence by punishment" orientation to a more prominent focus on "deterrence by denial." Many of these new elements sparked interest and debate in the 2000s, which served only to push forward the boundaries of strategic thought on nuclear power and deterrence.

Conventional deterrence

One aspect of the New Triad that sparked debate was placing nuclear and conventional forces into the same leg of a strategic force posture. The views of scholar Stephen Cimbala are representative of the concerns that this raised. "The conmingling of conventional, long range precision strike with intercontinental nuclear weapons," he argued in a 2005 work, "might erode the firebreak between nuclear and conventional operations." For Cimbala, the new conceptual approach implied that nuclear weapons would no longer be treated as a separate form of warfare, reserved for deterrent missions only. Dangerously, "nuclear weapons were part of a new military synergy and no longer a door opener to world war," with the implication that they were therefore more likely to be used.[13]

Proponents countered that integrating the Cold War triad with new non-nuclear strategic capabilities was intended for precisely the *opposite* reason: to reduce reliance on nuclear weapons. The 2001 NPR expresses a Pentagon view that a strategic posture that relies solely on offensive *nuclear* forces would be inappropriate—that is, not credible—for deterring the full range of twenty-first-century threats. During the Cold War, US nuclear threats against the Soviet Union were deemed credible because US survival was at stake. But in the contemporary period, in those regional contingencies where the stakes at risk for the US do not involve survival or the survival of allies, some may view US nuclear deterrent threats as incredible. Writing in the wake of the 1991 Gulf War, which first revealed America's dramatic advancements in conventional long-range precision strike, William Perry (later US Secretary of Defense in the Clinton administration) pointed out: "This new conventional military capability adds a powerful dimension to the ability of the United States to deter war. While it is certainly not as powerful as nuclear weapons, it is a more credible deterrent, particularly in regional conflicts vital to U.S. national interests."[14]

Conventional long-range precision-strike capabilities were seen to enhance the credibility of deterrence for two basic reasons. First, it was felt that conventional capabilities had become so powerful and precise that they could now impose unacceptable costs, such as destroying an adversary's strategic and high-value targets, and thereby be employed for missions once reserved for nuclear forces. Second, they were more "usable" because whereas limited nuclear war was an oxymoron, limited conventional war was clearly possible. In its 1998 Strategic Defence Review, for example, Britain argued that deterrence involves several capabilities in addition to nuclear weapons, and that it was especially advantageous to employ "conventional weapons with a capacity for precision and penetration so as to minimize incidental damage."[15] Ever more precise yet powerful precision weapons fit well with the Western world's growing aversion to causing "collateral" damage. Moreover, history suggests that non-nuclear nations are not intimidated by a country's nuclear capabilities (e.g. Vietnam by the United States or Argentina by Britain in the Falklands War), but many view US conventional capabilities as credible because of its demonstrated ability to use them.

Others are careful to stress that however powerful, precise, and "usable" conventional weapons are, they cannot replace nuclear weapons for strategic deterrence. "It is illusory and dangerous to claim that such technologies could have the effect of preventing war as nuclear weapons do," France argued in its defense White Paper of 1994. "Far from substituting for nuclear deterrence, a so-called conventional deterrent could only complement it."[16] Anecdotal evidence on North Korea seems to support this claim: US congressmen report that during a visit to North Korea in 2005 the only US weapon system that North Korea was truly interested in was the nuclear-armed "bunker buster" (see below), despite the range of powerful precision-force options that the United States has available. Payne underscores that US *nuclear* threats have deterred past opponents who otherwise would have been resistant to US non-nuclear threats, and that this could be because a challenger may believe it can withstand even "the most devastating conventional punishment" for an extended period.[17] Moreover, deterring regional conflict or aggression is not the same as deterring nuclear attack. After the 1991 Gulf War Perry pointed out that while the advanced conventional systems revealed by the war "will add a new dimension to deterrence, it also has significant limitations. It will not add to the ability of the United States to deter a nuclear attack; for the foreseeable future that [form of] deterrence will depend on the strength of U.S. nuclear forces."[18]

These differing perspectives on the value of conventional weapons for strategic deterrence focus primarily on their use for deterrence by punishment. Others argue that their utility lies in deterrence by denial, and in particular in the ability of advanced conventional weapons to deny an adversary its best chance of success on the battlefield, a *fait accompli*. This refers to an enemy striking quickly and achieving battlefield objectives (such as seizing territory) before the opponent has time to act. Payne notes that a challenger's expectation of achieving a *fait accompli* is considered a primary factor behind conventional deterrence failure. The role of conventional forces in denying battlefield objectives is one that was first examined in detail by scholar John Mearsheimer during the Cold War, who determined that conventional deterrence is less likely to fail in circumstances where it is not possible for the aggressor to achieve a quick and decisive victory.[19]

Dissuading a *fait accompli* attempt can depend on particular types of military capability. For example, in his 1996 work Payne stressed the value of rapid, decisive force projection using highly mobile, expeditionary forces—the kinds of units being developed as part of what was called the Revolution in Military Affairs at the time (see Chapter 4)— for dispelling adversary beliefs that a *fait accompli* is obtainable. In the years since, the US military has continued to emphasize these capabilities, now in the context of a Prompt Global Strike mission, which seeks to develop conventional capabilities that can strike targets anywhere in the world within one hour (just as nuclear-armed ICBMs can). The JOC includes force projection, or "[t]he capability to project U.S. military power globally and conduct operational maneuver from strategic distances," as a direct means for influencing an adversary's decision calculus.[20] It highlights highly valued adversary assets like weapons of mass destruction (WMD) production, storage, and delivery systems; and adversary decision makers, leadership power bases, and command and control facilities as especially important targets for global strike. For some analysts, the pursuit of a Prompt Global Strike capability "demonstrates how hard the United States is working to preclude having to use nuclear weapons in any contingency short of a response to a nuclear attack."[21]

Strategic thinking in this area has also progressed beyond rapidly deployable forces and long-range "smart" weapons to include forward-deployed combat power that can all but guarantee that substantial US forces are able to arrive quickly in theater. The JOC speaks of "forward presence," that is, "forward-stationed and forward-deployed multipurpose combat and expeditionary forces," as a key enabler for deterrence (by denial).[22] It also stresses the imperative of security cooperation with allies. By providing basing for US forces, or even their own extensive ground forces, partner nations can reduce the potential benefits to be reaped from a surprise adversary attack before US forces are fully deployed in theater. Still, some adversaries, should they deem the stakes critical enough to their national security, will not be deterred by removing the *fait accompli* option. In these circumstances, rather than denying the prospect of a quick victory, the United States must be able to credibly threaten defeat—something for which forward-deployed forces will also be well suited.

Nuclear deterrence

Nuclear deterrence also figured centrally in the first leg of the NPR New Triad, as would be expected, but its particular form provoked debate. It was then US Defense Secretary Les Aspin who, in 1993, first set out the demands of a deterrence-by-denial strategy, should it be pursued by the Clinton administration. These included: the ability to locate and target hardened and deeply buried underground (nuclear) sites, particularly with reference to North Korea; to do the same with respect to mobile missiles armed with WMD; and to defend against, i.e. shoot down, any enemy missiles that should survive a counterforce attack.[23] Ballistic Missile Defense (BMD) will be discussed below. What is useful to consider here is the contribution of nuclear counterforce to deterrence. As one scholar has put it,

> There is little disagreement that the United States should deter nuclear attacks by threatening to inflict unacceptably high costs with nuclear retaliation. But should it also plan to destroy with nuclear weapons an adversary's nuclear and other weapons of mass destruction and related facilities?[24]

Although classified, leaked portions of the NPR indicate that it included within its pages the need to be able to "hold at risk," i.e. directly target, hard and deeply buried underground sites containing WMD or command and control facilities. The reasoning behind this approach can best be understood by considering the views of Payne and of another notable strategic theorist of deterrence, Colin Gray. In his 1999 book, *The Second Nuclear Age*, Gray points out that in contrast to the first nuclear age of bipolar rivalry, the second nuclear age is characterized by a number of regional foes that are less risk averse than was the Soviet Union. As a result, deterrence is likely to fail—or fail to apply—more often in the second nuclear age than in the first. This is a theme that was picked up by the George W. Bush administration in its 2002 National Security Strategy, which argues that deterrence based on the threat of retaliation made sense with a status quo, risk-averse adversary that saw WMD as weapons of last resort, but is far less likely to work against rogue-state leaders who are willing to takes risks, gamble with the lives of their people, and who see WMD as weapons of choice.

For Gray, in the face of rogue states intent on acquiring WMD, "there are measures states can take, especially with respect to the provision of robustly layered offensive and defensive counterforce capabilities" that could well address the threat.[25] As regards offensive counterforce, he does not "shy away" from incorporating general war-fighting roles and the military uses of nuclear weapons into strategic thought on nuclear power. During the Cold War there was no realistic possibility of either superpower being able to disarm the other of its nuclear arsenal. But when it comes to the NBC arsenals of regional enemies, Gray stated in 1999, "in a phrase, the job generally is doable." Counterforce has become feasible. A decade later he echoed these themes, arguing that a contemporary application of the theory of deterrence should involve *deterring* and *coercing* those who we can and *defeating* those who remain irreconcilable. "The default option for strategy today vis-à-vis [rogue states] with nuclear weapons should not be to seek a stable condition of mutual deterrence. Instead, we can plan and attempt actually to defeat … by brute force … a state that has few WMD."[26] In terms of actual capabilities, Gray finds that one strategic mission of US nuclear forces should accordingly be to "[p]rovide 'niche' war fighting denial options against very hard, elusive, or dispersed targets." Gray suggests the use of offensive conventional strikes and nuclear forces tailored "to effect the kind of damage to targets that other U.S. forces cannot impose reliably." Moreover, to address America's casualty concerns, such nuclear strike capabilities would have to be as precise and discriminating as possible.[27]

Payne arrives at a similar conclusion—the need to develop low-yield, accurate, earth-penetrating nuclear weapons—albeit through a different logic process. The centerpiece is the credibility of deterrence. To the extent that the United States can hope to apply the logic of deterrence to rogue-state decision makers, the US must be able to credibly threaten those assets most valued by the opponent, including WMD sites in buried and hardened bunkers. To convince adversaries that they cannot "ride out" a US retaliatory strike by going underground, the requirement is for a weapon that can target and destroy these sites. Moreover, because opponents are well aware of the West's extreme reluctance to cause high levels of civil destruction, the weapon also had to be discriminate enough to address America's concern for collateral damage. "In the post-Cold War era," he argued, when national survival is not at stake, "the credibility of the U.S. deterrent may rest not on how much damage to the opponent's society is threatened but rather on how little."[28] Payne, a principal architect of the 2001 NPR, argued in favor of the robust nuclear earth-penetrator, soon dubbed the "bunker buster," which was pursued for several years by the Bush administration but ultimately failed to secure congressional funding.

A central critique of the bunker buster was that its pursuit appeared to connote a rejection of deterrence in favor of war-fighting, counterforce roles (perhaps along the lines envisaged by Gray). Thus Cimbala, who raised a general concern about integrating nuclear and conventional forces into one leg of the strategic triad (noted above), is doubly concerned about the creation of accurate, low-yield nuclear weapons because such advances could lower the nuclear threshold by making nuclear weapons more attractive to a US president. But for Payne, such arguments reflect a basic confusion between ensuring the credibility of a threat in the eyes of an opponent, and a US president's actual willingness to use a nuclear weapon. Low-yield tactical nuclear weapons were part of the Cold War landscape, and occupied several rungs on the escalation ladder of Flexible Response, but this effort to increase the credibility of deterrence did not translate into a lower nuclear threshold on the part of the US president. That is to say, weapons that can hold enemy sanctuaries at risk with minimal unintended damage may make deterrent threats more credible from an opponent's perspective (recall the North Korean interest in the bunker buster, noted above), but their availability would not simplify or increase the likelihood of nuclear employment decisions. A president's decision calculus is impacted on by a far greater range of factors—including the severity of the circumstances, the nature of the provocation, broader US goals, allied considerations, and foreign, domestic, and moral considerations—than the specific capability of a weapon system.

US allies, too, have discussed the deterrent value of low-yield, accurate nuclear weapons. In 2001, France took issue with the Bush administration's view, later expressed in the 2002 National Security Strategy, that rogue leaders could not be deterred. "The Americans judge that deterrence does not work with 'rogue states' that are considered irrational," former French President Jacques Chirac stated upon releasing France's new nuclear deterrence strategy; "[h]owever, the leaders of these states are sensitive to threats exerted against their centre of power." To this end, France would be acquiring "more accurate, less powerful, longer-range [nuclear] weapons" to reach "above all the political, economic, and military power centres of a possible aggressor."[29] The French goal was to acquire precise, discriminate nuclear strike options that could destroy bunkers without destroying cities, thereby increasing the credibility of French threats and strengthening deterrence.

Consistent with the American approach, France maintains a distinction between deterrence credibility and the willingness to authorize the use of nuclear weapons. Even as it pursued an option that lay between "the total annihilation of a country and doing nothing,"[30] France stressed that its overall nuclear doctrine is one of "non-use." Notes one scholar, "[t]he French have repeatedly affirmed since the mid-1980s that they do not regard nuclear arms as 'tactical' for battle but as political and strategic instruments."[31] Far from promoting war-fighting, French officials emphasize, more operationally useful and discriminate nuclear weapons would enhance deterrence credibility, thereby bolstering the "non-use" principle.[32] Box 7.1 highlights one perspective on contemporary requirements for deterrence.

Box 7.1 "The nukes we need"

- Contemporary scholars argue that the only way for the United States to determine the nuclear arsenal it needs for deterrence in the twenty-first century is to work through the "grim logic of deterrence": what actions need to be deterred, what threats need to be issued, and what capabilities are needed to make the threats credible.

- Actions may include the introduction of nuclear weapons by countries like North Korea, Iran, or China during a conventional war with the United States as a means of compelling a cease-fire or denying the US access to allied military bases. Nuclear escalation would be rational from the adversary's perspective because of his conventional inferiority as compared to the United States, just as NATO strategy rested on nuclear escalation throughout the Cold War because of its conventional inferiority vis-à-vis the Soviet Union.

- The least-bad threat that could be issued to deter escalation would be to be able to launch a counterforce attack that destroyed an enemy's nuclear forces, while the worst and least credible approach would be to threaten to destroy enemy cities. The latter would be a vastly disproportionate response to, say, a nuclear strike against a US carrier.

- Capabilities for a disarming counterforce strike include a mix of conventional and nuclear weapons, specifically, low-yield precision nuclear weapons and conventional counterforce weapons, such as the United States is pursuing with its prompt global strike capability. Finally, a limited number of traditional high-yield nuclear weapons must be retained in the event of circumstances "so dire that collateral damage was not a major concern."

See Keir A. Lieber and Daryl G. Press, "The Nukes We Need: Preserving the American Deterrent," *Foreign Affairs* 88, no. 6 (November/December 2009).

Questions of nuclear pre-emption

A related concern within this overall debate is that the pursuit of more accurate, low-yield nuclear weapons could be part of an overall shift in nuclear doctrine toward pre-emptive nuclear strikes. Early supporters of the 2001 NPR interpreted the US approach in the following way:

> Recent trends present a challenge. On the one hand, there is a strategic capability optimized for a danger that no longer exists ... On the other, failures in non-proliferation confront planners with relatively small-scale threats that could become serious problems with little warning ... America accepts that it cannot prevent proliferation. Instead, it is preparing to target [NBC] arsenals with conventional and, if necessary, nuclear forces.[33]

Although it is difficult to justify the use of nuclear weapons to prevent enemy use of nuclear weapons, for some this is a necessary card to hold in order to maintain escalation dominance. A high-level report prepared by retired NATO generals in 2008 argued that the alliance must be able to resort to pre-emptive nuclear attack to halt the "imminent" spread of nuclear weapons, and that the "first use of nuclear weapons must remain in the quiver of escalation as the ultimate instrument to prevent the use of [WMD]."[34] Nor was this approach confined to NATO: in a 2008 speech the chief of the general staff of the Russian armed forces stated that Russia was prepared to use pre-emptive nuclear strikes to uphold its interests in a variety of situations.

Throughout atomic history the United States and its allies have maintained the option for the first use of nuclear weapons, refusing to adopt a doctrine of "no first use" (NFU). Meanwhile, the Cold War declaratory policy of the Soviet Union was NFU, but post-Cold War Russia reversed this, including in its military doctrine the option of nuclear first use China is also thought to be abandoning its Cold War NFU policy in favor of the first-use option. NFU opponents argue that the potential, however remote, for a scenario to arise in which the only option is to use nuclear weapons first to forestall enemy use necessitates reserving the first-use option. But some scholars have made the case that retaining the first-use option in the contemporary period undermines crisis stability because the fear of a disarming first strike on the part of the United States increases the possibility of rogue-state escalation. Others note that an acknowledgment of the peril created by the acquisition of nuclear weapons by a rogue state can reasonably lead to the requirement for a pre-emptive strike, but it does not necessarily lead to a *nuclear* pre-emptive strike. In 2003 the commander of STRATCOM stated that precision-guided conventional munitions could do just as good a job as any nuclear penetrator in sealing off underground facilities. Still others have pointed out that earth-penetrating nuclear weapons may be useful for destroying moderately deep and precisely located nuclear bunkers, but this value would disappear as soon as an adversary responded by digging deeper or adopting a strategy of dispersion or mobility.

For proponents of the 2001 NPR, of course, all this points to the value of including long-range precision conventional weapons in the first leg of the New Triad. The Obama administration's 2010 NPR does not use the term "New Triad," reverting instead to the old terminology of a "nuclear triad" comprising ICBMs, SLBMs, and bombers. But while the New Triad terminology is gone, its content remains largely intact. In line with the US objective of reducing the role of nuclear weapons in deterrence, there is no mention in the 2010 NPR of new, low-yield weapons. The document does, however, place significant emphasis on the value and role of conventional precision force, missile defenses, and a robust infrastructure in America's strategic-force posture.

Pre-emption and biological and chemical weapons

Questions have also been raised about what role strategic weapons, whether conventional or nuclear, may have in deterring adversary use of chemical and biological weapons. Under the Nuclear Non-Proliferation Treaty (NPT)—which divides the world into nuclear weapons states and non-nuclear weapons states—the United States has extended a long-standing (since 1978) "negative security guarantee" stating that it would not target, with nuclear weapons, non-nuclear weapons states that are in compliance with its NPT obligations. But this negative security assurance did not extend to states brandishing chemical and biological weapons. Up until recently, the US had always maintained a "calculated ambiguity" doctrine of refusing to say whether or not it would respond to chemical or biological threats with nuclear weapons, given that it has no chemical or biological weapons of its own. In the past Britain and France have also left open the option of threatening nuclear retaliation against adversaries employing chemical and biological weapons, even if the adversary had no nuclear weapons and was not allied with a nuclear-weapons state.

The Obama administration's 2010 NPR was the first to explicitly rule out the use of nuclear weapons in response to chemical and biological weapons threats. Advances in US conventional military capabilities, it argued, as well as continued improvements in missile defenses, were enabling the US to continue to reduce the role of nuclear weapons in deterrence—a trend that had begun with the 2001 NPR. The United States reiterated its negative security assurance, noted above, but went further to state that it "affirms that any state eligible for the assurance that uses chemical or biological weapons against the United States or its allies and partners would face the prospect of a devastating *conventional* response" (emphasis added). The threat of a nuclear response is eliminated. That said, the administration does leave open the right to make a future "adjustment" in its stance, i.e. to return to America's previous policy of strategic ambiguity, if warranted by developments in proliferation and US capacities to counter the threat.

The Obama administration's less than firm position on whether conventional or nuclear forces should be used to deter chemical and biological weapons threats reflects the mixed views that exist within strategic thought on this issue. In a 2000 article, scholar Scott Sagan argued that America's calculated ambiguity policy placed the United States in a "commitment trap."[35] The reputation costs of not following through on threats increased the probability, in the event of deterrence failure, that US leaders would respond with nuclear weapons where it might otherwise have retaliated with conventional weapons only. Sagan and other scholars recommended an unambiguous commitment to retaliate with a devastating conventional response to the use of unconventional weapons. In fact, soon after the 1991 Gulf War Perry had raised the idea that conventional precision force could "serve as a credible deterrent to a regional power's use of chemical weapons."[36] But others dispute the deterrent value of conventional responses to WMD threats. For Payne, indicating what is militarily necessary to target biological or chemical weapons sites misses the fundamental point that deterrence involves exploiting an opponent's fears and sensitivities—and these may have little or no connection to America's conventional combat capabilities.

Ballistic missile defense

The second leg of the Bush administration's New Triad for deterrence, the integration of passive and active defenses, marked a substantial development in the evolution of strategic thought on deterrence. Cold War deterrence relied almost exclusively on the threat of punishment in kind. This was partly because conservative, status quo superpowers were particularly amenable to the logic of deterrence, but also because—notwithstanding the vision of US President Ronald Reagan's Strategic Defense Initiative—it was not possible to defend against the ballistic missile threat, which numbered in the thousands. In the contemporary period both elements have changed, and this is reflected in the strategic thought of several scholars. Colin Gray, for example, argued early on for defensive counterforce capabilities (noted above) as part of an overall "national military strategy that looks with favor upon denial options."[37] In his view, defense against some forms of WMD delivery had become both necessary and feasible: necessary because deterrence against rogue states was far more difficult and likely to fail; feasible because the challenge is to be able to defeat missile threats much more modest in scale and sophistication than was the case during the Cold War. "With the arguable exception of the … Russian nuclear arsenal," he argued, "there are no missile-armed groups in the world today [1999] … whose WMD capabilities should prove beyond defeat by U.S. offensive and (especially) *defensive* counterforce means" (emphasis in original).[38]

Other scholars and strategic thinkers have similarly focused on the current necessity of incorporating the defense into strategic thought on deterrence and nuclear policy.

"Defense, not deterrence," argues Sagan, will "be necessary when confronting irrational enemies who either welcome a nuclear apocalypse or are, for whatever reason, oblivious to any level of threatened destruction."[39] Meanwhile Payne predicted soon after the end of the Cold War that in the second nuclear age missile defense would be viewed more sympathetically, even essential, as a "safety" net against deterrence failure when a challenger is armed with a relatively small arsenal of missiles. BMD could provide protection for US urban areas while its sister, theater missile defense, could protect deployed troops, thereby increasing the credibility of conventional deterrence using force-projection capabilities. On the home front BMD "should now be seen ... as wise insurance against the near-certainty that at some future point deterrence will unexpectedly fail";[40] abroad, without defensive capabilities "the risk of significant American and allied casualties resulting from projecting force abroad could be too great for any President to accept."[41] Payne neatly summarized at the end of the 2000s that in the contemporary environment "we must seek not only to deter, we also must prepare to defend our society, our expeditionary forces, and our allies in the event deterrence fails."[42]

Critics contend that incorporating defensive measures into the US strategic posture is inherently destabilizing. During the Cold War the logic behind no missile defenses was twofold: first, establishing defenses would spark an arms race as one side sought to overcome the other side's defenses with more offensive power; second, missile defenses could make nuclear weapons more usable in the eyes of a country that was, by virtue of having defenses, no longer vulnerable to nuclear retaliation. Similarly, in the contemporary period it has been argued that BMD could motivate an arms build up by new and old nuclear powers to offset the defense, and that "[t]he deployment of effective missile defenses ... returns us to a condition in which victory is thought to be possible."[43] But for Payne and others these arguments have the effect of applying Cold War logic to twenty-first-century circumstances. New actors are not invariably deterrable; contemporary deterrence is more fallible. Today "[d]eterrence may fail, and U.S. damage-limiting capabilities may be the *only* means for mitigating the catastrophic consequences of nuclear or other WMD attack" (emphasis in original).[44]

Conceptually, then, active defenses are included as part the US strategic posture for two related yet discrete reasons. First, to enhance defense for the sake of defense, i.e. to minimize potential US and allied losses; second, to strengthen deterrence by denial by convincing an adversary that an attack against US territory could not succeed, and that the US would have the will to deploy [conventional] power protection forces. In this way, missile defenses are expected both to offer a hedge against deterrence failure, and to contribute to the functioning of deterrence itself. Meanwhile, passive defenses, such as improved homeland security measures, operate in the same fashion—strengthening deterrence and minimizing losses. For the latter, passive defenses like efficient consequent management capabilities reduce the effectiveness of attacks that active defenses fail to defeat. As for strengthening deterrence, if the police, customs, immigration, and other government services are better able to deal with the consequences of an attack, this might send the message that the homeland is a "hard target."

Deterrence and terrorism

A final area of strategic thought on nuclear power and deterrence that has emerged in the contemporary period (particularly, of course, since 9/11) is its relevance to terrorism. The primary issue here is the applicability of the concept of deterrence writ large with respect to terrorism, with the unspoken assumption that we are talking about conventional deterrence. Few would entertain nuclear strikes against terrorist sites, but this does not mean that the relevance of nuclear deterrence in the face of these attacks has not been discussed in the literature. Soon after 9/11, France responded to the seeming irrelevance of nuclear deterrence to contemporary threats with the point that "these attacks have in no way ... affected the credibility of nuclear deterrence. It was never designed to work against individuals or terrorist groups. It is aimed at states."[45]

Whether we are talking about nuclear or conventional deterrence, the original post-9/11 thought was that non-state actors were not deterrable. This was certainly the perspective of the Bush administration, which stated in its 2002 National Security Strategy that "[t]raditional concepts of deterrence will not work against a terrorist enemy whose avowed tactics are wanton destruction and the targeting of innocents; whose so-called soldiers seek martyrdom in death and whose most potent protection is statelessness." America's National Research Council pointed out at the time that there are problems in using traditional threats of punishment against terrorists because they do not control particular territories; they may not believe direct threats against them can be readily carried out in the short run; their leadership is elusive; it is hard to identify targets; in any case, it can be difficult to know what terrorists "value" and therefore what should be targeted; there are often no established channels of communication with such a diffuse adversary; clearly communicating credible warnings and threats is thus of limited utility if not entirely impossible; and some terrorists may actually wish for an overwhelming response against them because this will radicalize potential supporters.[46]

"Does that mean [deterrence] can be written off as a strategy of historical interest but no contemporary application?"[47] Freedman asked in the early post-9/11 period. For some this was initially thought to be true, but sober second thought indicates otherwise. Freedman challenges the argument that deterrence does not work with terrorism, and his writings in this regard, as well as those of others, comprise an evolution in strategic thought surrounding the concept. The core of this thought is that while it may be true that terrorists cannot be deterred in an immediate sense, it is also the case that even suicide terrorists want to die to accomplish something. Therefore, focusing on deterrence by denial—denying terrorists the accomplishment of the "benefits" of their actions—may be an avenue for applying the deterrence concept to non-state actors.

If it transpires that suicide terrorism rarely succeeds in achieving the strategic effects so desired, then terrorists may, in the long run, be deterred. Freedman recommends a strategy that isolates terrorists rather than rooting them out through force, stigmatizing their ideas amongst sympathetic communities. Payne argues that less emphasis should be placed on punitive threats than on "measures to frustrate their planning, operations and goals—actions which compel them to move and hide, put pressure on their societal network and state sponsors, demoralize their personnel, and deny their aims."[48] The National Research Council, too, makes the case for indirect deterrence measures as a supplement to more direct brute-force threats, while stressing the value of establishing communication with third parties, including other states, that have contact with terrorist supporters and may be able to influence their behavior.

Conclusion

Strategic thought on nuclear policy and deterrence evolved considerably in the two decades following the end of the Cold War. Scholars such as Keith Payne and Colin Gray have taken to task the applicability of Cold War deterrence tenets to contemporary circumstances. US policy documents, especially the 2001 NPR and the Pentagon's 2006 Deterrence Operations Joint Operating Concept, transformed the official US approach to deterrence and this new approach remained largely in place in the 2010 NPR. Ideas presented by these scholars and documents have been challenged and debated, and this has served to further push forward the boundaries of strategic thought.

Taken together, these views reveal a contemporary theory of nuclear power and deterrence that may include the following tenets: the foundation of strategic deterrence today is to first "know your enemy"; this involves accounting for intangible factors like values, culture, perceptions, and risk tolerance *and* tangible things like assets, capabilities, and vulnerabilities; based on these things deterrence strategies must be tailored to the specific adversary in mind; whereas the defense did not figure in Cold War deterrence, contemporary strategic deterrence involves a combination of offensive and defensive measures; offensive responses may be nuclear or precision conventional (some would also argue for precision nuclear); as compared to the Cold War's fall-back baseline of nuclear deterrence by punishment, the contemporary starting-point is deterrence by denial through precision conventional weapons and missile defenses; nuclear weapons figure less in contemporary strategic deterrence; that said, in a world in which nuclear weapons exist, they remain the penultimate deterrent; pre-empting the use of nuclear weapons would involve conventional precision strike (again, some would also argue for precision nuclear strike); deterrence by brute-force punishment has little bearing on terrorism but deterrence by denial can be effective; finally, conventional weapons, nuclear weapons, and missile defenses form only the military component of a far broader deterrence menu that now includes political, economic, and informational measures.

The study of nuclear power is quintessentially theoretical in nature and, one hopes, will remain so. Nuclear power is particularly amenable to being discussed in the context of something *not* happening, and therefore to the deterrence concept. Not surprisingly, the Cold War was a heyday of theorizing about deterrence and nuclear power, but the strategies that were associated with it, along with many of its underlying tenets, were rendered obsolete by the end of the Cold War, even if much of the language it spawned remained pertinent. Since that time a whole range of ideas have emerged and been debated as to how nuclear power and deterrence relate to the new era, with the result being no less than a transformation of ideas about how best to effect strategic deterrence. Yet old ideas should be shelved but not discarded. If, as Colin Gray argues, the second nuclear era is to be followed by a third that looks not unlike the first,[49] yesterday's tenets on nuclear power and deterrence may have to be dusted off and given new life.

Notes

1 Lawrence Freedman, "The First Two Generations of Nuclear Strategists," in Peter Paret, ed., *Makers of Modern Strategy from Machiavelli to the Nuclear Age* (Princeton, NJ: Princeton University Press, 1986), 735.
2 As quoted in Keith B. Payne, *Deterrence in the Second Nuclear Age* (Lexington, KY: The University Press of Kentucky, 1996), 5.
3 Michael Mullen, "It's Time for a New Deterrence Model," *Joint Forces Quarterly* 51 no. 4 (4th quarter 2008), 2.
4 M. Elaine Bunn, "Can Deterrence Be Tailored?" *INSS Strategic Forum* (January 2007), 2.

5 Payne, *Deterrence in the Second Nuclear Age*, 123.
6 Keith B. Payne, *The Fallacies of Cold War Deterrence and a New Direction* (Lexington, KY: The University Press of Kentucky, 2001), 99. See also Keith B. Payne, *The Great American Gamble: Deterrence Theory and Practice from the Cold War to the Twenty-first Century* (Fairfax, VA: National Institute Press, 2008), 305–6.
7 Department of Defense, *The 2006 Quadrennial Defense Review* (Washington, DC: Office of the Secretary of Defense, February 2006), 49.
8 Department of Defense, *Deterrence Operations Joint Operating Concept* (Washington, DC: Office of the Secretary of Defense, December 2006), 25, 29–30.
9 Keith Payne, "The Continuing Roles for U.S. Strategic Forces," *Comparative Strategy* 26 (2007), 270.
10 Department of Defense, *Deterrence Operations*, 35, 42.
11 Keith B. Payne, "The Nuclear Posture Review and Deterrence for a New Age," *Comparative Strategy* 23, no. 4 (2004), 415.
12 Donald H. Rumsfeld, Foreword to the Nuclear Posture Review, January 8, 2002, found at www.fas.org accessed May 2, 2011, 3.
13 Stephen J. Cimbala, *Nuclear Weapons and Nuclear Strategy: U.S. Nuclear Policy for the Twenty-first Century* (London: Routledge, 2005), 21, 69–70.
14 Willam J. Perry, "Desert Storm and Deterrence," *Foreign Affairs* 70, no. 4 (Fall 1991), 80.
15 As quoted in David S. Yost, "New Approaches to Deterrence in Britain, France and the United States," *International Affairs* 81 (2005), 86.
16 French Ministry of Defense, as quoted in ibid., 87.
17 Payne, *Deterrence in the Second Nuclear Age*, 136.
18 Perry, "Desert Storm and Deterrence," 81.
19 John J. Mearsheimer, *Conventional Deterrence* (Ithaca, NY: Cornell University Press, 1983), 203, 212.
20 Department of Defense, *Deterrence Operations*, 36.
21 Michael S. Gerson, "No First Use: The Next Step for U.S. Nuclear Policy," *International Security* 35, no. 2 (Fall 2010), 34.
22 Department of Defense, *Deterrence Operations*, 33.
23 "US Military Options Against Emerging Nuclear Threats: The Challenges of a Denial Strategy," *IISS Strategic Comments* 12, no. 3 (April 2006), 1.
24 Charles L. Glaser and Steve Fetter, "Counterforce Revisited: Assessing the Nuclear Posture Review's New Missions," *International Security* 30, no. 2 (Fall 2005), 84.
25 Colin S. Gray, *The Second Nuclear Age* (Boulder, CO: Lynne Rienner Publishers, 1999), xii.
26 Colin S. Gray, "Gaining Compliance: The Theory of Deterrence and its Modern Application," *Comparative Strategy* 29 (2010), 281–82.
27 Gray, *Second Nuclear Age*, 120, 145–48, 161.
28 Keith B. Payne, "The Nuclear Posture Review: Setting the Record Straight," *Washington Quarterly* 28, no. 3 (Summer 2005), 144.
29 As quoted in Yost, "New Approaches to Deterrence," 88 and 90.
30 Ibid., 89.
31 David S. Yost, "France's Evolving Nuclear Strategy," *Survival* 47, no. 3 (Autumn 2005), 128.
32 Ibid., 121.
33 James J. Wirtz and James A. Russell, "A Quiet Revolution: Nuclear Strategy for the 21st Century," *Joint Forces Quarterly* (Winter 2002–3), 10 and 14.
34 As quoted in Stephen J. Cimbala, "Nuclear First Use: Prudence or Peril?," *Joint Force Quarterly* 51, no. 4 (2008), 28.
35 See Scott D. Sagan, "The Commitment Trap: Why the United States Should not Use Nuclear Threats to Deter Biological and Chemical Weapons Attacks," *International Security* 24, no. 4 (Spring 2000).
36 Perry, "Desert Storm and Deterrence," 66.
37 Gray, *Second Nuclear Age*, 148.
38 Ibid., 102.
39 Sagan, "The Commitment Trap," 106.
40 Payne, *The Fallacies*, 195.

41 Payne, *Deterrence*, 144.
42 Payne, "The Nuclear Posture Review and Deterrence for a New Age," 416.
43 Cimbala, *Nuclear Weapons*, 33.
44 Payne, *Great American Gamble*, 293.
45 Former French President Jacques Chirac as quoted in Yost, "New Approaches," 89.
46 National Research Council, *Discouraging Terrorism: Some Implications of 9/11* (Washington, DC: The National Academies Press, 2002), 8–14.
47 Lawrence Freedman, *Deterrence* (Cambridge, UK: Polity Press, 2004), 25.
48 Payne, *Great American Gamble*, 302.
49 Gray, *Second Nuclear Age*, 170.

Further reading

Cimbala, Stephen J. *Nuclear Weapons and Nuclear Strategy: U.S. Nuclear Policy for the Twenty-first Century* (London: Routledge, 2005).
Department of Defense. *Deterrence Operations Joint Operating Concept* (Washington, DC: Office of the Secretary of Defense, December 2006).
Freedman, Lawrence. *Deterrence* (Cambridge, UK: Polity Press, 2004).
Gray, Colin S. *The Second Nuclear Age* (Boulder, CO: Lynne Rienner Publishers, 1999).
Mearsheimer, John J. *Conventional Deterrence* (Ithaca, NY: Cornell University Press, 1983).
National Research Council. *Discouraging Terrorism: Some Implications of 9/11* (Washington, DC: The National Academies Press, 2002).
Payne, Keith B. *Deterrence in the Second Nuclear* Age (Lexington, KY: The University Press of Kentucky, 1996).
——. *The Fallacies of Cold War Deterrence and a New Direction* (Lexington, KY: The University Press of Kentucky, 2001).

8 Spacepower

With the launch of *Sputnik I* in October 1957, space joined air, land, and sea as a potential fourth domain of warfare. Over the next three decades hundreds of satellites were sent into orbit, including among them communications satellites in high earth orbit, navigation satellites in medium earth orbit, and earth observation satellites in low earth orbit. The combination of communication and navigation satellites enabled the dramatically increased precision in force application, and speed of information transmission, that figured so prominently in the 1991 Gulf War. These attributes have led many to characterize the Gulf War as "the first space war," while others—fewer in number—claim that the distinction belongs to the Cold War. But "both claims are dubious," argues one of a handful of spacepower theorists that have emerged in the period since the end of the Cold War. "Though replete with examples of space support for terrestrial forces, these conflicts were devoid of confrontation in space. It is doubtful history will remember either as space wars."[1] Indeed, the organizing principle of examining strategic thinking on the *conduct of war* in this particular domain is (fortunately) limited by the lack, so far, of empirical examples. Yet this doesn't mean that there has not been discussion of the parameters and character of spacepower, and the potential role and mission of space forces acting both in and from space.

This chapter examines strategic thought on spacepower. It begins by discussing what is meant by "space" and the particular attributes unique to space, out to the geostationary belt around earth, that impact on its use. It then goes on to define spacepower, only one component of which is military, before drawing out some of the defining features of what might be the character of war in this dimension. Specific theorists are found largely in the United States defense community. They include the authors of official government and Pentagon documents, and also, and more notably, military and civilian scholars associated with the US Air Force. Despite their institutional affiliation, these thinkers are paradoxically united in the view that far from being an extension of airpower, as the term "aerospace" would indicate, space is a domain deserving and requiring its own tradition of strategic thought.

What is space?

In 1958 the Chief of Staff of the US Air Force, General Thomas White, declared: "There is no division ... between air and space. Air and space is an indivisible field of operations."[2] Thus was set the post-Sputnik tone under which air and space are seen as a seamless medium, unconstrained by altitudinal demarcations. Yet despite the fact that the atmosphere gradually rather than abruptly disappears the further one moves away from earth, there are important markers. "Air" extends upward from earth's surface to the highest point at which air-breathing engines can operate, about 50 kilometers, while "space" begins above the surface of earth at the lowest altitude at which a satellite can sustain a circular orbit, roughly 150 kilometers. Between the "ceiling of aviation" and the "floor of astronautics," notes spacepower theorist Colonel M. V. Smith of the US Air Force, there is a 100-kilometer-wide band called the transverse region, within which neither aerodynamic flight nor orbital rotation is possible.[3] The region divides the air from space, calling into question the idea of an aerospace continuum.

The "aerospace fallacy" of an aerospace continuum, perpetuated over decades and reflected, for example, in the official name of the North American Aerospace Defense Command (NORAD), has had the effect of hindering the development of spacepower theory. Despite Sputnik's launch in 1957, the first substantive work on spacepower, David Lupton's *On Space Warfare*, did not appear until the closing days of the Cold War.[4] The first dedicated effort on the part of the United States to craft a spacepower theory "similar to that of other domains, for example, sea power" was launched in 2006 but was unable in the timeframe given—and in part because of the little empirical evidence available to aspiring theorists—to develop a coherent theory of spacepower.[5]

The topography of space

At first glance, space appears to be simply a vast expanse. But a closer look reveals that as a result of the laws of physics it is as demarcated and bounded a domain as are the land and sea environments by earth's geographic features. Terrestrial orbits have been categorized into four, depending on their altitude and mission utility. Low earth (or altitude) orbit extends from 150 to 800 kilometers upward from earth and, being relatively close to earth, is particularly useful for earth-observation satellites, as well as manned space flights and the international space station. Medium earth orbit ranges from 800 to 35,000 kilometers and includes, most notably (as mentioned above), navigational satellites like the Global Positioning System at 20,000 kilometers up. The lower the satellite, the faster it moves in relation to earth: satellites in low earth orbit travel around earth between 14 and 16 times a day, while those in high earth orbit go around it between 2 and 14 times a day.

High earth orbit lies above 35,000 kilometers, and satellites here travel around earth no more than once a day. If a satellite's orbital period is exactly the same as the earth's (at a height of just under 36,000 kilometers) the satellite is considered geosynchronous and appears fixed above one spot of earth. With only three such satellites carefully placed equidistant from one another directly above the equator, in geostationary orbit, all points of earth between 70 degrees north and 70 degrees south are in constant view. As a result, this orbit is the preferred location for military and civilian communications satellites, as well as those that detect ballistic missile launches. Finally, satellites in highly elliptical orbit do not stay at the same altitude as they go around earth, but rather travel as close as 250 kilometers and as far out as 40,000 kilometers, allowing them to "see" the polar regions of earth. Today there are about 1,000 operating satellites in orbit, most in low earth and geostationary orbits. In theory, a satellite could be placed as far out as 900,000 kilometers, the limit of earth's gravitational field and just over twice the distance to the moon, at one time earth's only satellite.

Our concern here is space out to about 40,000 kilometers. The most important factor in the topography of this area around earth is gravity, which has the effect of creating strategic narrows and celestial lines of communication no less important than the maritime chokepoints and sea lines of communication on earth. The first strategic narrow is low earth orbit, a narrow band of space around earth that is relatively "easy" to reach because satellites going this distance do not need a third-stage rocket boost to go into orbit. The second obvious strategic narrow is the geosynchronous altitude, especially the geostationary belt above earth's equator, where satellites are stable relative to a position on earth, thereby allowing for fixed antennae on earth.

Apart from orbits, the topography of space around earth also features common pathways. In theory, maneuvering between orbits is possible anywhere in space, but this requires enormous amounts of very limited onboard fuel. Earth's gravitational pull is such that anything done close to earth requires exponentially more energy or, in space-travel terms, "total velocity effort." It takes twice as much effort to propel a satellite from earth out to 100 kilometers as it does from that altitude to the moon. The most effort-efficient way to move from one orbit to another is via a two-step engine boost, the first to accelerate the spacecraft into a higher orbit (or decelerate into a lower orbit) and a second, once the new orbit is intersected, to circularize and stabilize the destination orbit. The concave line traveled between orbital levels is known as the Hohmann Transfer Orbit. Because of their advantages in fuel efficiency, notes one scholar, "The future lanes of commerce and military lines of communications in space will be the Hohmann transfer orbits between stable spaceports."[6] Beyond this, the trajectory of satellites in or on the way to orbit must also account for the Van Allen radiation belts. These are two donut-shaped regions of space, one straddling low and medium earth orbit and another straddling (and going beyond) medium and high earth orbit, that are dangerous to space vehicles and must be avoided.

Strategic areas for spacepower are also found on the surface of earth. Launch trajectory impacts on the effort required to place a satellite into orbit. The fact that earth rotates west to east gives a "boost" to satellites launched upward in an eastward direction. Since booster rockets fall to earth once expended, launch sites are best located on the eastern seaboard of an ocean (Cape Canaveral, Florida) or in the middle of a vast, unpopulated area (Baikonur, Kazakhstan). Launch latitude also matters. Because the boost from earth's rotation peaks at the equator, where the speed of its rotation is greatest, a country that has territory straddling the equator or close to it (Kourou, French Guinea) has a decided edge in launching satellites into geostationary orbit. Twice the payload for the same energy can be launched into geostationary orbit from the equator as from Kazakhstan. Strategic areas for spacepower are also found on earth wherever there are satellite ground stations to receive the electromagnetic information from the satellite and pass it on to the user.

Thus the physical characteristics of space create a number of strategic elements and terrain-like features, including common routes, chokepoints, celestial lines of communication, and hubs or bases of operations. Common routes in space-going terms are the orbital paths used for most standardized missions and functions, such as low earth orbit for weather satellites and geosynchronous satellites for communications; chokepoints are limited-access locations through which large volumes of traffic must pass, including space launch facilities, passage through low earth orbit to medium and high earth orbit, Hohmann Transfer Orbits, and common pathways to avoid the Van Allen belts; celestial lines of communication are those from, into, and through space, including information links between satellites and their operators and among satellites; hubs or bases of operations are the satellites in orbit and the communication relay stations on earth, continually passing information back and forth. Today there are certain desirable orbits, but future strategic locations for space vehicles could also include the so-called Lagrange Libration Points. First postulated in the 1700s, these are five points in space where it is theoretically likely that the gravitational pull of the moon and earth cancel each other out, and where a space vehicle could therefore remain permanently fixed and stable with no fuel expenditure.

The character of spacecraft

Global presence and access

The defining features of space mean that spacecraft have some significant environmentally influenced characteristics. One is that such platforms, unlike those in any other domain, have global presence and coverage, with line-of-sight view to large portions of earth and the ability to sustain this presence, once in orbit, with little or no use of fuel. Spacecraft are unique in that they are able to "see" within the boundaries of sovereign states, whereas air forces, for example, must normally get over-flight permission. Space-power's global presence means that, as with and even more so than airpower, it is flexible and versatile, in that it can shift from one campaign objective to another very quickly. With global presence, space forces can also produce both global and theater effects simultaneously.

Space, strategic thinkers have noted, is the ultimate "high ground" that military doctrine from time immemorial has advised commanders to seek and to hold. Forces on high ground or an elevated position are at an advantage because they can look down on enemy forces and because they are harder to reach and therefore less vulnerable to enemy fire. Similarly, British scholar Colin Gray argues that space can be considered a (dramatically) new variant of the familiar high ground concept. Space systems have a global vantage point and at the same time are, notwithstanding the advent of ground-based anti-satellite weapons, relatively difficult to reach because of earth's gravity well.[7]

A corollary to global presence is global access: a space vehicle can be observed from the ground and accessed for information throughout large portions of the day, and in the case of geostationary satellites, all day. Moreover, with relatively few assets all locations on earth can be accessed simultaneously. The Iridium Satellite Company in low earth orbit with 66 satellites, GPS in medium earth orbit with 24 satellites, and a handful of satellites in geosynchronous orbit, are indicative of the number of assets required at each level to ensure that all points on earth are in view at all times. A fundamental reason, then, to migrate capabilities in other domains—for example, those of Joint Surveillance and Target Attack Radar System aircraft that pin-point targets on the ground—to space would be to exploit the global presence and global access attributes of spacepower.

Non-maneuvering

A further characteristic of spacecraft is that they are "quasi-positional" rather than maneuvering platforms. Once in orbit they are in non-stop motion at high velocity, and they cannot maneuver, stop, or reverse course in the manner of terrestrial vehicles. As Gray notes, "laws of motion that must govern celestial bodies are a permanent constraint upon the flexibility with which spacepower can be employed."[8] Celestial objects cannot persist in an area of operations in the way, for example, that naval vessels can. Spacecraft "persistence" comprises repetitive over-flights of a given region, much as is done by aircraft in the air domain. Uniquely, however, celestial objects move in a predictable trajectory. Objects in space are in regular, unceasing motion around the world, an attribute that is useful for reliable global presence and access, but that also presents vulnerabilities because friendly and enemy parties alike know the location of space platforms. (This is one reason, apart from cost, not to migrate earthly capabilities to space.)

Spacecraft are also congregational. The topography of space dictates that there are certain desirable orbits and areas of operation, and this in turn creates cluster points. The geostationary belt is especially crowded because of its utility, and space is limited by the fact that satellites must be sited far enough apart to avoid broadcast interference in the electromagnetic spectrum. Competition for space in geostationary orbit is so tight that it has required regulation by the International Telecommunication Union since the late 1970s.

Spacepower

It is against this backdrop of space and spacecraft characteristics that we can examine strategic thinking on spacepower. Lupton defined spacepower as "the ability of a nation to exploit the space environment in pursuit of national goals and purposes and includes the entire astronautical capabilities of the nation." By contrast, in his 1999 volume, *Modern Strategy*, Gray defines spacepower in narrower terms as "the ability to use space and to deny such use to a foe."[9] This is an understanding that is closer to that of "space control" (see below), although elsewhere he broadens his definition to "the ability to use space for military, civil, or commercial purposes and to deny the ability of an enemy to do the same."[10]

Official US publications have consistently reflected the more comprehensive approach to spacepower. The Joint Doctrine for Space defines spacepower as "the total strength of a nation's capabilities to conduct and influence activities to, in, through and from space to achieve its objectives."[11] As such, space is a nationwide endeavor and can include, depending on the country, up to four distinct yet overlapping areas of space activity: civil (like the space station); commercial (like telecommunications); intelligence (like surveillance and reconnaissance); and military (like military communications and ballistic missile detection). This is the approach taken in the 2001 *Report of the Commission to Assess United States National Security Space Management and Organization*, a bipartisan commission chaired by Donald Rumsfeld before he became secretary of defense, where the same four sectors of space activity are identified. And it appeared far earlier in Lupton's work, which is also careful to stress that not all four sectors need to be covered for a country to be a spacepower.

A number of spacepower theorists have highlighted conditions that influence whether a country will become a spacepower, much as Alfred Thayer Mahan (see Chapter 1) drew out important conditions influencing seapower. Indeed, of the terrestrial forms of power, spacepower is seen as being most like seapower; it is an analogy that appears often in the literature. For Mahan, the six conditions that define a nation's seapower potential are geographical position, physical conformation, extent of territory, number of population, character of the people, and character of the government. They are conditions that also ring true for spacepower. One spacepower theorist has identified the basic traits of most spacefaring nations as being geographical size and location, national wealth, a large and well-educated population, a popular appetite for technology, and, above all, political will. Geographical size and location determine whether there are suitable launch locations; wealth provides resources to focus on space endeavors; and a large population is more likely to have a critical mass of well-educated, technologically oriented people. But there are spacefaring countries that defy one or more of these traits, indicating that "[w]hen all layers are peeled away what is left is a state's political will."[12] In addition, a national character that includes a commercial orientation and a popular appetite for technology is particularly important in the post-Cold War period.

Space forces and space missions

The military component of spacepower is called "space forces." These may be capable of destructive acts themselves or, just like many land, sea, and air platforms, provide support to such destructive elements. Benjamin Lambeth, an airpower theorist who has also written extensively on spacepower, divides the spectrum of space force missions into four: space support, force enhancement, space control, and space force application. Space support involves things like launching satellites, the daily management of on-orbit systems, and replenishing lost or malfunctioning satellites.

Force enhancement

It is force enhancement with which we are most familiar. When we say the 1991 Gulf War was the "first space war," what we are really referring to is the force-enhancement mission—enhancing the effectiveness of terrestrial systems through the synergistic support of space systems. Thus communications satellites enable the near-real-time transmission of voice, data, and even images from, for example, unmanned aerial vehicles (UAVs); navigation satellites pin-point coordinates for the application of precision air-, sea-, and, increasingly, landpower; and imaging satellites significantly augment the sensory picture provided by manned aircraft, UAVs, and on-ground intelligence.

   Gray characterizes the force-enhancement attributes of spacepower as providing the next "layer" of increased force capability. "Spacepower augments the military effectiveness of air power, just as air power augmented the potency of sea power, and as air power and sea power worked synergistically and 'jointly' to enable land power."[13] Spacepower is thus quintessentially joint in nature, in that its value lies in its synergistic application in concert with other military domains. In the decades since the end of the Cold War, spacepower assets have been fully integrated into the sensor-to-shooter loop of active combat operations. Box 8.1 highlights some of the space-based force-enhancement capabilities available today.

Box 8.1 Space force enhancement

The force-enhancement mission of space forces, that is, the contribution that space-based assets make to terrestrial operations, dates to the Cold War. But it has become increasingly apparent and part of the public consciousness with every international conflict from the 1991 Gulf War onward. Force-enhancement functions and representative assets include:

- *Missile warning.* The original space force-enhancement mission was to detect the launch of intercontinental ballistic missiles. In 1970 the United States launched the first of about eight to ten satellites in geosynchronous orbit at any one time that are part of the Defense Support Program (DSP) satellite system, with the most recent launched in 2007. Designed to warn of strategic missile launches, DSP's first operational test came with the detection of tactical Scud missiles during the Gulf War. The system is to be replaced over the coming years with a new Space Based Infrared System.

- *Satellite communications.* The ability to transmit voice, data, and now images (for example from UAVs to decision makers) in near-real time half-way around the world is central to the conduct of modern war. Located in geosynchronous orbit, America's dedicated military satellite communications systems include MILSTAR, launched in the 1990s and early 2000s, and the next-generation Advanced Extremely High Frequency system, the initial satellite of which was launched in 2010. Countries like Britain and France also have dedicated military satellite communications systems, but it is more common for militaries to rent space on commercial satellites.

- *Navigation.* The application of satellite-guided precision force by air forces, navies, and, increasingly, armies is dependent on America's Global Positioning System. Located in medium earth orbit, GPS is the world's only fully functioning satellite navigation system, but others are in the process of being established. They include Russia's Global Navigation System (GLONASS) and China's Beidou Satellite Navigation and Positioning System, both of which already have many satellites in orbit. The European Union (EU) is also pursuing a satellite navigation system, called Galileo, but political differences among the various EU countries on costs and funding have hindered progress.

- *Earth observation.* Intelligence, surveillance, and reconnaissance information— the ability to "see over the next hill"—can come from manned and unmanned aircraft, but the most strategic picture is provided by satellites. America's Landsat earth observation system has been operating in low earth orbit since the 1970s, providing an uninterrupted picture of earth's surface. France and Germany also have military surveillance earth-imaging satellites, the Helios II and SAR Lupe systems respectively, while other countries receive dedicated imagery from commercial satellites. Canada's RADARSAT, for example, gives 1-meter resolution of most of earth's land mass every several hours, while a follow-on RADARSAT constellation will provide an almost continuous capability to monitor ships approaching North America from the Atlantic, Pacific, and Arctic oceans.

Space control

Spacepower theorists within the US Air Force define space control as measures to "ensure freedom of action in space for the United States and its allies and, when directed, deny an adversary freedom of action in space."[14] Along these lines, the US Air Force officially refers to space-control missions as "counterspace operations," the objective of which is "space superiority"—"the freedom *to* attack as well as freedom *from* attack."[15] The idea that controlling space, or at least precluding control by a hostile power, could be just as critical in the future as air and sea control first appeared in the scholarly military literature in the 1970s, ironically by the US Army. Yet perhaps because of the lack of US competitors in the early post-Cold War period, throughout much of the 1990s space control was not an area of focus for the Pentagon. In 1995 one space analyst prophesized that "Today the United States is the undisputed leader in space-assisted warfare ... [but] [w]hen an enemy can use the orbital highways over-head at will, or interfere with U.S. space missions critical to the course or outcome of a war, space control will no doubt receive the attention it deserves."[16] Gray underscored at the time that the space-control concept had to be assigned "master status" if America's ideas for the military use of spacecraft were not to be rendered irrelevant.[17]

By the early 2000s the United States was more heavily invested in, and dependent on, its on-orbit assets than ever before, while potential adversaries were closing in on the ability to disrupt those assets. Strategic thinkers associated with the US Air Force began to stress the quintessential importance of space control: "*Space control is not optional*," wrote Smith in 2002. "A growing reliance on spacepower assets by govern-mental agencies and the business community makes it essential to secure access to satellite services. It is equally important to deny access to unfriendly users" (emphasis in original).[18] Benjamin Lambeth argued that potential opponents would soon be able to threaten US space-based assets by means ranging from harassment to neutralization, to outright destruction. A watershed and clear demonstration of potential future threats was China's early 2007 destruction of one of its obsolete weather satellites in low earth orbit using a ground-based anti-satellite missile.

Official US strategic thinking on space control is found in the 2004 Air Force Doctrine Document on *Counterspace Operations*, the 2006 Air Force Doctrine Document on *Space Operations*, and, at the Joint Chiefs of Staff level, the 2009 Joint Publication on *Space Operations*. For the Air Force, the space-control or counterspace mission includes several components. The first is "space situational awareness," or knowing about space-related conditions and capabilities in, from, toward, or through space. The idea here is that it is necessary to monitor what sorts of space vehicles are in orbit at any given moment, where they are going, what they are capable of doing, and what they are relaying to their operators. In addition, space control involves defensive counterspace operations; that is, passive and active measures to protect friendly systems from attack. System hardening and the simple dispersal of space systems can be passive measures, while more active measures include maneuvering in orbit or changing frequencies to deny an adversary the ability to track or target a satellite.

Space control also includes offensive counterspace operations designed to actively preclude an adversary from exploiting space. For the US Air Force, offensive space-control strategy involves "deception" by manipulating or distorting information; "dis-ruption" by temporarily impairing system capability, without physical effects; "denial" by temporarily eliminating system capability, without physical effects; "degradation" by permanently impairing system capability, with physical damage; and "destruction" by permanently eliminating system capability with physical damage. Targets include on-orbit satellites, communications links between ground stations and satellites, ground stations themselves, and launch facilities. It is immediately apparent that when it comes to offensive space control, much of what is being controlled is not physically in space. Indeed, Coalition air attacks against Iraqi satellite ground stations during the 1991 Gulf War have been considered in hindsight as a successful first-generation attempt at offensive space control. Offensive space control includes the full range of capabilities "to disrupt, delay, or deny enemy access to space by launching air attacks or ground assaults against ground nodes and terminals, jamming enemy satellite links, introducing viruses into computer programs, and destroying hostile satellites."[19]

Some experts argue that the best way to negate adversary satellites is in orbit. The physical, i.e. kinetic, destruction of satellites using ground-based anti-satellite capabilities is one way of doing this. Both the United States and the Soviet Union pursued such a capability during the Cold War but the only successful anti-satellite test was by the United States against one of its own low earth-orbit satellites in 1985. The satellite which China shot down in 2007 was also in low earth orbit. However, strategic thinkers have long theorized that by virtue of the fact that satellites are so predictable in their orbits there is no apparent reason why, with the use of a larger launch vehicle, intercepts could not be accomplished up to geosynchronous orbit. In future, space-based kinetic-energy anti-satellite capabilities could also be used to physically destroy satellites. The United States and other countries are thought to be developing microsatellites that could be used for this purpose. In the mid-2000s America's Missile Defense Agency worked on a space-based kinetic-energy weapon designed to destroy ballistic missiles in their mid-course phase, and experts noted at the time that such weapons could also be used as a space-based anti-satellite weapon.

A major problem with the kinetic destruction of satellites is debris. Indeed, one outcome of the 2007 Chinese anti-satellite demonstration, which created thousands of pieces of dangerous debris in low and medium earth orbit that could orbit for infinity, may have been to definitively confirm that the kinetic destruction of anything in space, whether a satellite or a mid-course ballistic missile, is not a viable option. The unique physical attributes of space, specifically the lack of gravity, mean that, unlike sea, land, or air forces, future space forces cannot—or at least should not—kinetically engage one another. "Battlefields in space are ... fundamentally different from those on land, at sea, or in the air," note some spacepower scholars. "Battlefield debris in space ... can last for decades, centuries, or even millennia, thereby constituting an indiscriminate lethal hazard" to the very high-value satellite systems the satellite warfare was meant to protect.[20]

Thus it is likely that to the extent the United States and other countries pursue anti-satellite capabilities in the future, these will be of the non-kinetic variety. Apart from electromagnetic jamming, ground-based lasers may be an option. But more likely are microsatellites that render adversary satellites inoperable by firing paintball-like material at them, or by burning out their wiring with lasers. Along these lines, a maneuverable satellite carrying laser weapons was first foreseen in the 1970s. Others have suggested somehow non-kinetically dislodging a satellite from its orbit. "[A] bump or a push in the wrong direction is all that is necessary to send [a satellite] spinning off into a useless or uncontrollable orbit."[21]

Space force application

A fourth space force mission is "space force application," first raised in the US context by the Rumsfeld Commission in early 2001. "Many think of space only as a place for passive collection of images or signals or a switchboard that can quickly pass information back and forth over long distances," the commission pointed out, "[but] [i]t is also possible to project power through and from space."[22] The US Joint Chiefs of Staff define space force application as "combat operations in, through, and from space to influence the course and outcome of conflict *by holding terrestrial targets at risk*" (emphasis added).[23] The US Air Force Doctrine Document on *Space Operations* similarly speaks of operations "in, through, or from space which hold terrestrial-based targets at risk" and gives examples of the weapons systems involved as being intercontinental ballistic missiles (ICBMs), ballistic missile defense, and force projection.[24] Thus ICBMs, which reach well into medium earth orbit (about 1,500 kilometers up) in their mid-course phase travel "through" space; ballistic missile defense systems that intercept missiles in the mid-course phase would operate "in" space; and any future space-to-terrestrial power-projection capability would operate "from" space.

The emphasis above on terrestrial targets is necessary in order to draw a distinction between, on the one hand, space force application, and on the other, offensive counter-space missions involving the use of force in space. That said, the space force application concept also speaks of operations "in" space, raising some confusion as to the distinction between space force application and offensive counter-space missions. For good reason, spacepower theorists argue that "The line between space control and force applications has been increasingly blurred" since the US Air Force released its 2004 doctrine statement on *Counterspace Operations*.[25]

Space force application weapons

An early attempt at a space-to-ground capability was the Soviet Union's Fractional Orbit Bombardment System (FOBS), an ICBM that was to go into low earth orbit and be called on to de-orbit for ground attack. The 1967 Outer Space Treaty banned the placing of WMDs in space, but the Soviets continued to test the FOBS without the warhead for over a decade. More recently, both the United States and China are thought to be exploring space-to-ground attack weapons. Indeed, US Space Command considered the force application mission as far back as in its 1998 Long Range Plan, which discussed, among other things, the technology areas that required attention if a spacecraft were to be able to reliably hit terrestrial targets. One of the four operational concepts included in the Long Range Plan (of which there is no more recent unclassified version) is "global engagement," a concept that is given the explicit 2020 end-state objective of "A robust and fully integrated suite of space ... capabilities providing ... the ability to identify, track, and hold at risk designated high value terrestrial targets."[26]

Advocates of space-to-ground weapons argue that they may be uniquely able to strike two types of terrestrial target: those that are time critical, for example, mobile scud missiles or biological weapons laboratories; and those that are considered "denied access," that is, geographically remote, hardened, or deeply buried. To this list we might add the value (for avoiding space debris) of using space-based weapons to destroy ballistic missiles in their launch or terminal phases within the atmosphere, rather than ground- or sea-based interceptors designed for interceptions in the mid-course, exoatmospheric stage. Critics counter that non-space weapons such as UAVs, cruise missiles, and ICBMs with conventional payloads provide greater capability and at a lower cost.

The weaponization debate

The Space Command Long Range Plan also underscored that "the notion of weapons in space is not consistent with US national policy" and that planning was being done only in case the government "should later decide the application of force from space is in the [US] national interest."[27] Thus was raised the elephant in the room behind all discussions of the force application mission—whether space is or should be weaponized, or whether space can somehow be sanctuarized. The latter, sanctuary school of space-power thought seeks to preserve space as a weapons-free zone to prevent states from threatening other states, and to prevent triggering of security dilemmas. The basic tenet of the school, which has its basis in the Cold War, is that non-offensive spacepower helped to prevent nuclear war and create strategic stability by providing each super-power with the means to see within the other's sovereign boundaries and to detect a nuclear attack. In the post-Cold War era the sanctuary school has argued that the United States, as the country most dependent on space assets both militarily and commercially, has the most to lose should space be militarized and its own assets be put at risk.

But many spacepower thinkers come from the perspective that while the weaponization of space is probably undesirable, it is nonetheless inevitable. "Can humans transcend their power urges and instincts to engage in cooperative behaviour?" asks Robert Pfaltzgraff. "Will earthly competition inevitably be expanded into space? There is little, if any, evidence to support the proposition that human behaviour in space would differ substantially from that on earth."[28] In its 2001 report the US commission on space stated this perspective directly: "We know from history that every medium—air, land and sea—has seen conflict. Reality indicates that space will be no different."[29] Indeed, strategist Norman Friedman draws a direct link between the force-enhancement attributes of space-based assets and space's eventual weaponization. Information gathered and distributed by satellites has become central to victory on land, he notes. "It follows that eventually war will be fought in space. After all, air warfare began with reconnaissance. The first fighters were designed to deny enemies that information."[30]

Although the timing is not known, at some point in the future it can be expected that the nature of the international system of sovereign states and the nature of mankind will combine to put weapons into orbit. Thinkers predict that space-based weapons will eventually be used against targets on land, sea, and in the air. Lambeth, for example, expects that the force application mission "will eventually entail the direct defensive and offensive imposition of kinetic and non-kinetic measures from space in pursuit of joint terrestrial objectives," including the range of hardened bunkers, surface vessels, armored vehicles, and enemy leadership targets.[31] Others argue that space forces will become directly engaged in traditional combat—killing targets and receiving hostile fire—adapted for the unique environment of space, while at the same time retaining the spacepower role of force enhancement. Space-based weapons may fill specific niches, ideal for some missions during certain phases of operations.

Some theorists argue that space is the dominant theater for military operations and that force application from space could have decisive effects on terrestrial conflicts. From this perspective, spacepower could succeed in coercing leaders by holding high-value, well-defended targets at risk from space attack. But most strategic thinkers concede that, as with airpower, spacepower alone is insufficient to control the outcome of terrestrial conflict or to ensure the attainment of political objectives. Gray approaches the debate in the context of space as a "leading edge" military force, under which "leading edge" can mean the military capability that takes the war to the enemy (as airpower did in the 1991 Gulf War), or that determines the outcome of a conflict even if that capability is not of the combat sort.[32] From this perspective, spacepower can decide the course and outcome of some conflicts, even though space forces may not be combat ones with offensive capabilities. "No claim is made that spacepower by itself can be decisive in conventional warfare," Smith similarly argues, "but it may help set the conditions for victory under some circumstances."[33]

The conduct of war

For Lambeth, only once it is possible to directly inflict harm on adversaries from space against space-based, air-breathing, and terrestrial targets, will it become possible to truly speak of "spacepower." Today, military space activity remains limited to enabling rather than actually conducting combat operations and this, combined with concerns about weaponizing space, has meant that there has been only limited strategic thinking on how and why combat operations might be conducted in and from space.

... *from space*

Combat operations *from* space, that is, the force-projection component of the space force application mission, may be considered conceptually analogous to air-to-ground warfare. Strategic thinking on its use and value, when it comes, may parallel or at least have some similarities to strategic thought by airpower theorists on the use and value of strategic bombing (see Chapter 3). Against the argument that spacepower could coerce leaders by holding high-value targets at risk, for example, future space force application theorists may determine that force application from space "doesn't matter" and that achieving political objectives still requires "boots on the ground." Alternatively, and again echoing the airpower debate, it may be determined that force application from space can reduce the casualty costs of warfare, doing much of the battlefield work prior to introducing ground forces. These debates are still many years off, but it is not difficult to foresee their likely future facets.

... *in space*

It is with respect to combat operations *in* space that the most innovative ground will eventually be broken on spacepower strategic thought. Theorists speak of space warfare as involving not only attacking terrestrial nodes (similar to striking any other building) and disrupting lines of communication between earth and space assets, but also targeting the satellites themselves. Already thinkers within the US Air Force and Navy have put forward some ideas about the conduct of war in space.

Strategic thought on combat in the space domain discusses the difficulty of the defense. Despite the protection of earth's gravity well, space forces are vulnerable. They are bright objects against a dark background, they travel in predicable orbits, and, unlike terrestrial forces, do not have sovereign barriers behind which they can find refuge. Space forces are like ships on the open, ungoverned seas, with the added circumstance that they cannot seek protection by returning to friendly waters. (The exception here would of trans-atmospheric vehicles. China is thought to be exploring in theoretical research space planes that can transit and fight up and down between the upper atmosphere and space.) Smith has characterized satellites as "delicate, fragile devices" that can easily fall prey to lasers, radio-frequency jamming, brute-force weapons, and ground-launched anti-satellite kinetic-kill vehicles. Satellites in low earth orbit are most vulnerable to anti-satellite measures, yet "satellites all the way out to the geostationary belt and in highly elliptical orbits share a universal vulnerability to radio frequency jamming and electromagnetic brute force attacks."[34] It is possible to arm satellites against some types of electromagnetic interference, but arming a satellite against physical attack as one would, say, a tank, is not feasible. The cost limitations of propelling extra weight into space mean that satellites have little carrying capacity beyond that which is necessary to carry out their mission.

In its official doctrine the US Air Force includes the dispersal of space systems as one possible defensive counter-space measure. Strategic thinkers in the US Navy concur, provided such forces retain the flexibility to combine dispersal with concentration. "Space forces and systems should in general be dispersed to cover the widest possible area yet retain the ability to concentrate decisive force. Dispersal of forces will allow the protection of a nation's space assets ... [but] [t]o defend against or neutralize a significant threat ... space forces should quickly concentrate firepower."[35] Lupton goes further on the defensive side, proposing that space force clustering—a predominant tendency in any case because of the topography of space—could actually be advantageous because it might simplify the defensive problem: "High value assets might be defended individually, whereas strategic chokepoints might be provided an area defense."

The difficulty of the defense in space means that many emphasize the importance of the offense: "The first and most enduring mission of space forces is to gain relative space control over enemies, enabling the space offensive."[36] Strategists caution that an offensive space force "looking for a decisive victory will likely not find it," and the force must be careful not to throw away space assets on "ill-considered attacks."[37] But offensive counter-space does not have to be total to be effective, since an adversary will likely have satellites that do not especially affect its warfighting capability. "Circumstances and strategy will dictate the degree of offensive space control required."[38] The choice of offensive measures is limited by concern for space debris, which impacts on friendly and enemy forces equally, but some theorists have proposed tactical measures that could address this battlefield problem. The pace of technological development in microsatellites may allow a major spacefaring nation to launch enough independent kinetic-kill vehicles in the lowest of low earth orbits—where it is physically likely that any debris from a kinetic destruction would fall through the atmosphere—to effectively deny entry to space of any other state. In future, this orbital band could become central to an anti-access strategy in the space domain.

Strategists also argue that offensive and defensive operations in space are mutually complementary: a country wanting to initiate limited war in space needs a defensive capability against any unlimited counter-attack. Moreover, some aspects of space weigh equally on the offense and defense. While electromagnetic waves travel unimpeded throughout space, kinetic and laser interactions between objects must involve either aligning or intersecting orbital paths. Changing direction at orbital speeds can be difficult or impossible because of the limited fuel available. Thus spacecraft, whether attacking or evading, cannot rely on maneuverability to conduct their operations or increase their survivability, and to the degree that they do maneuver they do so in relatively predictable transfer orbits.

Although the offense is considered the dominant form of war in space today, this may not necessarily always be the case. Satellites are getting smaller, and therefore stealthy because space surveillance networks are less and less able to track them;

avoiding tracking is starting to include maneuvering satellites to undisclosed wartime orbits; space systems involve a growing number of cheaper satellites, thereby building in redundancy and creating a "swarming" effect; and satellites increasingly include a mix of civilian and military applications, making them a complicated target for adversaries. In this context, "The best defense for a space system in the 21st century may be the dual use system that is owned, operated and used by broad international partners."[39]

Conclusion

Strategic thought on spacepower is relatively new and, at least in the unclassified domain, limited only to some types of spacepower missions. Sparked by the 1991 Gulf War, much has been written from the mid-1990s onward about the value of force enhancement through space-based assets, that is, of enhancing the military effectiveness of land, sea, and air forces through the integration of space-based capabilities. During the early post-Cold War period the force-enhancement capability was dominated by the United States. But as new spacepower players emerged, thereby raising the potential for threats to US capabilities, strategic thinking evolved. The focus expanded to encompass space control and the imperative, during a conflict or crisis, of maintaining access to space-based assets while denying such access to adversaries. In the post-9/11 period the US Air Force and scholars associated with it have written quite extensively on space control or counter-space operations, including defensive and offensive measures. Because strategies associated with the latter range from relatively benign deception and denial, through to hostile destruction, certain aspects of the offensive counter-space mission start to look a lot like combat operations "in" space, blurring the line between counter-space and space force application, a fourth military mission that appears within spacepower strategic thought.

For some spacepower thinkers, true spacepower will arrive only when it is possible to directly inflict harm on an adversary's sea, land, air, or space forces using space-based assets, in essence a space-to-space or space-to-terrestrial capability. Although strategic thought in the open literature has yet to emerge on space force application against earthly targets, it seems likely that the value and use of such capabilities will have some resonance with debates about the value and use of strategic airpower. Strategic thinking on space-to-space combat, by contrast, promises to be wholly unique from that which we have seen before, largely because of the most important topographical aspect of space: its lack of gravity and resulting orbital dynamics.

Already theorists have put forth some ideas about what may be the impact of space's topographical features on combat operations in space. They include an emphasis on the vulnerability of space forces; the difficulty of the defense; the relative advantage of the offense; some fledgling anti-access ideas; the limited ability to maneuver, whether on the offense or defense; the tendency toward cluster points and chokepoints, which, depending on one's perspective, makes space forces either harder or easier to defend; and the measures that are being taken to increase the defense. This is not an extensive list. Notwithstanding the weaponization debate, in the future, space warfare is bound to occur between two or more warring states if space is a critical medium for at least one side and the other side has the capacity for space combat. Before then, much more strategic thinking will need to be done on the conduct of war in the space domain.

Notes

1 James E. Oberg (US Air Force), *Space Power Theory* (Colorado Springs, CO: US Air Force Academy, Department of Astronautics, March 1999), 123.
2 As quoted in Mark E. Harter (US Air Force), "Ten Propositions Regarding Space Power," *Air & Space Power Journal* (Summer 2006), fn 13.
3 M. V. Smith (US Air Force), *Ten Propositions Regarding Spacepower* (Maxwell Air Force Base, AL: Air University Press, 2002), 5.
4 David E. Lupton (US Air Force), *On Space Warfare: A Space Power Doctrine* (Maxwell Air Force Base, AL: Air University Press, 1988). Quotes by Lupton are directly attributed to him in the text but are not footnoted because the document has no page numbers.
5 Charles D. Lutes et al., *Toward a Theory of Spacepower* (Washington, DC: National Defense University Press, 2011), xv–xvii.
6 Everett C. Dolman, "Geostrategy in the Space Age: An Astropolitical Analysis," *Journal of Strategic Studies* 22, no. 2 (1999), 96.
7 Colin S. Gray, *Modern Strategy* (Oxford: Oxford University Press, 1999), 260.
8 Colin S. Gray, "The Influence of Space Power upon History," *Comparative Strategy* 15 (1996), 301.
9 Gray, *Modern Strategy*, 244.
10 Gray, "The Influence," 299.
11 US Air Force, *Space Operations* (Washington, DC: Air Force Doctrine Document 2–2, November 27, 2006), 1.
12 Oberg, *Space Power Theory*, 136.
13 Gray, "The Influence," 300.
14 Smith, *Ten Propositions*, 72.
15 US Air Force, *Counterspace Operations* (Washington, DC: Air Force Doctrine Document 2–2.1, August 2, 2004), 1.
16 Steven Lambakis, "Space Control in Desert Storm and Beyond," *Orbis* (Summer 1995), 418.
17 Gray, "The Influence," 306.
18 M. V. Smith, "Some Propositions on Spacepower," *Joint Force Quarterly* (Winter 2002–3), 57.
19 Lambakis, "Space Control in Desert Storm," 431.
20 Michael Krepon et al., "Preserving Freedom of Action in Space: Realizing the Potential and Limits of U.S. Spacepower," in Lutes et al., *Toward a Theory of Spacepower* (Washington, DC: National Defense University Press, 2011), 121 and 128.
21 Everett C. Dolman and Henry F. Cooper, Jr., "Increasing the Military Uses of Space," in ibid., 107.
22 *Report of the Commission to Assess United States National Security Space Management and Organization* (Washington, DC: January 2001), 33.
23 US Joint Chiefs of Staff, *Space Operations* (Washington, DC: Joint Pub 3–14, January 6, 2009), II-10.
24 US Air Force, *Space Operations*, 5.
25 Joan Johnson-Freese, *Space as a Strategic Asset* (New York: Columbia University Press, 2007), 83.
26 Howell M. Estes III, "The Aerospace Force of Today and Tomorrow," in Peter L. Hays et al., *Spacepower for a New Millenium* (New York: McGraw-Hill, 2000), 171.
27 *US Space Command Long Range Plan*, April 1998, http://fas.org, accessed June 2011.
28 Robert L. Pfaltzgraff, Jr., *Space and U.S. Security: A Net Assessment* (Cambridge, MA: Institute for Foreign Policy Analysis, January 2009), 3.
29 *Report of the Commission to Assess United States National Security Space Management and Organization*, 10 and 100.
30 Norman Friedman, *Seapower and Space* (London: Chatham Publishing, 2000), 311.
31 Benjamin S. Lambeth, "Airpower, Spacepower, and Cyberwar," *Joint Force Quarterly* 60, no. 1 (2011), 48–49. See also Benjamin S. Lambeth, *Mastering the Ultimate High Ground: Next Steps in the Military Uses of Space* (Santa Monica, CA: RAND, 2003), 113.
32 Gray, "The Influence", 303.
33 Smith, "Some Propositions," 64.
34 M. V. Smith, "Spacepower and Warfare," *Joint Force Quarterly* 60, no. 1 (2011), 43.

35 John J. Klein, "Corbett in Orbit: A Maritime Model for Strategic Space Theory," *Naval War College Review* 57, no. 1 (Winter 2004), 69.
36 Smith, "Some Propositions," 61.
37 Klein, "Corbett in Orbit," 67.
38 Smith, "Some Propositions," 61.
39 Smith, "Spacepower and Warfare," 44.

Further reading

Lambeth, Benjamin S. *Mastering the Ultimate High Ground: Next Steps in the Military Uses of Space* (Santa Monica, CA: RAND, 2003).

Lupton, David E. *On Space Warfare: A Space Power Doctrine* (Maxwell Air Force Base, AL: Air University Press, 1988).

Lutes, Charles D. et al. *Toward a Theory of Spacepower* (Washington, DC: National Defense University Press, 2011).

Oberg, James E. *Space Power Theory* (Colorado Springs, CO: US Air Force Academy, Department of Astronautics, March 1999).

Pfaltzgraff, Robert L., Jr. *Space and U.S. Security: A Net Assessment* (Cambridge. MA: Institute for Foreign Policy Analysis, January 2009).

Smith, M. V. *Ten Propositions Regarding Spacepower* (Maxwell Air Force Base, AL: Air University Press, 2002).

United States Air Force. *Counterspace Operations* (Washington, DC: Air Force Doctrine Document 2–2.1, August 2, 2004).

——. *Space Operations* (Washington, DC: Air Force Doctrine Document 2–2, November 27, 2006).

United States Joint Chiefs of Staff. *Space Operations* (Washington, DC: Joint Pub 3–14, January 6, 2009).

Conclusion

The period since the end of the Cold War has been one of almost continual conflict or war at some level in the international system. The prevalence of wars between states or, more often, between a state and a non-state actor has meant that the conduct of war remains one of the most important acts of the state. Strategic thought on the conduct of war can help us to manage and contend with crises by shedding light on the contemporary role and contribution of military force in and to a nation's security policy.

In the two decades after the Cold War, civilian academics and military practitioners produced a substantial literature pertaining to one or more of the warfare domains—sea, land (conventional and irregular), air, space, and cyber—as well as on military topics that do not fit neatly into one domain or another, including joint theory, nuclear warfare, and deterrence. In some cases their scholarship is explicitly structured around statements or principles about the conduct of war, with one example being the US Army/Marine Corps counterinsurgency manual. In most cases, however, it has been necessary to pull these themes together from various parts of their works. Doing so for a range of notable scholars within a domain of warfare reveals a set of principles or statements that may collectively be considered a modern, albeit partial, theory of war.

A modern theory of seapower tells us that seapower should work in conjunction with land forces to achieve strategic effects. It should be used to gain sea control in the littorals to impact on the course of intra-state conflicts and in the open ocean to maintain open the sea lanes of communication. In addition, navy expeditionary warfare, through forward presence and things like sea basing, is necessary to respond to distant crises. Landpower should be employed using small, mobile units that are dispersed on the battlefield and are linked together through information technology. It should feature simultaneous and synchronized operations that are nonlinear in nature, seek massed effects with precision technologies, and operate at all times in close conjunction with sea, air, and space forces. Airpower should be applied in conjunction with friendly landpower; rarely be used in a strategic bombing "decapitation" strategy; not be used in a punishment strategy against population centers; be employed against economic and other critical nodes to achieve strategic effects in war; work in conjunction with indigenous forces to reduce friendly casualties; be applied in counterinsurgency missions to a degree that is inversely proportional to the proximity of insurgents to civilian population centers; and be relied on to contribute to situational awareness in forms of warfare from conventional to counterinsurgency. All services, whether navy, army, or air force, should be fully interoperable in practical and technological terms; operate in conjunction with at least one other service; be assigned missions according to requirement, not service; and work increasingly with non-military instruments.

A modern view of counterinsurgency reveals that counterinsurgents should strive to secure the population using non-kinetic means; use highly discriminate, direct combat strikes against some insurgents; secure the population in large urban areas first and then spread security and stability outward from consolidated areas; seal off safe havens and porous borders; and integrate economic, political, and social measures as soon as feasible. Meanwhile cyber strikes should be employed offensively in the opening phases of a conflict, even pre-emptively; be targeted at specific high-value nodes deemed to be a center of gravity; be closely synchronized with or conducted in parallel or simultaneously with conventional strikes; be employed as a one-time bolt from the blue; or, conversely, be deployed over a long period of time, surreptitiously, stealthily, and patiently to manipulate information. Deterrence strategies must be tailored to the specific adversary in mind; use a combination of offensive and defensive approaches and nuclear and conventional threats; focus in the first instance on deterrence by denial whether vis-à-vis a state or non-state actor; and integrate the military component of deterrence with comprehensive measures. Spacepower should be used to gain space control, thereby securing global presence and an ultimate high-ground picture for the other services, while denying these to the adversary. Space control should be secured offensively through non-kinetic means and with a growing emphasis on defensive measures. Principles of force application from space will likely mirror airpower themes, while principles of combat in space may include anti-access strategies and the defense of cluster and chokepoints.

Each set of principles above may be considered as representing, or at least approaching, a partial theory of warfare within each warfare domain. They indicate how a particular kind of military power should be employed to affect the course of a conflict. But what can we say about warfare as a whole? Clausewitz's theory of war remains relevant today because it was based on principles and statements about the conduct of war that were not bounded by time or domain. After discussing the enduring nature of war, the character of which does not change, Clausewitz argued that war plans should be based on principles like applying force proportional to the political goal; directing efforts at an enemy's center of gravity; acting with the utmost concentration and utmost speed; and directly engaging the enemy through the shortest route possible, rather than engaging in maneuver. These are ideas that were meant for landpower but could easily be, and have been, applied to other dimensions of warfare.

From our partial theories above it may be possible to draw out some general themes about warfare today that similarly are not bounded by domain, or at least are applicable across two or more domains. These include: achieving strategic effects in war today (including irregular war) is a joint effort; plans must be drawn up that account for sea, land, air, space, and cyber forces working together to achieve the political objective of the war; military force from all domains must be employed in synchronized, parallel, and simultaneous fashion; force should be applied with utmost precision; the offensive use of force holds the upper hand in most scenarios; that said, the patient accumulation of intelligence is imperative across several domains (cyber, deterrence, and irregular), as is the honing of non-kinetic war-fighting skills (space and irregular); and war efforts must be planned with a comprehensive approach in mind, incorporating a wide range of non-military elements.

This is an admittedly short list of statements and principles. But collectively they may comprise the beginnings of a modern, general theory of war. That war is a continuation of politics by other means and that force must be applied against the enemy's center of gravity are enduring and undisputed aspects of war. They remain in a modern theory of war. Nor is the nature of war any different; it still, for example, resembles a game of cards. But some things have changed. There *are* contemporary strategic thinkers, both military and civilian. New elements in the conduct of war *have been* drawn out and recorded in their scholarship. It *is* possible to detect some common themes that cut across domains. These principles and statements mark the initial signposts in a twenty-first-century understanding of the role of military forces in a nation's security policy, that is, in modern strategy.

Glossary

4GW	fourth-generation warfare
BMD	Ballistic Missile Defense
C4I	communications, computers, command, control and intelligence
CNA	Computer Network Attack
CNE	Computer Network Exploitation
COIN	counterinsurgency
EBO	effects-based operations
ICBM	Intercontinental Ballistic Missile
ISR	intelligence, surveillance and reconnaissance
JOC	Joint Operating Concept
LCS	Littoral Combat Ship
MTR	military technical revolution
NCW	network-centric warfare
NFU	no first use
NPR	Nuclear Posture Review
NPT	Nuclear Non-Proliferation Treaty
ONA	Office of Net Assessment
PGM	precision-guided munitions
PLA	People's Liberation Army
PSYOPS	psychological operations
RDO	rapid decisive operations
RMA	Revolution in Military Affairs
SLBM	Submarine-Launched Ballistic Missiles
STRATCOM	Strategic Command
TRADOC	Training and Doctrine Command
UAV	Unmanned Aerial Vehicle
WMD	Weapons of Mass Destruction

Bibliography

"A Cyber-riot: Estonia and Russia," *Economist*, May 12, 2007.

Adams, James. "Virtual Defense," *Foreign Affairs* 80, no. 3 (May/June 2001).

Alexander, Keith. "Warfighting in Cyberspace," *Joint Force Quarterly* 46, no. 3 (4th quarter 2007).

Arquilla, John and David Ronfeldt. "Cyberwar Is Coming!," *Comparative Strategy* 12 (1993).

——. *The Advent of Netwar* (Santa Monica, CA: RAND Corporation, 1996).

Baer, George. *One Hundred Years of Seapower: The US Navy, 1890–1990* (Stanford, CA: Stanford University Press, 1994).

Bayles, William J. "The Ethics of Computer Network Attack," *Parameters* (Spring 2001).

Biddle, Stephen. "Afghanistan and the Future of Warfare," *Foreign Affairs* 82, no. 2 (March/April 2003).

——. "New Way of War? Debating the Kosovo Model," *Foreign Affairs* 81, no. 3 (May/June 2002).

——. "Strategy in War," *Political Science & Politics* 40, no. 3 (July 2007).

——. "Victory Misunderstood: What the Gulf War Tells Us about the Future of Conflict," *International Security* 21, no. 2 (Fall 1996).

Blaker, James. "Arthur K. Cebrowski: A Retrospective," *Naval War College Review* 59, no. 2 (Spring 2006).

——. *Understanding the Revolution in Military Affairs* (Washington, DC: Progressive Policy Institute, January 1997).

Blank, Stephen J. "Preparing for the Next War: Reflections on the Revolution in Military Affairs," *Strategic Review* (Spring 1996).

Brodie, Bernard. *A Guide to Naval Strategy* (Princeton, NJ: Princeton University Press, 1965).

——. *War and Politics* (New York: Macmillan Publishing Co., Inc., 1973).

Bunn, M. Elaine. "Can Deterrence Be Tailored?," *INSS Strategic Forum* (January 2007).

Byman, Daniel L. and Matthew C. Waxman. "Kosovo and the Great Airpower Debate," *International Security* 24, no. 4 (Spring 2000).

Callwell, C. E. *Small Wars: Their Principles and Practice*, 3rd edition (Lincoln, NE: University of Nebraska Press, 1996, first published 1906).

Castex, R. *Strategic Theories* (Annapolis, MD: US Naval Institute Press, 1993).

Cavas, Christopher P. "Cebrowksi's Legacy: Think outside the Pentagon," *Defense News*, November 21, 2005.

——. "Spanning the Globe: U.S. Floats Fleet Cooperation Concept to Allies," *Defense News*, January 8, 2007.

Cebrowski, Arthur K. and John J. Garstka. "Network-centric Warfare: Its Origins and Future," *U.S. Naval Institute Proceedings* 124, no. 1 (January 1998).

Cimbala, Stephen J. "Nuclear First Use: Prudence or Peril?," *Joint Force Quarterly* 51, no. 4 (2008).

——. *Nuclear Weapons and Nuclear Strategy: U.S. Nuclear Policy for the Twenty-first Century* (London: Routledge, 2005).

Clarke, Richard. *Cyber War: The Next Threat to National Security and What to Do about It* (New York: HarperCollins, 2010).

Clausewitz, Carl von. *On War*, ed. Michael Howard and Peter Paret (Princeton, NJ: Princeton University Press, 1976).

Cohen, Eliot A. "A Revolution in Warfare," *Foreign Affairs* 75, no. 2 (March/April 1996).

Corbett, Julian S. *Some Principles of Maritime Strategy* (New York: Longmans, Green and Co., 1911).

Corum, James S. "The Air Campaign of the Present and Future—Using Airpower Against Insurgents and Terrorists," in Allan D. English, *Air Campaigns in the New World Order* (Winnipeg, MB: University of Manitoba Centre for Defence and Security Studies, 2005).

Corum, James S. and Wray R. Johnson. *Airpower in Small Wars: Fighting Terrorists and Insurgents* (Lawrence, KS: University Press of Kansas, 2003).

Crowl, Philip A. "Alfred Thayer Mahan: The Naval Historian," in Peter Paret, ed., *Makers of Modern Strategy from Machiavelli to the Nuclear Age* (Princeton, NJ: Princeton University Press, 1986).

"Cyber war," *Economist*, July 3, 2010.

Dahl, Erik J. "Network Centric Warfare and the Death of Operational Art," *Defence Studies* 2, no. 1 (Spring 2002).

Defense Science Board Task Force. *Sea Basing* (Washington, DC: Department of Defense, 2003).

Department of Defense. *Deterrence Operations Joint Operating Concept* (Washington, DC: Office of the Secretary of Defense, December 2006).

——. *The 2006 Quadrennial Defense Review* (Washington, DC: Office of the Secretary of Defense, February 2006).

Deptula, David. "Effects-based Operations: A U.S. Commander's Perspective," *Journal of the Singapore Armed Forces* 31, no. 2 (2005).

——. *Effects-based Operations: Change in the Nature of Warfare* (Arlington, VA: Aerospace Education Foundation, 2001).

Dilanian, Ken. "Iran's Nuclear Program and a New Era of Cyber War," *Los Angeles Times*, January 17, 2011.

Dolman, Everett C. "Geostrategy in the Space Age: An Astropolitical Analysis," *Journal of Strategic Studies* 22, no. 2 (1999).

Dolman, Everett C. and Henry F. Cooper, Jr. "Increasing the Military Uses of Space," in Charles D. Lutes et al., *Toward a Theory of Spacepower* (Washington, DC: National Defense University Press, 2011).

Douhet, Guilio. *The Command of the Air*, trans. Dino Ferrari, ed. Joseph Patrick Harahan and Richard H. Kohn (Tuscaloosa, AL: University Of Alabama Press, 1942).

Earle, Edward Mead, ed. *Makers of Modern Strategy: Military Thought from Machiavelli to Hitler* (Princeton, NJ: Princeton University Press, 1943).

English, Allan D. *Air Campaigns in the New World Order* (Winnipeg, MB: University of Manitoba Centre for Defence and Security Studies, 2005).

Estes, Howell M. III. "The Aerospace Force of Today and Tomorrow," in Peter L. Hays et al., *Spacepower for a New Millennium* (New York: McGraw-Hill, 2000).

Foster, Gregory D. "Research, Writing, and the Mind of the Strategist," *Joint Forces Quarterly* (Spring 1996).

Freedman, Lawrence. *Deterrence* (Cambridge, UK: Polity Press, 2004).

——. "The First Two Generations of Nuclear Strategists," in Peter Paret, ed., *Makers of Modern Strategy from Machiavelli to the Nuclear Age* (Princeton, NJ: Princeton University Press, 1986).

Friedman, Norman. *Seapower and Space* (London: Chatham Publishing, 2000).

——. *Seapower as Strategy: Navies and National Interests* (Annapolis, MD: Naval Institute Press, 2001).

Galula, David. *Counterinsurgency Warfare: Theory and Practice* (New York: Praeger Publishers, 1964).

Geers, Kenneth. *Sun Tzu and Cyber War* (Tallinn, Estonia: Cooperative Cyber Defence Centre of Excellence (CCD CoE) Publications, 2011), http://www.ccdcoe.org.

Gerson, Michael S. "No First Use: The Next Step for U.S. Nuclear Policy," *International Security* 35, no. 2 (Fall 2010).

Glaser, Charles L. and Steve Fetter. "Counterforce Revisited: Assessing the Nuclear Posture Review's New Missions," *International Security* 30, no. 2 (Fall 2005).

Gordon, Michael R. and Bernard E. Trainor. *Cobra II: The Inside Story of the Invasion and Occupation of Iraq* (New York: Pantheon Books, 2006).

Gorshkov, Sergie. *Navies in War and Peace* (Annapolis, MD: US Naval Institute Press, 1974).

——. *The Seapower of the State* (London: Pergamon, 1979).

Gray, Colin S. "Gaining Compliance: The Theory of Deterrence and its Modern Application," *Comparative Strategy* 29 (2010).

——. *Modern Strategy* (Oxford: Oxford University Press, 1999).

——. *Strategy for Chaos: Revolutions in Military Affairs and the Evidence of History* (London: Frank Cass, 2002).

——. "The Influence of Space Power Upon History," *Comparative Strategy* 15 (1996).

——. *The Navy in the Post-Cold War World* (University Park, PA: The Pennsylvania State University Press, 1994).

——. *The Second Nuclear Age* (Boulder, CO: Lynne Rienner Publishers, 1999).

Hammes, Thomas X. *The Sling and the Stone: On War in the 21st Century* (St. Paul, MN: Zenith Press, 2004).

——. "War Evolves into the Fourth Generation," *Contemporary Security Policy* 26, no. 2 (August 2005).

Harter, Mark E. "Ten Propositions Regarding Space Power," *Air & Space Power Journal* (Summer 2006).

Hayes, Peter L. et al. eds. *Spacepower for a New Millennium: Space and U.S. National Security* (New York: McGraw-Hill, 2000).

Hinman, Ellwood P. IV. "Counterair and Counterland Concepts for the 21st Century," *Joint Force Quarterly* 48, 1st quarter (2008).

Hollis, David M. "Cyber War Case Study: Georgia 2008," *Small Wars Journal* (January 2011).

——. "USCYBERCOM: The Need for a Combatant Command Versus a Subunified Command," *Joint Force Quarterly* 58, no. 3 (2010).

Hughes, Wayne. *Fleet Tactics and Coastal Combat* (Annapolis, MD: US Naval Institute Press, 2010).

——. *Fleet Tactics: Theory and Practice* (Annapolis, MD: US Naval Institute Press, 1986).

Hundley, Richard O. *Past Revolutions, Future Transformations* (Santa Monica, CA: Rand Corporation, 1999).

Johnson-Freese, Joan. *Space as a Strategic Asset* (New York: Columbia University Press, 2007).

Jomini, Antoine Henri. *The Art of War*, ed. J. D. Hittle (Harrisburg, PA: Military Service Publishing Company, 1947).

Kaldor, Mary. *New and Old Wars: Organized Violence in a Global Era* (Stanford, CA: Stanford University Press, 1999).

Kilcullen, David J. "Countering Global Insurgency," *Journal of Strategic Studies* 28, no. 4 (August 2005).

——. "Counter-insurgency *Redux*," *Survival* 48, no. 4 (Winter 2006–7).

——. *The Accidental Guerrilla: Fighting Small Wars in the Midst of a Big One* (New York: Oxford University Press, 2009).

Klein, John J. "Corbett in Orbit: A Maritime Model for Strategic Space Theory," *Naval War College Review* 57, no. 1 (Winter 2004).

Krekel, Bryan. "Capability of the People's Republic of China to Conduct Cyber Warfare and Computer Network Exploitation," report prepared for The US–China Economic and Security Review Commission, October 9, 2009.

Krepinevich, Andrew F. "Cavalry to Computer: The Pattern of Military Revolutions," *National Interest* (Fall 1994).
——. *The Army and Vietnam* (Baltimore, MD: Johns Hopkins University Press, 1986).
——. *The Military Technical Revolution: A Preliminary Assessment* (Washington, DC: Center for Strategic and Budgetary Asssessments, 2002).
——. *The War in Iraq: The Nature of Insurgency Warfare* (Washington, DC: Center for Strategic and Budgetary Analysis, June 2, 2004).
——. *Transforming the Legions: The Army and the Future of Land Warfare* (Washington, DC: Center for Strategic and Budgetary Assessments, 2004).
Krepon, Michael et al. "Preserving Freedom of Action in Space: Realizing the Potential and Limits of U.S. Spacepower," in Charles D. Lutes et al., *Toward a Theory of Spacepower* (Washington, DC: National Defense University Press, 2011).
Krulak, Charles C. "Ne Cras: Not Like Yesterday," in Richard H. Shultz Jr. and Robert L. Pfaltzgraff, Jr., eds., *The Role of Naval Forces in 21st-century Operations* (Washington, DC: Brassey's, 2000).
——. "Operational Maneuver from the Sea," *Joint Force Quarterly* (Spring 1999).
Lambakis, Steven. "Space Control in Desert Storm and Beyond," *Orbis* (Summer 1995).
——. *On the Edge of the Earth: The Future of American Space Power* (Lexington, KY: University Press of Kentucky, 2001).
Lambeth, Benjamin S. "Air Force–Navy Integration in Strike Warfare," *Naval War College Review* 61, no. 1 (Winter 2008).
——. *Air Power against Terror: America's Conduct of Operation Enduring Freedom* (Santa Monica, CA: RAND Corporation, 2005).
——. "Air Power, Space Power and Geography," *Journal of Strategic Studies* 22, no. 2 (1999).
——. "Airpower, Spacepower, and Cyber power," *Joint Force Quarterly* 60, no. 1 (2011).
——. "Bounding the Air Power Debate," *Strategic Review* (Fall 1997).
——. *Mastering the Ultimate High Ground: Next Steps in the Military Uses of Space* (Santa Monica, CA: RAND, 2003).
——. *NATO's Air War for Kosovo: A Strategic and Operational Assessment* (Santa Monica, CA: Rand Corporation, 2001).
——. "The Technology Revolution in Air Warfare," *Survival* 39, no. 1 (Spring 1997).
——. *The Transformation of American Air Power* (Ithaca, NY: Cornell University Press, 2000).
Lawrence, T. E. *Seven Pillars of Wisdom: A Triumph* (London: Jonathan Cape, 1940).
——. "The 27 Articles of T. E. Lawrence," *The Arab Bulletin*, August 20, 1917.
Lever, Rob. "U.S. May Use Cyberhackers as War Weapon," *National Post*, February 17, 2003.
Lewis, James. *A Note on the Laws of War in Cyberspace* (Washington, DC: Center for Strategic and International Studies, April 2010).
Libicki, Martin. *Conquest in Cyberspace: National Security and Information Warfare* (New York: Cambridge University Press, 2007).
——. *Cyberdeterrence and Cyber War* (Santa Monica, CA: RAND Corporation, 2009).
——. *What Is Information Warfare?* (Washington, DC: National Defense University Institute for National Strategic Studies, ACIS Paper 3, August 1995).
Liddell Hart, B. H. *Strategy: The Indirect Approach* (London: Faber and Faber Limited, 1954).
Lind, William S. "Parting Thoughts, for Now," December 15, 2009, http://original.antiwar.com.
Lind, William S. et al. "The Changing Face of War: Into the Fourth Generation," *Military Review* (October 1989).
Lupton, David E. *On Space Warfare: A Space Power Doctrine* (Maxwell Air Force Base, AL: Air University Press, 1988).
Lutes, Charles D. et al. *Toward a Theory of Spacepower* (Washington, DC: National Defense University Press, 2011).
Luttwak, Edward N. "A Brief Note on 'Fourth-generation Warfare'," *Contemporary Security Policy* 26, no. 2 (August 2005).

Lynn, William J. III. "Defending a New Domain: The Pentagon's Cyberstrategy," *Foreign Affairs* 89, no. 5 (September/October 2010).

Macgregor, Douglas A. *"Breaking the Phalanx": A New Design for Landpower in the 21st Century* (Westport, CT: Praeger, 1997).

——. "Future Battle: The Merging Levels of War," *Parameters* (Winter 1992–93).

——. *Transformation under Fire: Revolutionizing how America Fights* (Westport, CT: Praeger Publishers, 2003).

Mahan, A. T. *The Influence of Sea Power upon History 1660–1783* (New York: Dover Publications, 1987).

Malik, J. Mohan. "The Evolution of Strategic Thought," in Craig A. Snyder, ed., *Contemporary Security and Strategy* (New York: Routledge, 1999).

Mao, Tse-Tung. *On Guerrilla Warfare*, trans. Samuel B. Griffith (New York: Praeger Publishers, 1961).

Marshall, Andrew W. "Some Thoughts in Military Revolutions," Office of Net Assessment Memorandum, July 27, 1993.

——. "The 1995 RMA Essay Contest: A Postscript," *Joint Forces Quarterly* (Winter 1995–96).

Matthews, William. "U.S. Faces Many Cyber Threats, Commander Warns," *Defense News*, September 27, 2010.

Mattis, James N. "USJFCOM Commander's Guidance for Effects-based Operations," *Joint Forces Quarterly* 51 (4th quarter 2008).

Mazarr, Michael J. *The Military Technical Revolution: A Structural Framework* (Washington, DC: Center for Strategic and International Studies, March 1993).

Mearsheimer, John J. *Conventional Deterrence* (Ithaca, NY: Cornell University Press, 1983).

Meilinger, Phillip S. "Douhet and Modern War," *Comparative Strategy* 12 (1993).

Mesic, Richard et al. *Air Force Cyber Command (Provisional) Decision Support* (Santa Monica, CA: RAND Corporation, 2010).

Mitchell, William. *Winged Defense* (Port Washington, NY: Kennikat Press, 1925).

Mullen, Michael. "A Global Network of Nations for a Free and Secure Maritime Commons," in John B. Hattendorf, ed., *Seventeenth International Seapower Symposium: Report of the Proceedings 19–23 September 2005* (Newport, RI: U.S. Naval War College, 2006).

——. "It's Time for a New Deterrence Model," *Joint Forces Quarterly*, 51 no. 4 (4th quarter 2008).

Mundy, Carl E. "Thunder and Lightning," *Joint Force Quarterly* (Spring 1994).

Munkler, Herfried. *The New Wars* (Malden, MA: Polity Press, 2002).

Murray, Williamson. "The Evolution of Joint Warfare," *Joint Forces Quarterly* (Summer 2002).

Murray, Williamson and Robert H. Scales, Jr. *The Iraq War: A Military History* (Cambridge, MA: Harvard University Press, 2003).

National Research Council. *Discouraging Terrorism: Some Implications of 9/11* (Washington, DC: The National Academies Press, 2002).

——. *Technology, Policy, Law and Ethics Regarding U.S. Acquisition and Use of Cyberattack Capabilities* (Washington, DC: National Academies Press, 2009).

Oberg, James E. *Space Power Theory* (Colorado Springs, CO: US Air Force Academy, Department of Astronautics, March 1999).

O'Hanlon, Michael. "A Flawed Masterpiece," *Foreign Affairs* 81, no. 3 (May/June 2002).

Owens, Mackubin Thomas. "Technology, the RMA, and Future War," *Strategic Review* (Spring 1998).

Owens, William A. *Lifting the Fog of War* (New York: Farrar, Straus and Giroux, 2000).

——. "The American Revolution in Military Affairs," *Joint Forces Quarterly* (Winter 1995–96).

——. "The Emerging System of Systems," *Military Review* (May–June 1995).

——. "The Once and Future Revolution in Military Affairs," *Joint Forces Quarterly* (Summer 2002).

Pape, Robert A. *Bombing to Win: Airpower and Coercion in War* (Ithaca, NY: Cornell University Press, 1996).

——. "The Limits of Precision-guided Air Power," *Security Studies* 7, no. 2 (Winter 1997/98).

——. "The True Worth of Air Power," *Foreign Affairs*, 83, no. 2 (March/April 2004).

Paret, Peter et al., eds. *Makers of Modern Strategy from Machiavelli to the Nuclear Age* (Princeton, NJ: Princeton University Press, 1986).

Payne, Keith B. *Deterrence in the Second Nuclear Age* (Lexington, KY: The University Press of Kentucky, 1996).

——. "The Continuing Roles for U.S. Strategic Forces," *Comparative Strategy* 26 (2007).

——. *The Fallacies of Cold War Deterrence and a New Direction* (Lexington, KY: The University Press of Kentucky, 2001).

——. *The Great American Gamble: Deterrence Theory and Practice from the Cold War to the Twenty-first Century* (Fairfax, VA: National Institute Press, 2008).

——. "The Nuclear Posture Review and Deterrence for a New Age," *Comparative Strategy* 23, no. 4 (2004).

——. "The Nuclear Posture Review: Setting the Record Straight," *Washington Quarterly* 28, no. 3 (Summer 2005).

Perry, William J. "Defense in an Age of Hope," *Foreign Affairs* 75, no. 6 (November/December 1996).

——. "Desert Storm and Deterrence," *Foreign Affairs* 70, no. 4 (Fall 1991).

Pfaltzgraff, Robert L. Jr. *Space and U.S. Security: A Net Assessment* (Cambridge, MA: Institute for Foreign Policy Analysis, January 2009).

Posen, Barry R. *The Sources of Military Doctrine* (Ithaca, NY: Cornell University Press, 1984).

Press, Daryl G. "The Myth of Air Power in the Persian Gulf War and the Future of Warfare," *International Security* 26, no.2 (Fall 2001).

Rattray, Greg. *Strategic Warfare in Cyberspace* (Cambridge, MA: MIT Press, 2001).

Report of the Commission to Assess United States National Security Space Management and Organization (Washington, DC: January 2001).

Roxborough, Ian. "From Revolution to Transformation: The State of the Field," *Joint Forces Quarterly* (Autumn 2002).

Rubel, Robert C. "The Navy's Changing Force Paradigm," *Naval War College Review* 62, no. 2 (Spring 2009).

Rumsfeld, Donald H. "Foreword" to the *Nuclear Posture Review*, January 8, 2002, found at www.fas.org accessed May 2, 2011.

——. "Transforming the Military," *Foreign Affairs* 81, no. 3 (May/June 2002).

Sagan, Scott D. "The Commitment Trap: Why the United States Should not Use Nuclear Threats to Deter Biological and Chemical Weapons Attacks," *International Security* 24, no. 4 (Spring 2000).

Scales, Robert H. Jr. "Return of the Jedi," *Armed Forces Journal* (October 2009).

——. "The Second Learning Revolution," in Anthony D. McIvor, ed., *Rethinking the Principles of War* (Annapolis, MD: Naval Institute Press, 2005).

——. *Yellow Smoke: The Future of Land Warfare for America's Military* (Lanham, MD: Rowman & Littlefield Publishers, Inc., 2003).

Schneider, James J. "T. E. Lawrence and the Mind of an Insurgent," *Army* (July 2005).

Schuurman, Bart. "Clausewitz and the 'New Wars' Scholars," *Parameters* (Spring 2010).

Sherman, Jason. "Pentagon Group Details Sea Base Concept," *Defense News*, October 27, 2003.

Shultz, Richard H. Jr. and Andrea J. Dew. *Insurgents, Terrorists and Militias: The Warriors of Contemporary Combat* (New York: Columbia University Press, 2006).

Shultz, Richard H. Jr. and Robert L. Pfaltzgraff, Jr., eds. *The Role of Naval Forces in 21st-century Operations* (Washington, DC: Brassey's, 2000).

Shy, John. "Jomini," in Peter Paret, ed., *Makers of Modern Strategy from Machiavelli to the Nuclear Age* (Princeton, NJ: Princeton University Press, 1986).

Shy, John and Thomas W. Collier. "Revolutionary War," in Peter Paret, ed., *Makers of Modern Strategy from Machiavelli to the Nuclear Age* (Princeton, NJ: Princeton University Press, 1986).

Smith, M.V. "Some Propositions on Spacepower," *Joint Force Quarterly* (Winter 2002–3).

——. "Spacepower and Warfare," *Joint Force Quarterly* 60, no. 1 (2011).

——. *Ten Propositions Regarding Spacepower* (Maxwell Air Force Base, AL: Air University Press, 2002).

Smith, Rupert. *The Utility of Force: The Art of War in the Modern World* (London: Allen Lane, 2005).

Sprout, Margaret Tuttle. "Mahan: Evangelist of Sea Power," in Edward Mead Earle, *Makers of Modern Strategy: Military Thought from Machiavelli to Hitler* (Princeton, NJ: Princeton University Press, 1943).

Stigler, Andrew L. "A Clear Victory for Air Power: NATO's Empty Threat to Invade Kosovo," *International Security* 27, no. 3 (Winter 2002/03).

Sumida, Jon. *Inventing Grand Strategy and Teaching Command: The Classic Works of Alfred Thayer Mahan Reconsidered* (Washington, DC: Johns Hopkins University Press, 1999).

Sun Tzu, *The Art of War*, trans. Samuel B. Griffiths (New York: Oxford University Press, 1963).

Tangredi, Sam J., ed. *Globalization and Maritime Power* (Washington, DC: National Defense University Press, 2002).

Thomas, Timothy. "China's Electronic Long-range Reconnaissance," *Military Review* (November/ December 2008).

Thompson, Robert. *Defeating Communist Insurgency* (New York: Praeger Publishers, 1966).

Till, Geoffrey. *Naval Transformation, Ground Forces, and the Expeditionary Impulse: The Sea-basing Debate* (Carlisle, PA: US Army War College Strategic Studies Institute, 2006).

——. "New Directions in Maritime Strategy? Implications for the U.S. Navy," *Naval War College Review* 60, no. 4 (Autumn 2007).

——. *Seapower: A Guide for the Twenty-first Century* (London: Routledge, 2009).

Toffler, Alvin and Heidi Toffler. *War and Anti-war* (New York: Warner Books, 1973).

Trimble, Stephen. "New Dawn for US Global Strategy?," *Jane's Navy International*, November 1, 2006.

——. "US Seeks Wider Seapower Definition," *Jane's Navy International*, July 1, 2006.

Ullman, Harlan K. and James P. Wade. *Shock and Awe: Achieving Rapid Dominance* (Washington, DC: National Defense University Press, 1996).

UN High-Level Panel on Threats Challenges and Change. *A More Secure World: Our Shared Responsibility* (New York: United Nations, 2004).

US Air Force. *Counterspace Operations* (Washington, DC: Air Force Doctrine Document 2–2.1, 2004).

——. *Global Engagement: A Vision for the 21st Century Air Force* (Washington, DC: Department of the Air Force, 1996).

——. *Space Operations* (Washington, DC: Air Force Doctrine Document 2–2, 2006).

US Army. *Concepts for the Objective Force* (Washington, DC: US Army, 2001).

——. *The Army Vision Briefing*, www.army.mil/armyvision/armyvis.htm, n.d.

——. *The US Army – Marine Corps Counterinsurgency Field Manual (FM 3–24)* (Chicago, IL: University of Chicago Press, 2007).

US Army Training and Doctrine Command. *Cyberspace Operations Concept Capability Plan 2016–2028* (Fort Monroe, VA: United States Army, February 2010).

US Joint Chiefs of Staff. "Joint Vision 2010: America's Military Preparing for Tomorrow," *Joint Force Quarterly* (Summer 1996).

——. *Joint Vision 2020* (Washington, DC: Joint Chiefs of Staff, 2000).

——. *National Military Strategy for Cyberspace Operations* (Washington, DC: Department of Defense, December 2006).

——. *Space Operations* (Washington, DC: Joint Pub 3–14, 6 January 2009).

US Joint Forces Command. *A Concept for Rapid Decisive Operations* (RDO Whitepaper Version 2.0), August 9, 2001.

US Joint Warfighting Center. "An Effects-based Approach: Refining how We Think about Joint Operations," *Joint Forces Quarterly* 44, no. 1 (1st quarter 2007).

"US Military Options against Emerging Nuclear Threats: The Challenges of a Denial Strategy," *IISS Strategic Comments* 12, no. 3 (April 2006).

US Navy. *Forward … from the Sea* (Washington, DC: Department of the Navy, 1994).

——. "The Navy Operational Concept," in John B. Hattendorf, ed., *U.S. Naval Strategy in the 1990s* (Newport, RI: Naval War College Press, 2006).

US Navy and US Marine Corps. "From the Sea: Preparing the Naval Service for the 21st Century," in John B. Hattendorf, ed., *U.S. Naval Strategy in the 1990s* (Newport, RI: Naval War College Press, 2006).

US Navy, US Marine Corps and US Coast Guard. *A Cooperative Strategy for 21st Century Seapower* (Washington, DC: The Pentagon, 2007).

US Office of Force Transformation. *Military Transformation: A Strategic Approach* (Washington, DC: Office of Force Transformation, Fall 2003).

——. *Transformation Planning Guidance* (Washington, DC: Office of Force Transformation, April 2003).

US Space Command Long Range Plan (1998) http://fas.org.

van Creveld, Martin. *The Transformation of War* (New York: The Free Press, 1991).

van Riper, Paul and Robert H. Scales, Jr. "Preparing for War in the 21st Century," *Parameters* (Autumn 1997).

"War in the Fifth Domain." *Economist*, July 3, 2010.

Warden, John. *The Air Campaign: Planning for Combat* (Washington, DC: Brassey's, 1989).

Warner, Edward. "Douhet, Mitchell, Seversky: Theories of Air Warfare," in Edward Mead Earle, *Makers of Modern Strategy: Military Thought from Machiavelli to Hitler* (Princeton, NJ: Princeton University Press, 1943).

Widen, J. J. "Julian Corbett and the Current British Maritime Doctrine," *Comparative Strategy* 28, no. 2 (March/April 2009).

Wirtz, James J. "Politics with Guns: A Response to T. X. Hammes," *Contemporary Security Policy* 26, no. 2 (August 2005).

Wirtz, James J. and James A. Russell. "A Quiet Revolution: Nuclear Strategy for the 21st Century," *Joint Forces Quarterly* (Winter 2002–3).

Work, Robert O. "Small Combat Ships and the Future of the Navy," *Issues in Science and Technology* (Fall 2004).

Work, Robert O. and Jan van Tol. *A Cooperative Strategy for 21st Century Seapower: An Assessment* (Washington, DC: Center for Strategic and Budgetary Assessments, March 2008).

Yost, David S. "France's Evolving Nuclear Strategy," *Survival* 47, no. 3 (Autumn 2005).

——. "New Approaches to Deterrence in Britain, France and the United States," *International Affairs* 81 (2005).

Zakaria, Fareed. "The General: An Interview with David Petraeus," *Newsweek*, January 4, 2009.

Name index

Subject index